DROGHEDA

DROGHEDA

JOE CURTIS

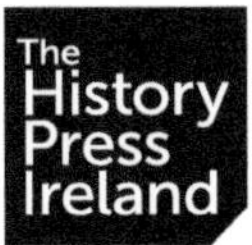

First published 2013

The History Press Ireland
50 City Quay
Dublin 2
Ireland
www.thehistorypress.ie

British Library Cataloguing in Publication Data.
A catalogue record for this book is available from the British Library.

ISBN 978 1 84588 798 8

Typesetting and origination by The History Press
Printed by TJ International Ltd

CONTENTS

ACKNOWLEDGEMENTS

Grateful thanks to: Sr Aine MacNamara (Daughters of Charity), Sr Catherine Dwyer (Medical Missionaries of Mary), Sr Carmel Curran (Presentation Sisters), Sr Clare Marie (Siena Monastery), Sr Evelyn Kenny (Sisters of Mercy), Paul Ferguson (Trinity College Map Library), Conor Keane (Drogheda Station Master), Michael McBrinn (Wilson & McBrinn), Tommy Leddy (TLT Concert Hall & Theatre), Matt Doolan (Porterhouse Ltd), Eddies Hardware/Grafton Group, John McCullen, Des Clinton, and all who allowed me to take photos, escorted me around their premises, told me their story, or assisted in numerous ways, including Drogheda Tourist Office, Highlanes Gallery, Droichead Arts Centre.

Liam Reilly, of Drogheda Museum Millmount, kindly afforded me access to their extensive library and museum.

Thanks to the excellent staff at the National Library, National Archives, Irish Architectural Archive, Office of Public Works, Valuation Office, Central Catholic Library, and Drogheda Library.

Where photos are not acknowledged, they were taken by the author.

INTRODUCTION

In the twelfth century, there were two towns: Drogheda-in-Meath on the south bank of the River Boyne, and the larger Drogheda-in-Louth on the north bank, both a few miles upstream of the river mouth. In 1412, the two towns were united, and the entire town is now in County Louth.

By the mid-thirteenth century the town was protected by a stone wall, 1½ miles long, with about twenty gates. Starting in the centre west and going clockwise, some well-known gates were West Gate, Fair Gate, Sunday Gate (Cow Gate), Tooting Gate, Tailors' Hall Gate, Pigeon Gate, St Laurence's Gate, Blind Gate, St Catherine's Gate, Dublin Gate, Duleek Gate, Butter Gate and John's Gate. In random locations around Drogheda, there are partial remains of the old walls, most notably on the south side of St Mary's Church of Ireland graveyard. Part of the base of the octagonal Butter Gate, to the west of Millmount, still remains – its name is due to the fact that butter entering the town was once taxed. Only St Laurence's Gate survives in full, which in fact is a protective barbican outside the original gate, the latter long gone. This barbican is 20 metres high, and consists of two towers, connected by a screen wall. An extra storey was added in the fifteenth century, and other alterations over the centuries.

The Irish Parliament sat in Drogheda in 1495, when Poyning's Law was passed, allowing the Irish Parliament to be ruled by the English King. Cromwell laid siege to the Royalists inside the walled town around 150 years later, in 1649, and thousands of Catholics and Protestants were killed. Some Catholics took refuge in the wooden steeple of St Peter's Anglican church, which was then burned by Cromwell, although the rest of the church was not badly damaged.

The Battle of the Boyne took place on 11 July 1691, at Oldbridge, a few miles to the west of Drogheda. The 25,000-strong Jacobite army (supporters of King James II) were beaten by the 36,000-strong Williamite army (King William III or William of Orange from Holland, grandson of Charles I). Oldbridge House, designed by George Darley, was built in the 1740s on the site of the battle, and is now a very interesting state museum. The nearby bridge over the River Boyne dates from 1869. A memorial obelisk was erected near the north side of this bridge in 1736, but was blown up in 1923, leaving only the base. A ceremonial mace and sword of state were given to the Corporation of Drogheda by King William shortly after the Battle of the Boyne, in 1691. The mace is of solid silver and weighs nearly 7 pounds.

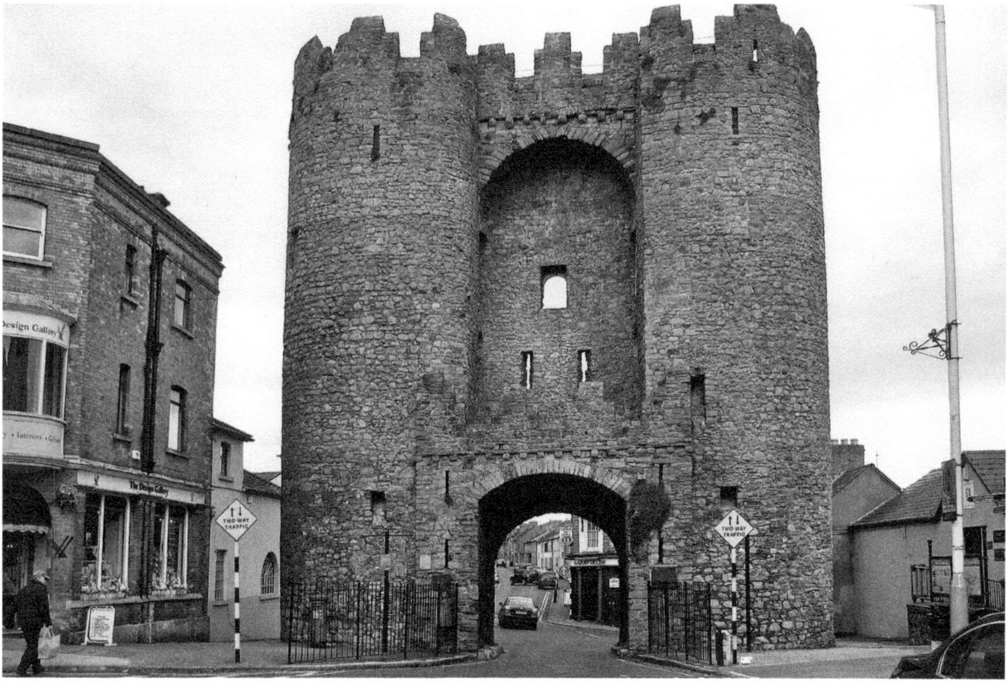

St Laurence Gate, looking east.

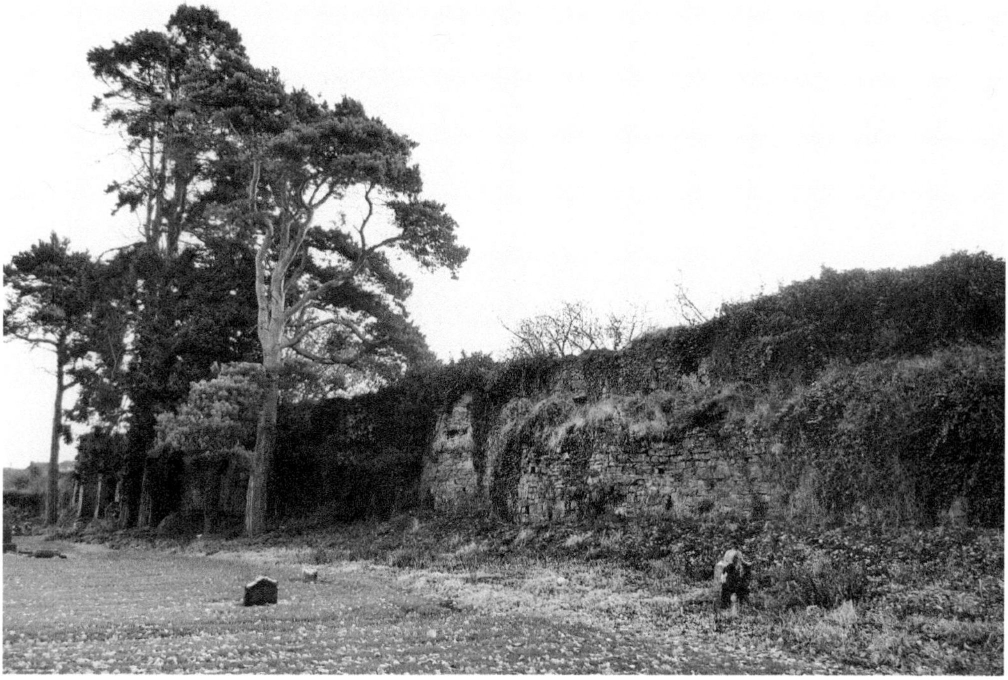

The high stone wall, which forms the south boundary of St Mary's C of I graveyard, is in fact a section of the original thirteen-century town wall which enclosed the entire town.

1

LAW AND ORDER

MILLMOUNT BARRACKS/RICHMOND FORT

Millmount Fort (Richmond Fort) dates from the twelfth century and was originally a motte-and-bailey built by Hugh de Lacy. The Martello Tower dates from 1808, and has two 9-pound canons on a movable wooden platform.

By a deed dated 1702, Drogheda Council sold 2 acres of land here with a covenant to build a barracks. By a lease dated 1830 another 21 perches were leased, and in 1913, an additional 1¼ acres adjoining the barracks were leased for ten years, with an option to purchase. The Barracks was built in 1714, with the canteen/hospital (a museum since 1974) added around the 1840s.

In the 1901 census, the only residents of the Barracks were a sergeant and his wife, who occupied two rooms. By the 1911 census there were 101 soldiers, six of them English. The rest were Irish, with many from Dublin, and the majority were around 17-19 years old.

Proposals in 1910/11 to accommodate the 5th Battalion of the Leinster Regiment allowed for one field officer, four officers, eighty-one non-commissioned officers and men (sixty-nine infantry and twelve artillery), and five others. The site layout in the proposal shows the previous uses of the different blocks, as follows, starting at the main barrack entrance:

(a) Guardroom: prisoner's room on ground floor, and married quarters on first. The west building alongside was for two officers' horses, with a small hay loft overhead.

(b) The present three-storey museum had a hospital on the first floor, canteen on ground, and armoury in basement. To the north was a handball alley.

(c) The main U-shaped soldiers' block had four staircases and fourteen small dormitories. Three little detached buildings alongside the west boundary comprised a Wash House, Cook House, and Bath House. The north-east addition to the main building was for a fire engine, and straw store.

(d) The L-shaped block opposite the present museum, comprised married soldiers quarters in the west wing, and officers' quarters in the east wing. To the east was a bread and meat store.

(e) To the west of the Martello Tower was the officers' quarters and mess, with a bedding store and married quarters in a rear block. Under the ramp up to the

tower was the machine-gun shed. This building is nowadays incorrectly called the Governor's House, a title more appropriate for a gaol/prison.
(f) The ground floor of the tower was used as artillery soldiers' quarters, with married quarters on the first floor.

When the British Army surveyed the barracks in 1919, the present museum building was listed as the 'Regimental Institute and Canteen'. Such institutes were provided for the improvement of the soldiers and to reduce their excessive drinking.

Just before the start of the Civil War, the Irregulars (Anti-Treaty army forces) took over the Martello Tower, but it was shelled and recaptured on 4 July 1922 by the Free State Army.

By August of 1922, two officers and thirty soldiers were in occupation, and J. Gogarty of No 87 West Street was engaged in essential repairs, to the value of £1,175. However, reports indicated that Blocks A and B (the blocks adjoining the ramp up to the tower) would have to be re-built and other blocks repaired, in addition to restoration of the Martello Tower. In fact, the tower was only rebuilt in 2000 by Drogheda Council.

INFANTRY BARRACKS, FAIR STREET

The infantry barracks is marked on the 1836 Ordnance Survey map. Lewis, writing in 1837, said that the barracks included a hospital with twenty beds. However, on the 1869 Ordnance Survey map, the barracks is marked 'Disused'.

For a short period prior to 1870, the property was occupied by the parish priest of St Peter's RC church, and he donated it to the Sisters of Charity of St Vincent de Paul in 1870. The nuns immediately built a red-brick industrial school (a special type of orphanage) in the parade ground, but they retained the main barrack building, with its limestone facade, as their convent.

FCA/ARMY RESERVE FORCE

Sluagh Hall, to the immediate west of St Peter's Cemetery, was opened by Eamon de Valera in 1938 and used by the FCA. The unit was disbanded in 2012.

GAOL, SCARLETT STREET

The old gaol was in James Street, on the site of the present St Mary's Roman Catholic church. The gaol in Scarlett Street was built in 1818. In his 1844 history of Drogheda, Dalton records that it comprised sixteen cells, a small chapel, and a hospital room. A Government Report, dated 1851, records that there were sixteen single cells, two solitary cells, four rooms with beds, five day rooms, and six yards.

According to the report, the average number of prisoners was nineteen males and ten females. The men worked at picking oakham and breaking stones. The women worked at knitting, sewing, and washing clothes. For breakfast there was stirabout (porridge) and buttermilk, and for dinner there was brown bread and buttermilk. The governor, James Hughes, earned £80 a year, the matron, Margaret McDonnell,

£6 a year, while the chaplain, Fr Hanratty, £40 a year – he also acted as the Local Inspector of Prisons. There were two turnkeys (warders).

The 1901 census recorded only three prisoners, who were minded by two warders and their families. By the time of the 1911 census, the gaol was unoccupied. The main buildings were later demolished, but the four high stone boundary walls remained. Eddie's Hardware (now owned by the Grafton Group) have occupied the premises since 1989, and have retained a few old stone features.

ROYAL IRISH CONSTABULARY

The three-storey over-basement Barlow House in West Street was designed by Richard Cassels in 1734, for Alderman James Barlow.

The Royal Irish Constabulary (RIC) were in the adjoining building on the east side (now a two-storey pub), before moving to Marlow House in 1861.

The 1901 census recorded John Carroll as the head constable, together with a sergeant and six constables. Two of the constables were Church of Ireland, and the other six were Catholics (including Carroll). Carroll's wife and four children also lived in the barracks.

In 1922, the RIC left Marlow House, and in 1925 the property was taken over by the newly established Garda Siochana, who remained here until moving to their new building in Fr Connolly Way in 1996. Since 1999, Marlow House, with its splendid timber staircase, has been used by Droichead Arts Centre.

There was another RIC barracks at No 3 South Quay. Two sergeants and five constables were in occupation in the 1901 census. All were Catholic, except one sergeant who was Presbyterian and one Church of Ireland constable.

The Gardai occupied the South Quay building from 1925 to 1931, when they united with Marlow House. A map of 1927 records that Revd J.J. Nulty, PP, owned the building, and leased it to the Gardai.

THOLSEL/TOWN HALL, WEST STREET

The Tholsel was constructed in 1770, to a design by George Darley, as a Court and Assembly Room. In 1889 a new Courthouse was constructed in Fair Street, on the site of the Corn Market. The Hibernian Bank occupied the former Tholsel from 1900 until recent years, and it is now the Tourist Office.

MAYORALTY HOUSE, NORTH QUAY

Otherwise known as the Mansion House, this limestone-faced building, designed by Hugh Darley in 1769, was intended for a Lord Mayor but was never used as such. Lewis, writing in 1837, records that the building was used as a public reading and news-room. The famous 'Sound Shop' acquired the building in 1976, but in recent years re-located to the East Coast Business Park.

CUSTOM HOUSE

The two-storey Custom House, to the immediate east of the Mayoralty House, was built in 1754, and collected taxes from the ships importing goods. It was demolished in recent decades.

COUNCIL OFFICES, FAIR STREET

The Corn Market was built in 1796, to a design by the famous architect Francis Johnston, and included a small office building fronting Fair Street. The rest of the south side, in addition to the east and west side, was an open colonnade. The Court was added to the office in the 1880s. The Council occupied the premises from 1889, and demolished the Courthouse just over a century later to make way for new offices. In 1991, the Court moved out to St Mary's Hall, where it was located until 2005. It is now in Dyer Street.

WATCH HOUSE

There was a 'fire look-out' about halfway up the east side of St Peter's Street, in a back garden, accessed by a covered archway. The Watch House is listed as No 13 Peter Street in the 1901 Census.

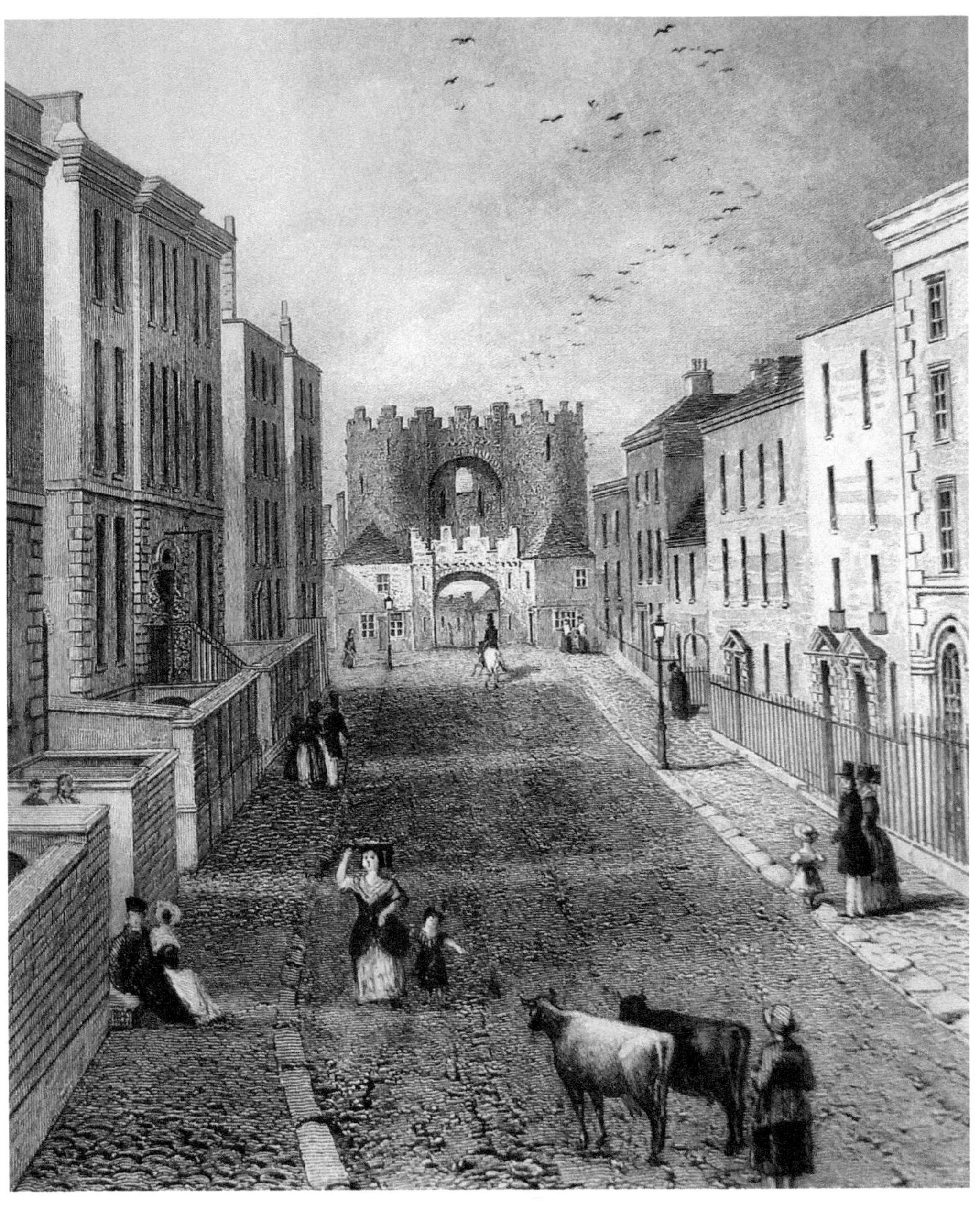

St Laurence Street. (From Dalton's *History of Drogheda*, 1844)

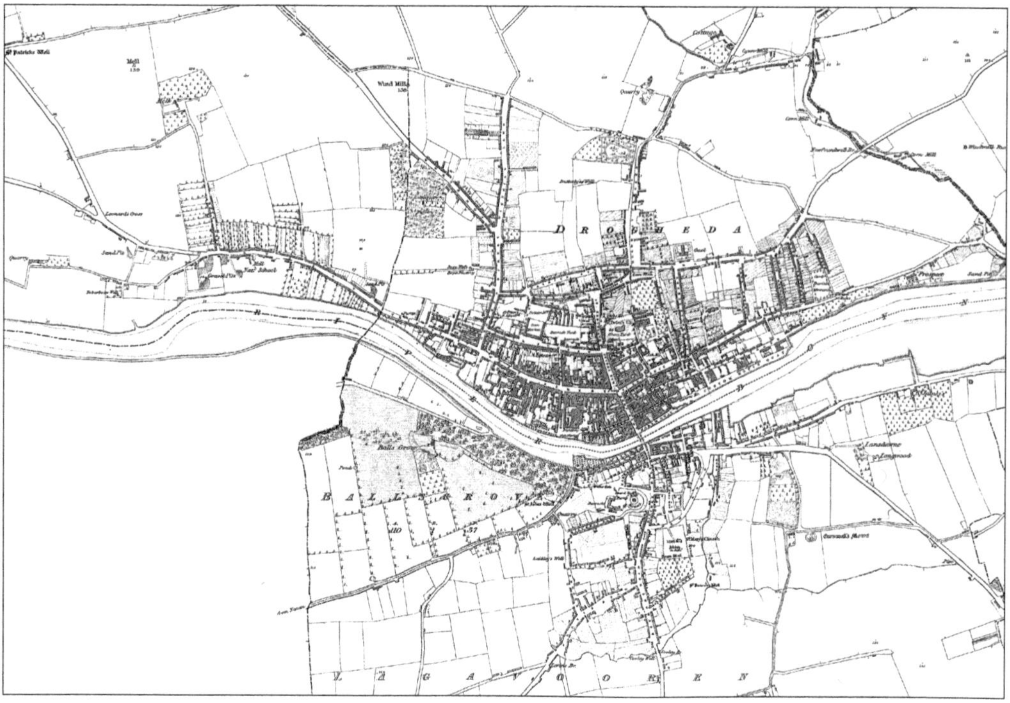

1836 Ordnance Survey map of Drogheda. (Courtesy of Trinity College Dublin Map Library)

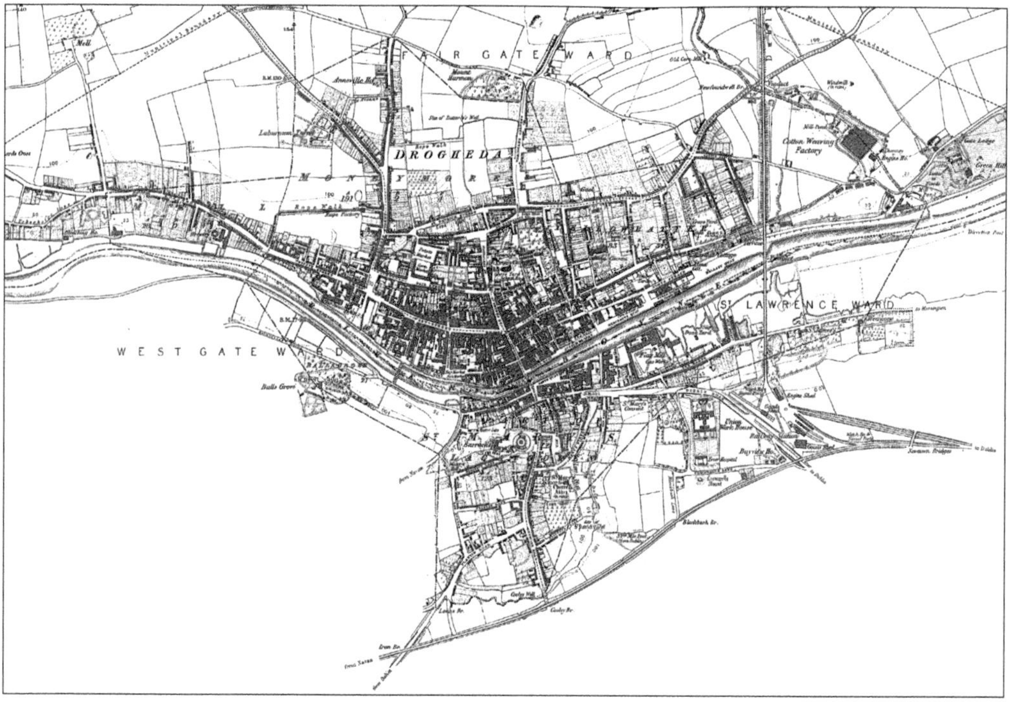

1869 Ordnance Survey map of Drogheda. (Courtesy of Trinity College Dublin Map Library)

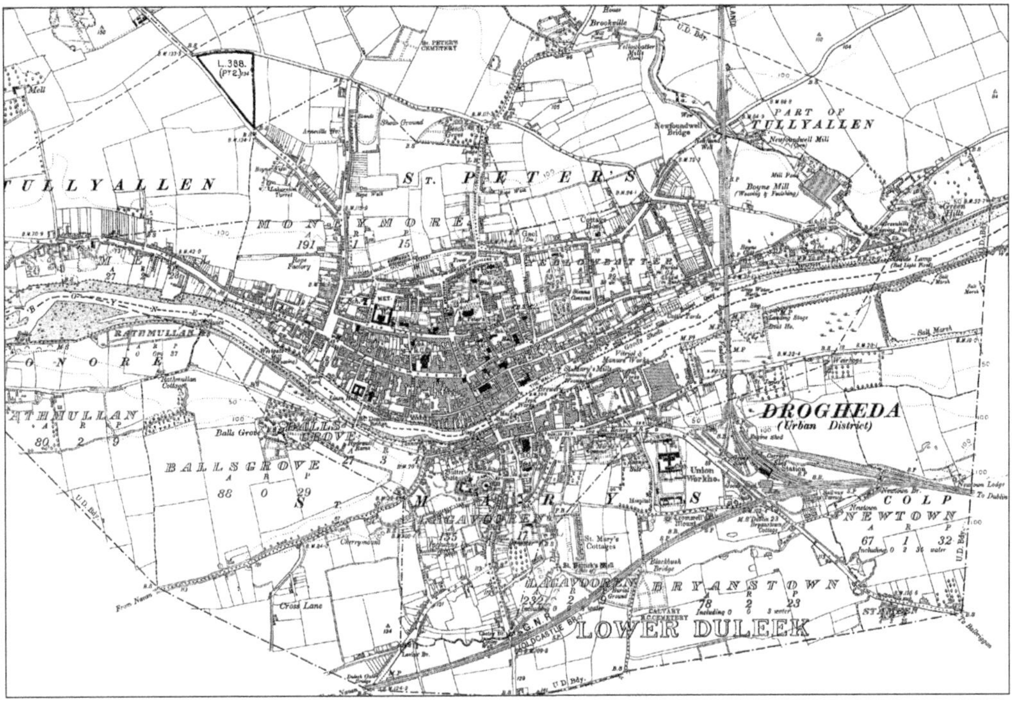

1912 Ordnance Survey map of Drogheda. (Courtesy of Trinity College Dublin Map Library)

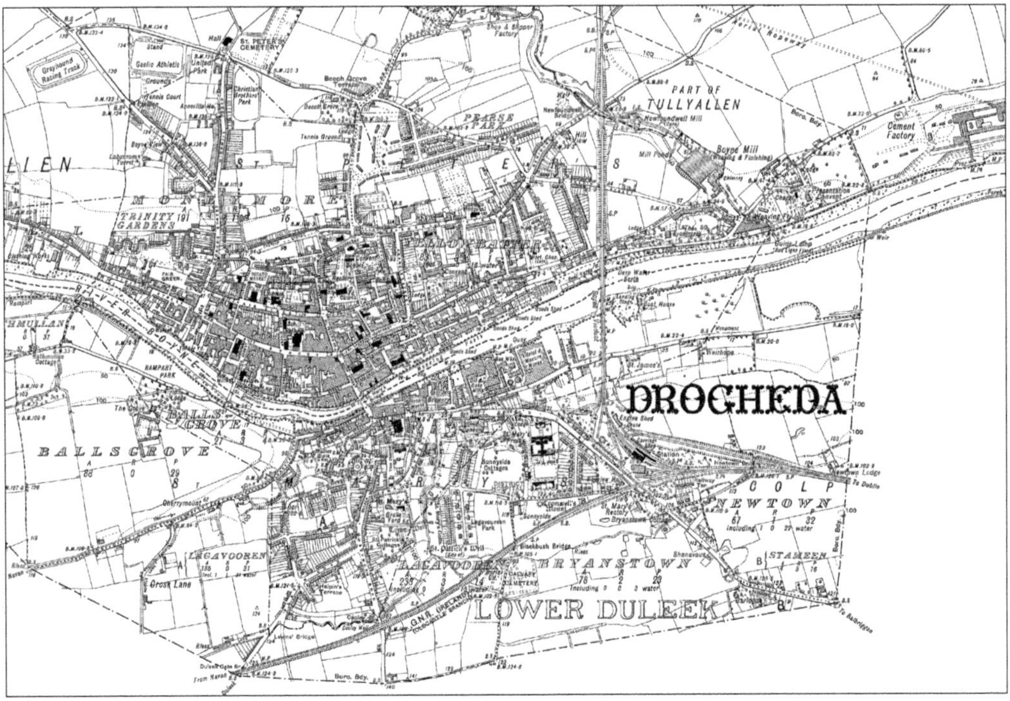

1948 Ordnance Survey map of Drogheda. (Courtesy of Trinity College Dublin Map Library)

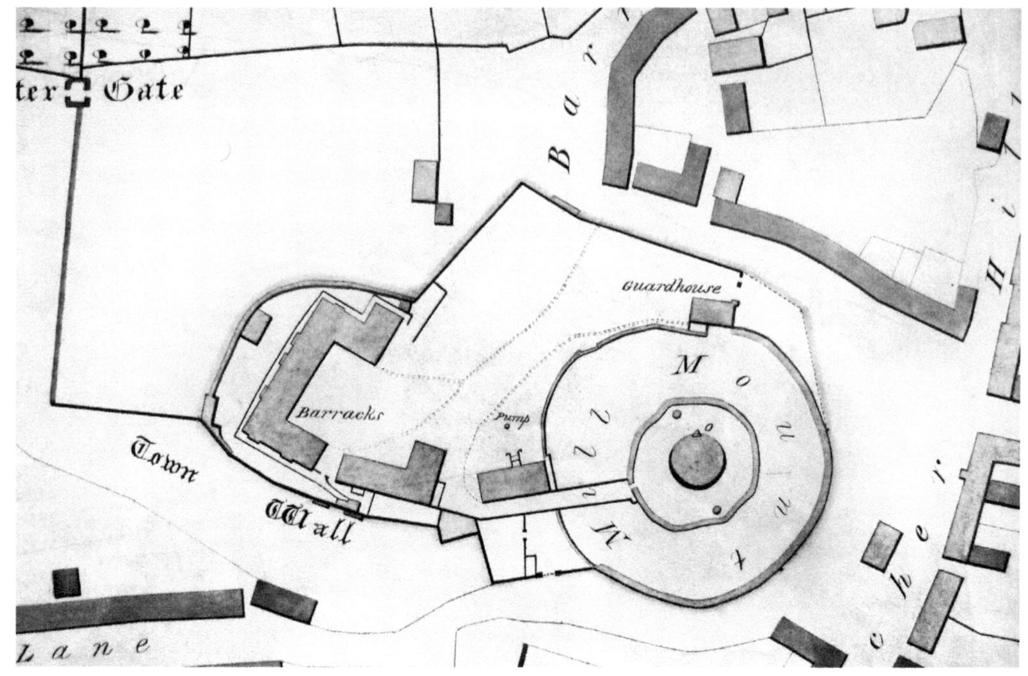

1835 Town Plan showing Millmount. (Courtesy of the National Archives)

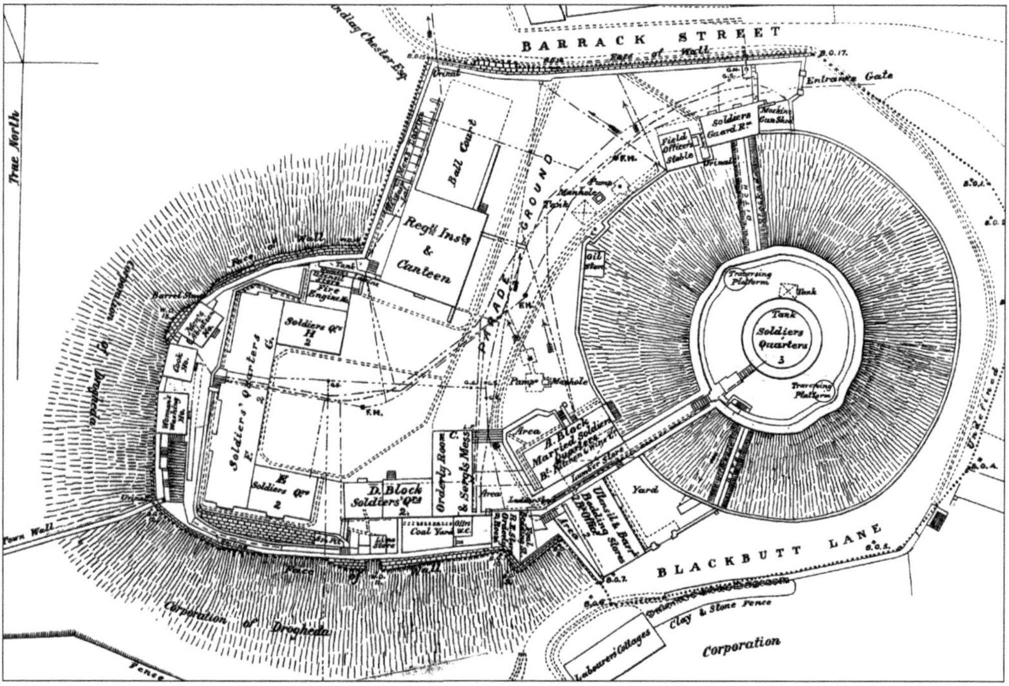

Millmount in 1919. (Courtesy of the Office of Public Works)

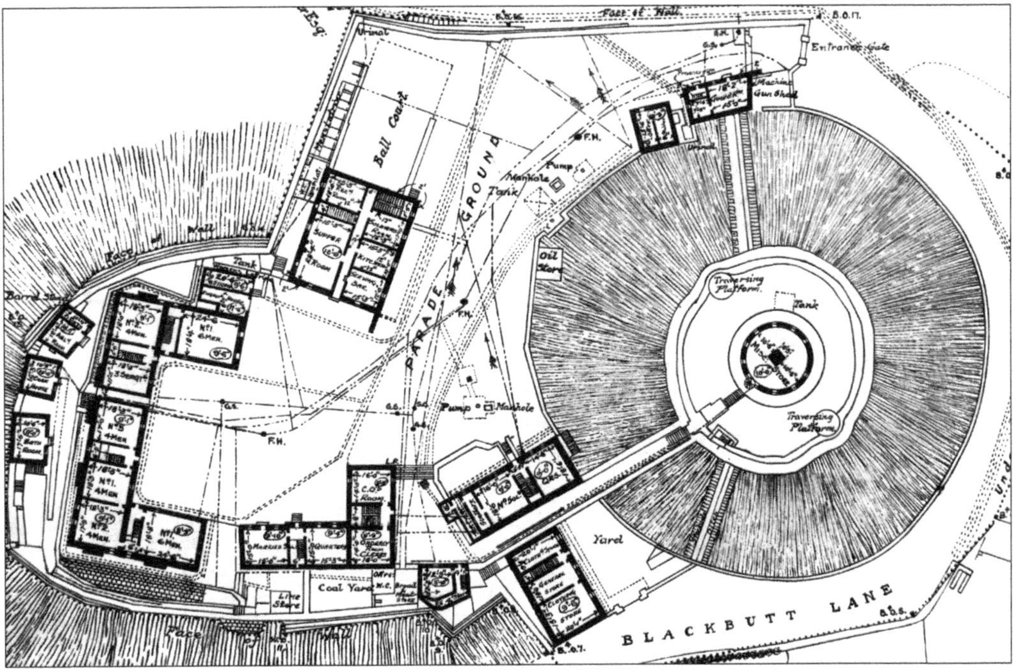

Above Millmount in early 1922.
(Courtesy of the Office of Public
Works)

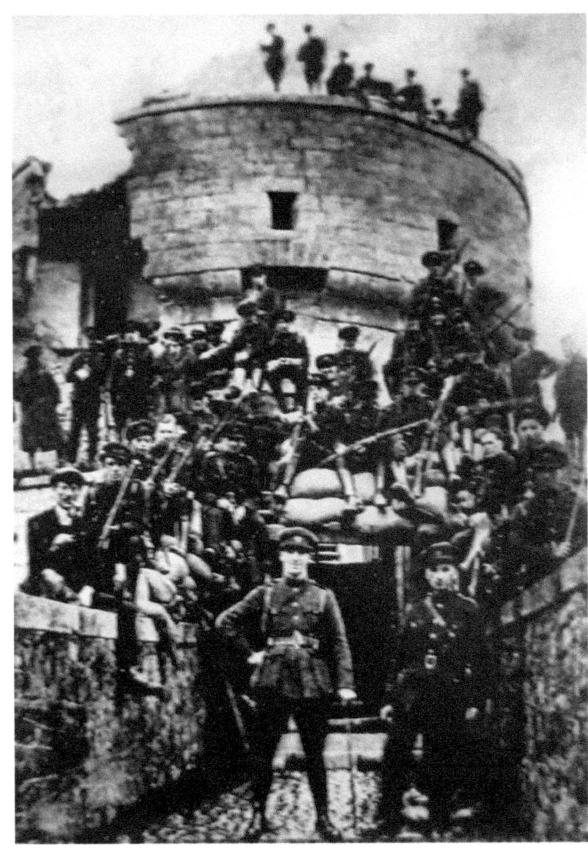

Right Damaged Millmount in
1922, following its re-capture by
Irish Free State soldiers. (Courtesy
of Drogheda Museum Millmount)

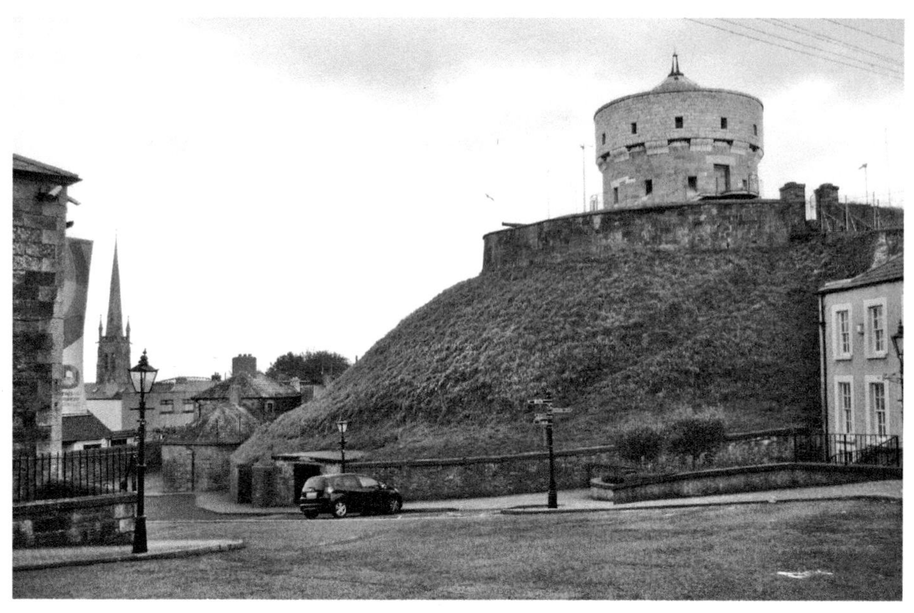

A current view of Millmount, with the side wall of the museum building on the left, part of the former officers' quarters on the right, the former barrack guard house at the base of the hillock, and St Mary's RC church spire in the distance.

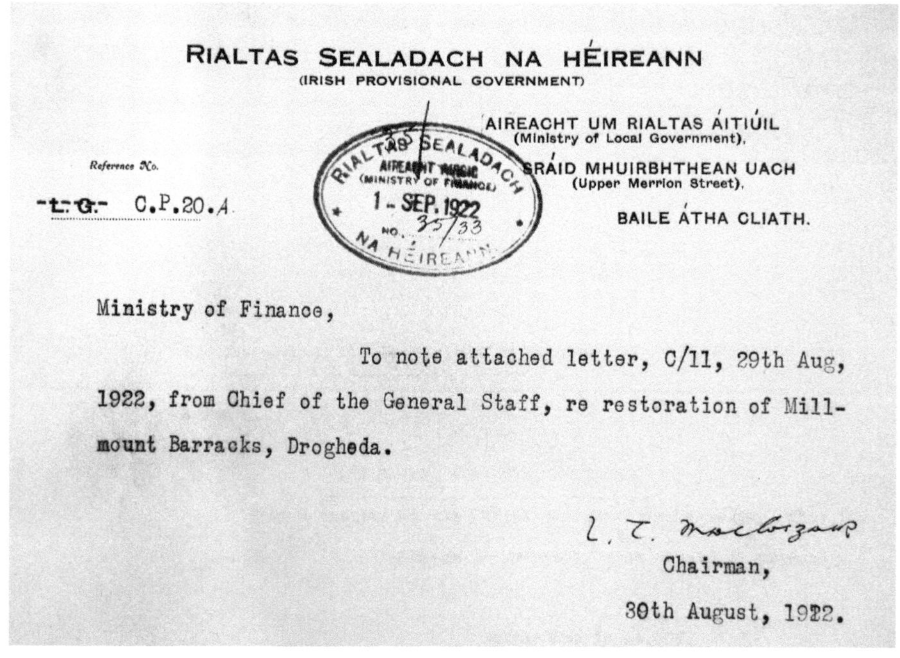

A letter about repairing Millmount after it was shelled in 1922. (Courtesy of the National Archives)

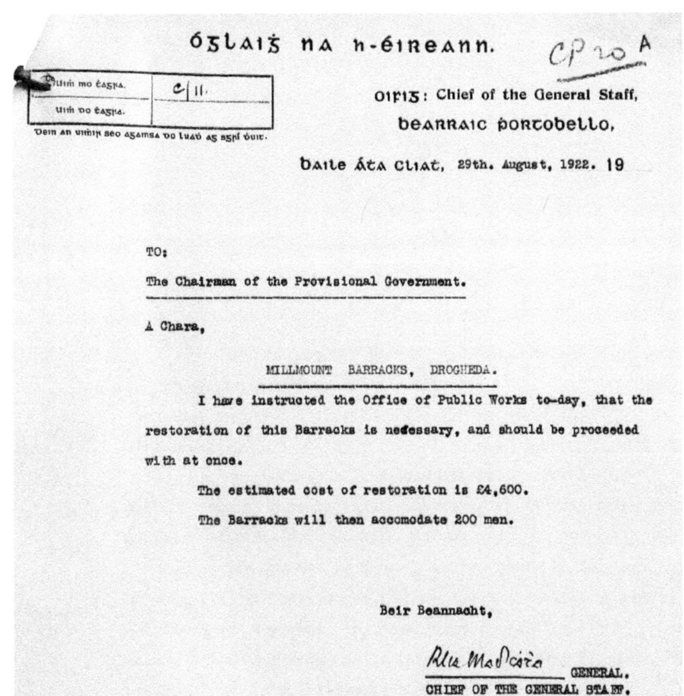

Óglaiġ na h-Éireann.

CP 20 A

Uiṁ mo Ċaṡḱa.   C 11.
Uiṁ do Ċaṡḱa.

Dein an uiṁiṙ seo aġamsa do luaḋ aġ aġḟ ḃuiṫ.

OIFIG: Chief of the General Staff,
bearraic Portobello,

baile Áta Cliat, 29th. August, 1922. 19

TO:

The Chairman of the Provisional Government.
____

A Chara,

        MILLMOUNT BARRACKS, DROGHEDA.
        ____

        I have instructed the Office of Public Works to-day, that the
restoration of this Barracks is necessary, and should be proceeded
with at once.

        The estimated cost of restoration is £4,600.
        The Barracks will then accomodate 200 men.

                    Beir Beannacht,

                    _______________ GENERAL,
                    CHIEF OF THE GENERAL STAFF.

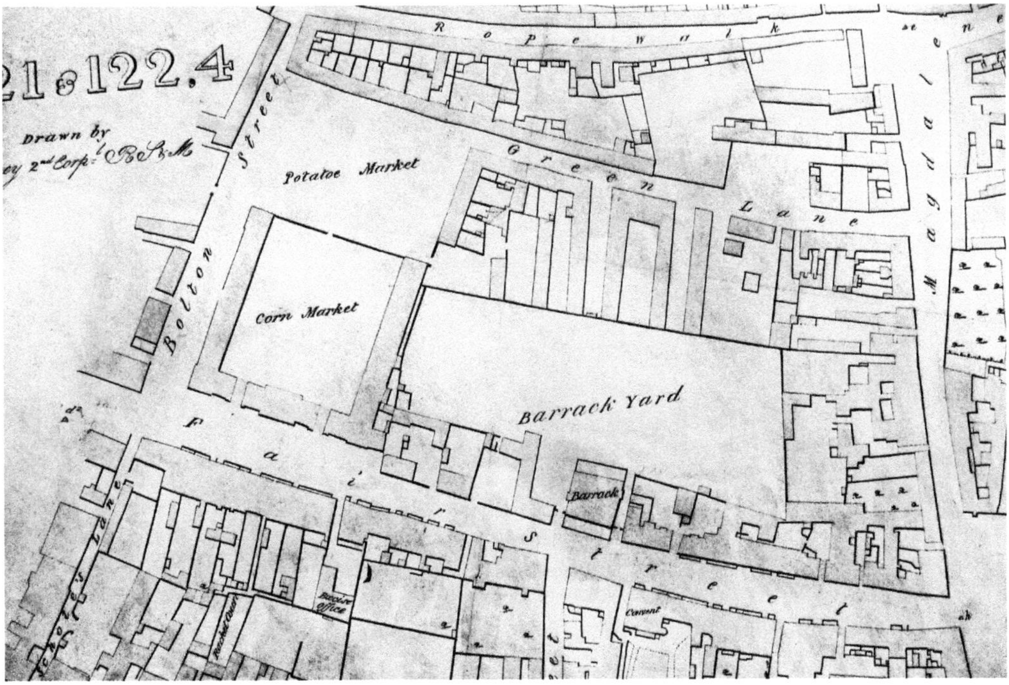

Fair Street Army Barracks in 1836. (Courtesy of the National Archives)

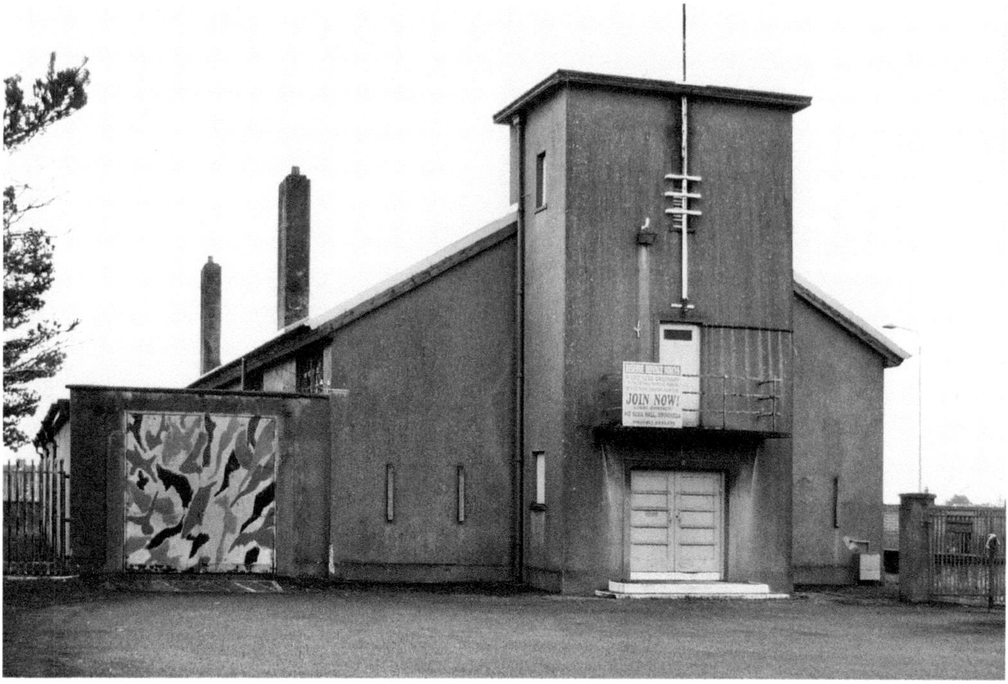

Sluagh Hall, west of St Peter's cemetery, was used by the FCA/Army Reserve Force.

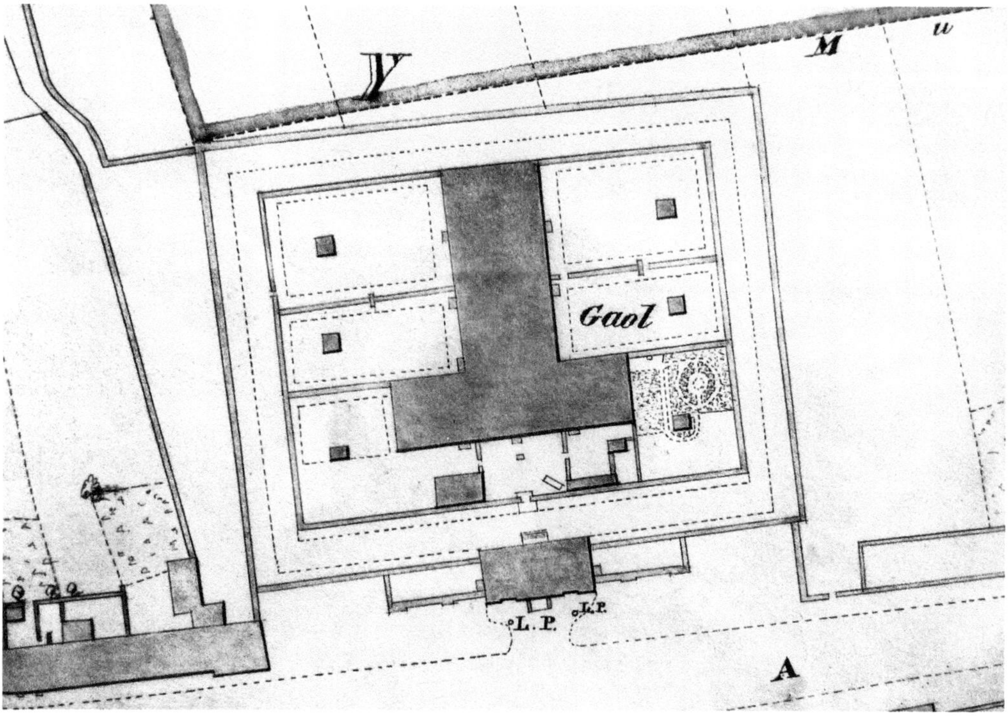

The gaol in Scarlett Street in 1836. (Courtesy of the National Archives)

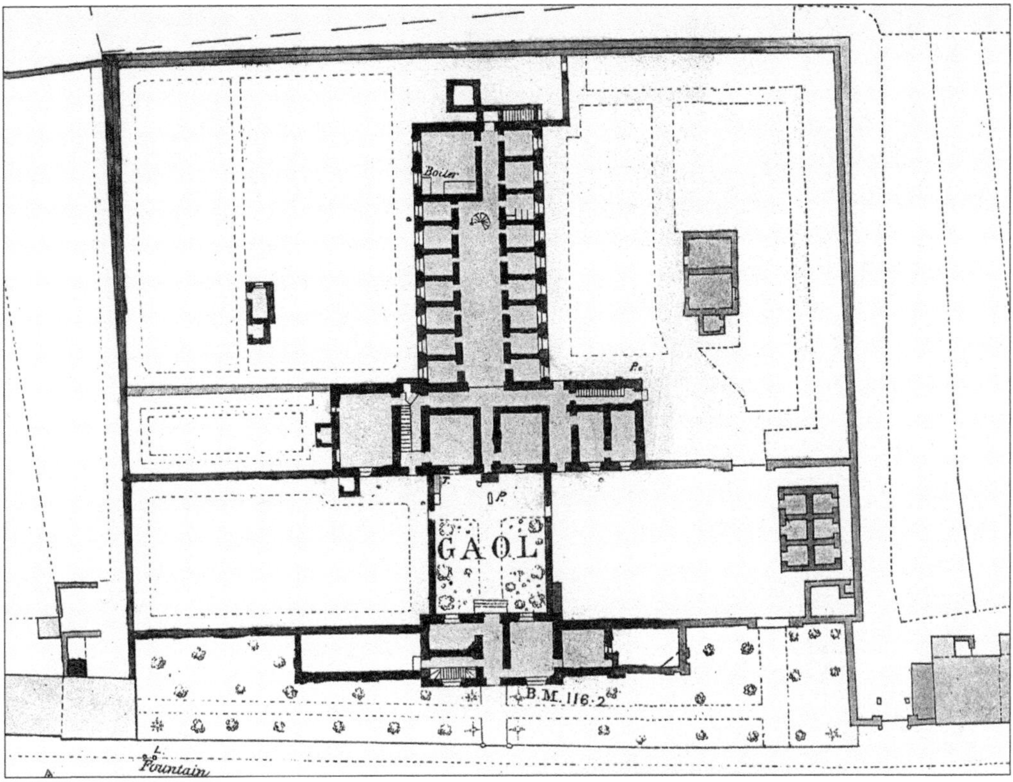

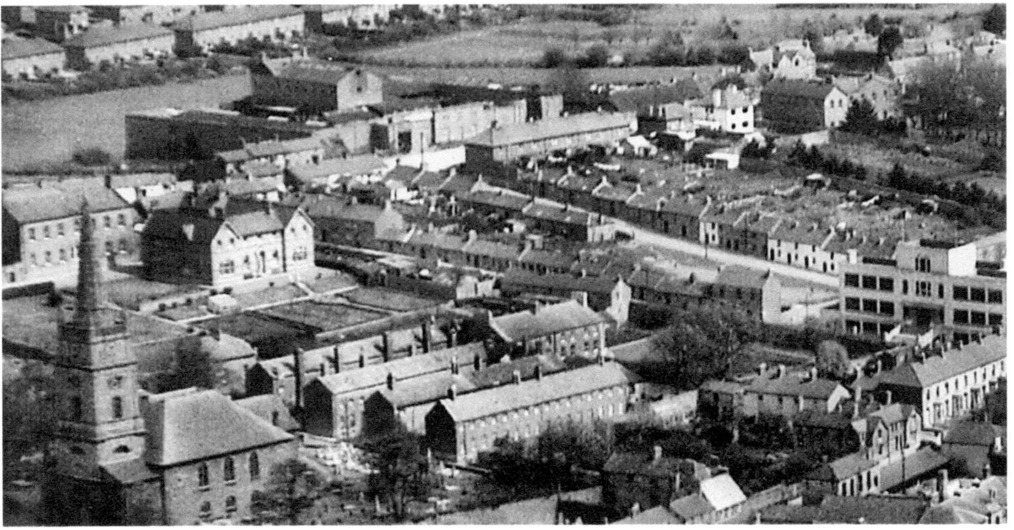

The gaol in Scarlett Street in 1870. (Courtesy of Trinity College Dublin Map Library)

1950s aerial photo, with the former gaol at the top, showing that the main cell block was three or four storeys high. St Peter's church is at bottom left, with The Alleys alongside, and the CBS monastery behind these almshouses. Eddie's Hardware now occupies the gaol site. (Courtesy of the National Library, Independent Collection)

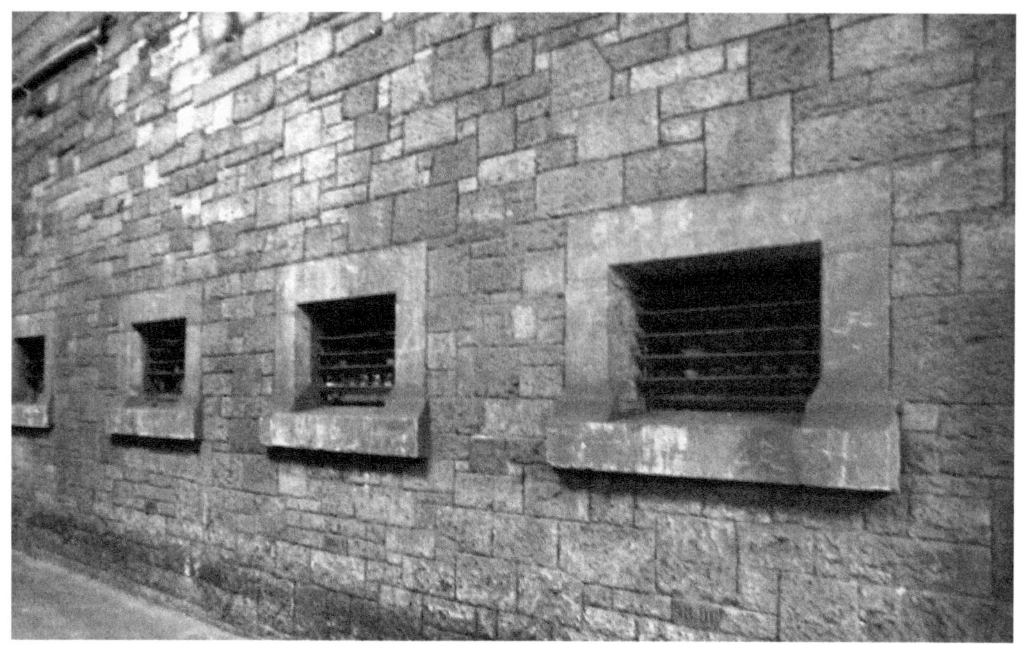

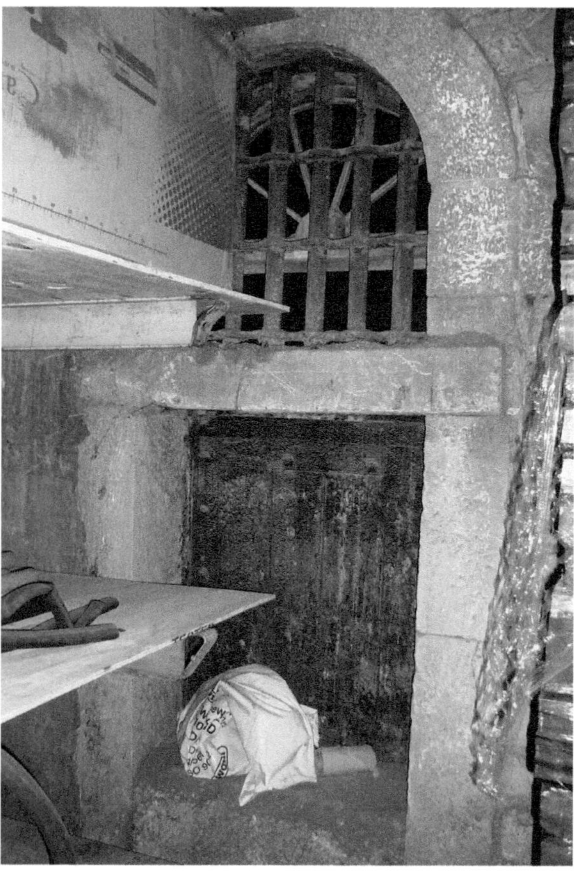

Above Parts of the former gaol are still visible inside Eddie's Hardware.

Left Another remnant of the gaol inside Eddie's Hardware.

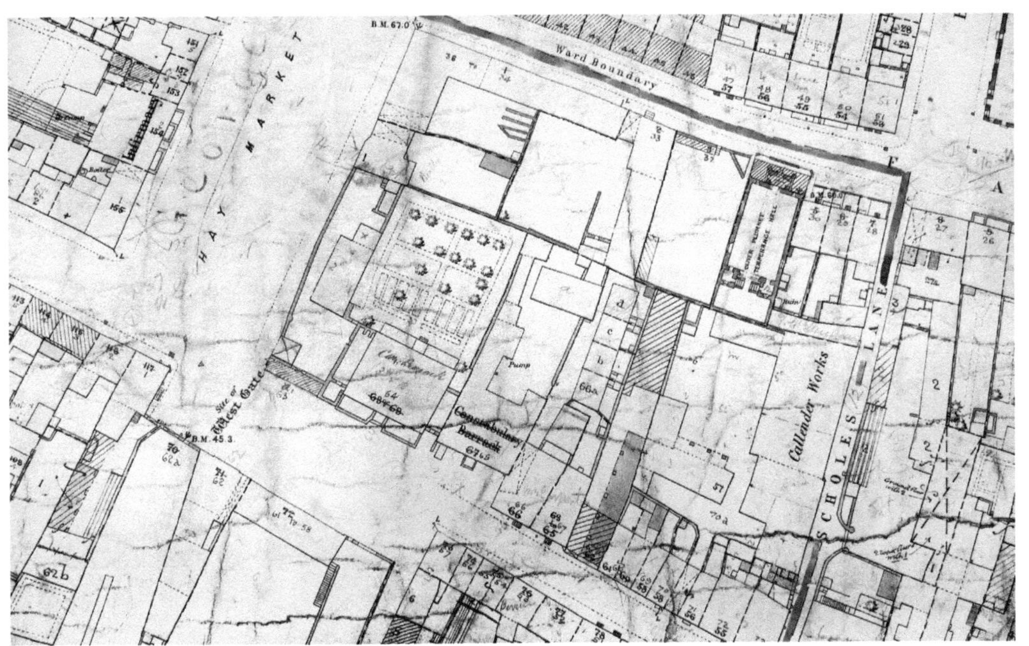

West Street, showing Marlow House. The building on its right was originally the Constabulary Barracks. Note St Mark's church in Fair Street visible at the top right. (Courtesy of the Valuation Office)

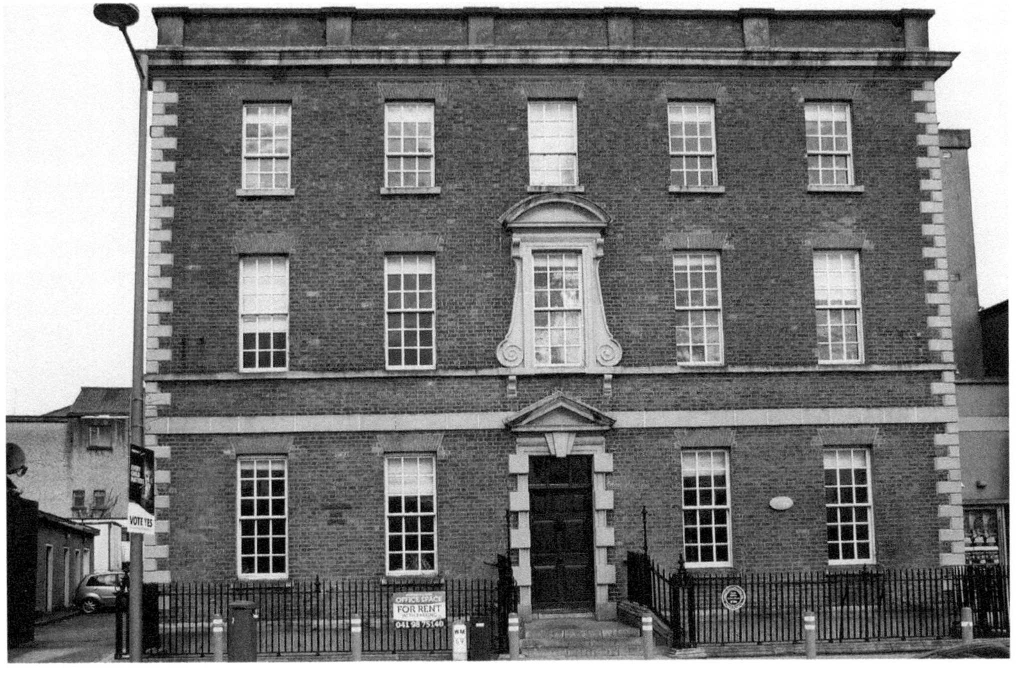

The red-brick Marlow House became the RIC Barracks, and then a Garda station. It is now used by Droichead Arts Centre.

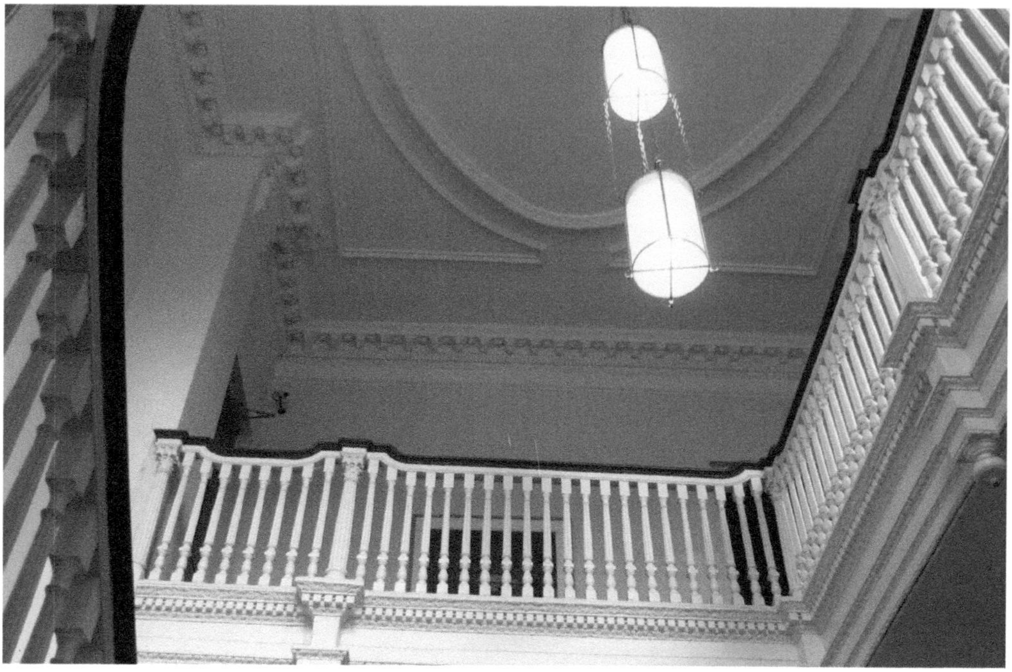

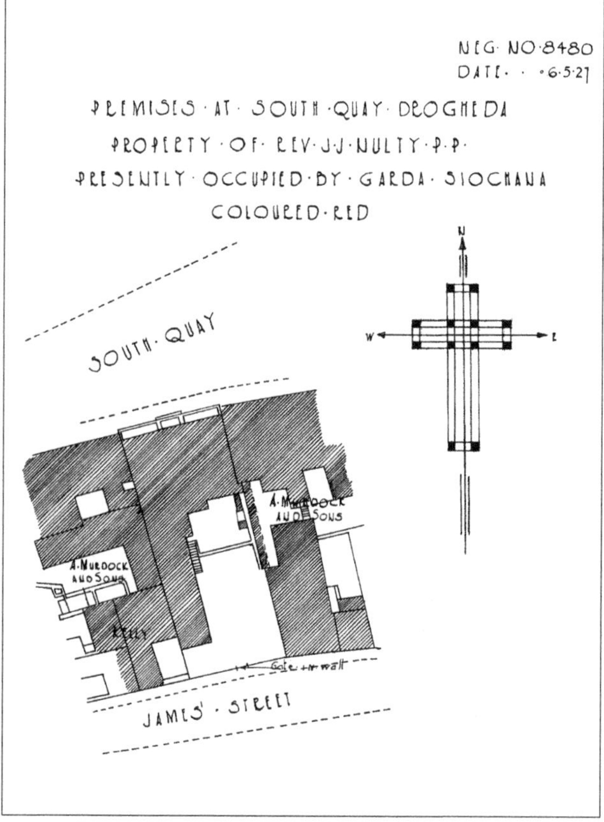

Above The grand staircase in Droichead Arts Centre/Marlow House.

Left A map showing the former RIC Barracks/Garda Station on South Quay, with Murdocks on both sides. (Courtesy of Office of Public Works)

The 1770 Tholsel (Town Hall) is
now the Tourist Office.

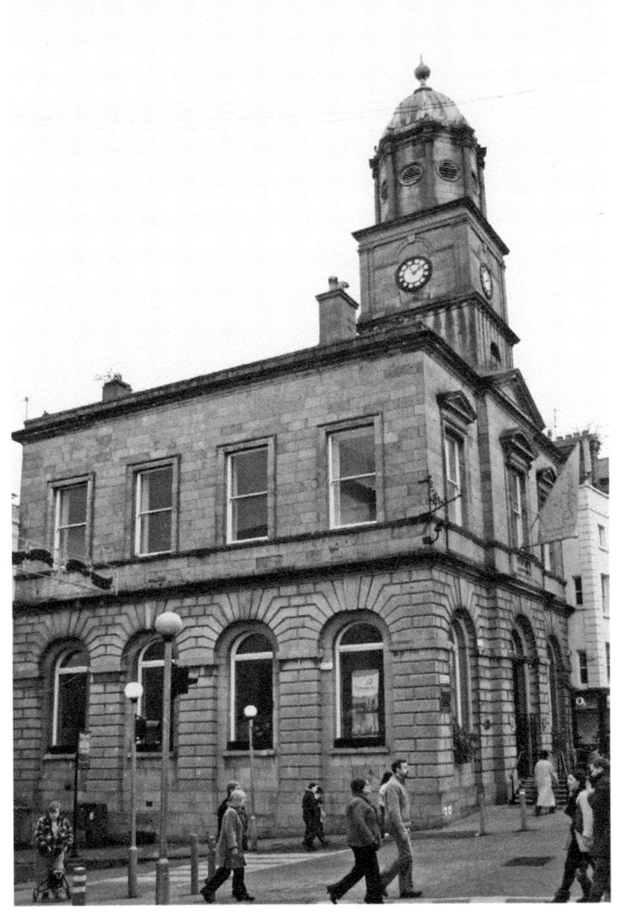

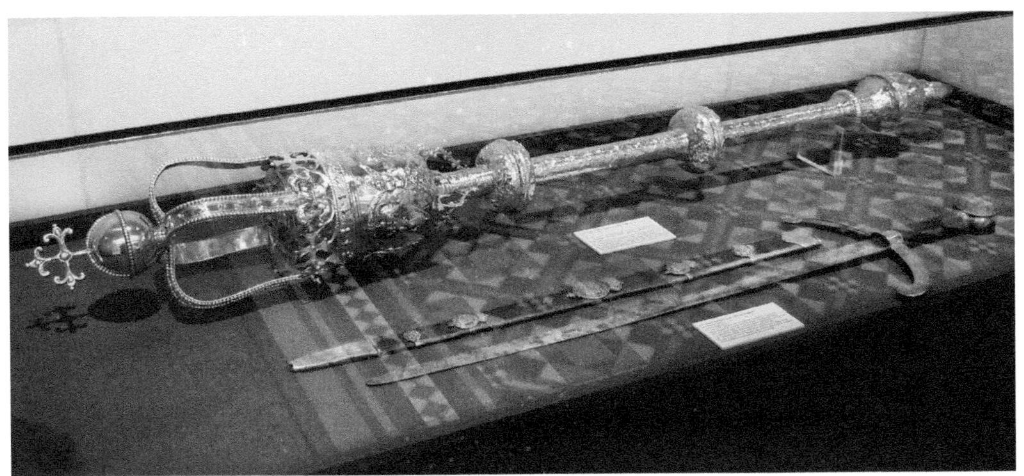

The ceremonial mace and sword of state given to the Corporation of Drogheda by King
William III, shortly after the Battle of the Boyne in 1691. The mace is of solid silver and weighs
nearly 7 pounds.

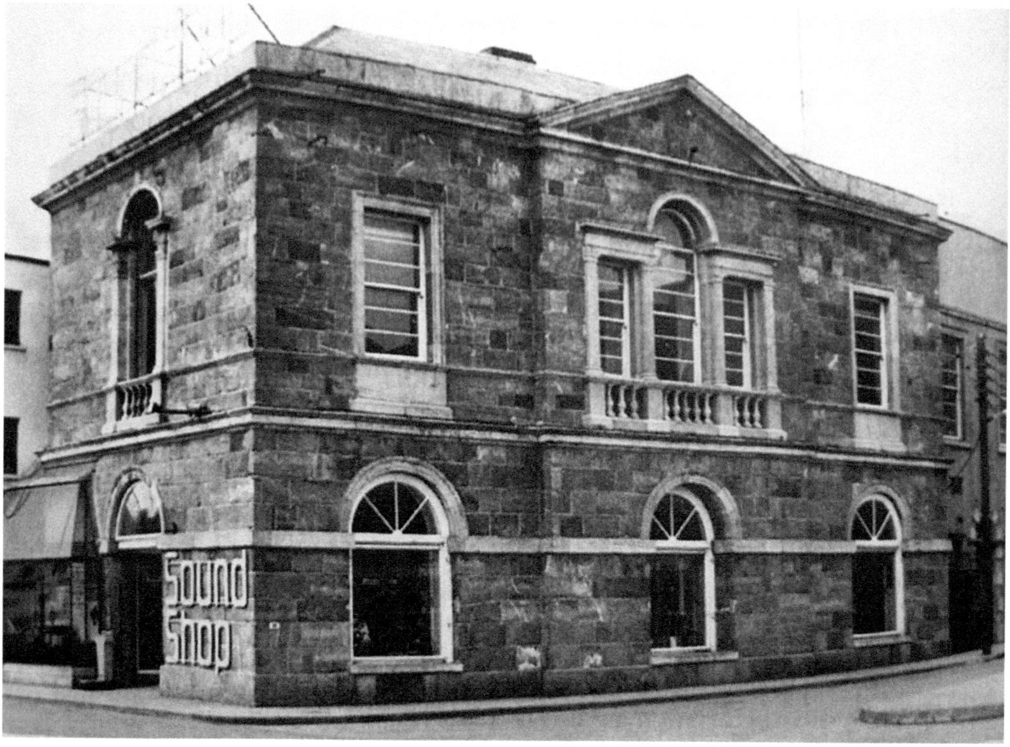

Above Mayoralty
House in the
mid-1980s.
(Courtesy of An
Foras Forbartha)

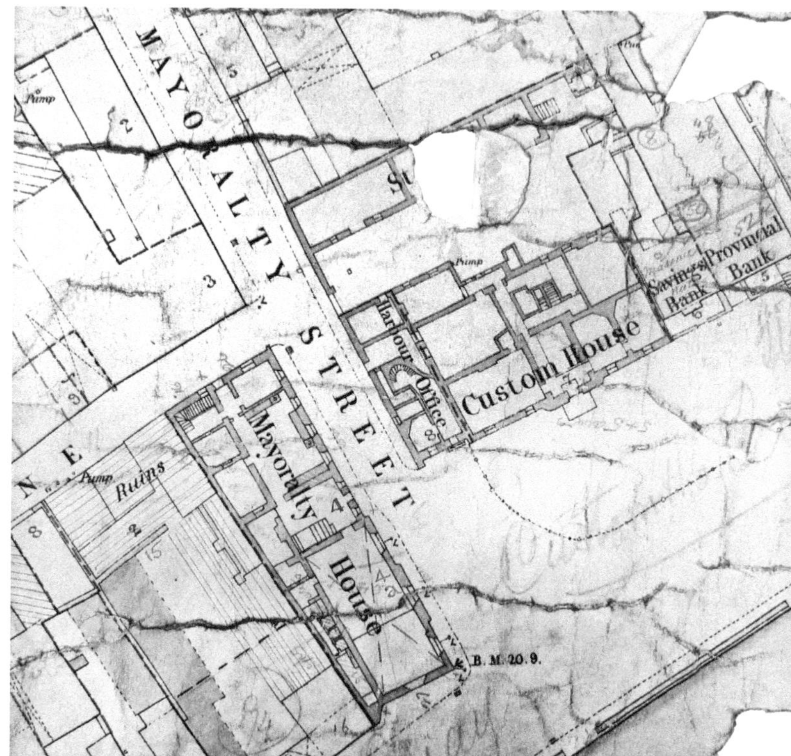

Right The Mall in the
nineteenth century.
(Courtesy of the
Valuation Office)

26

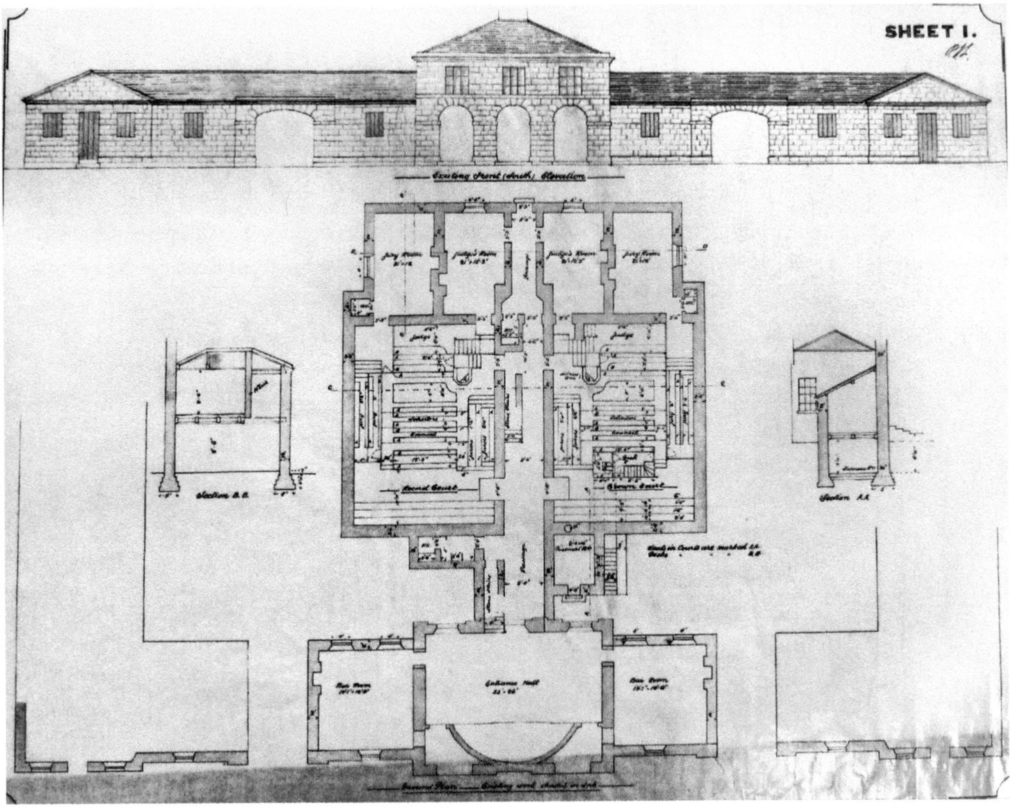

Above Courthouse, Fair Street, contained the Record Court, Crown Court, and barristers' rooms at front, with judges and jury rooms at rear. (Courtesy of the National Archives)

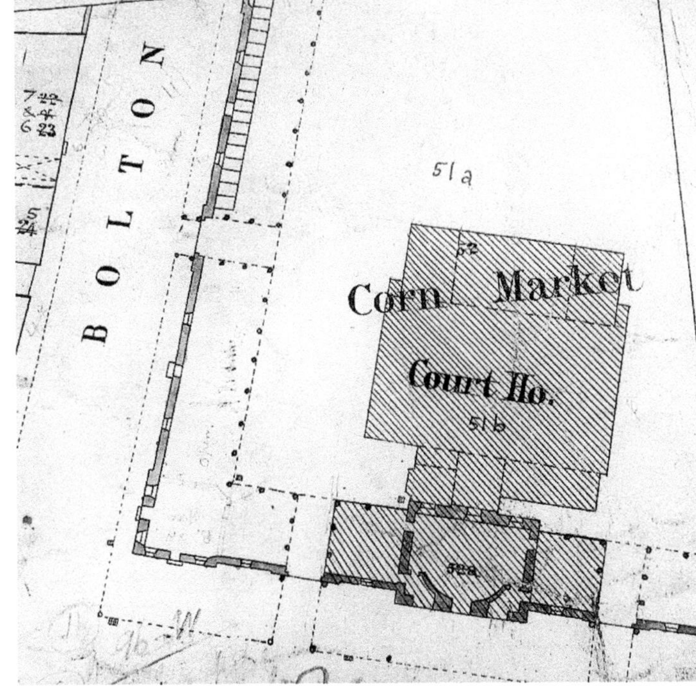

Right Courthouse, Fair Street. (Courtesy of the Valuation Office)

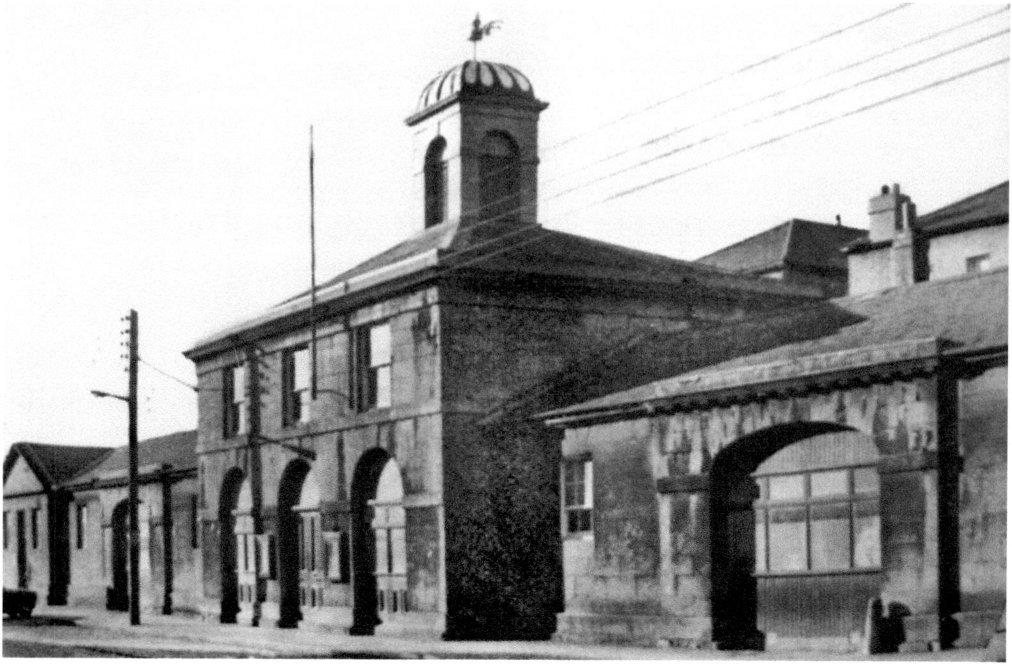

The Courthouse in the mid-1980s. Note the higher Courts building to the rear, which was demolished in recent decades. (Courtesy of An Foras Forbartha)

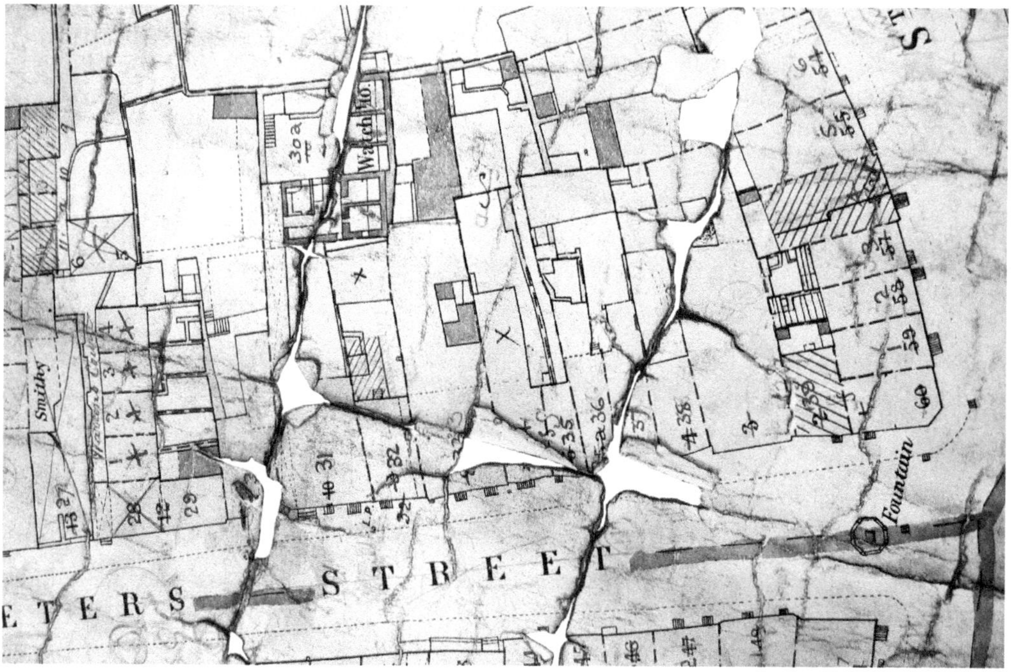

The Watch House, at the rear of No 32 St Peter's Street. Note the Whitworth Fountain in the centre of the road, lower right. (Courtesy of the Valuation Office)

2

RIVER BOYNE

SHIPPING

The Drogheda Steam Packet Co. service to Liverpool started in 1826 as the Drogheda Paddle Steamship Co. They were taken over by the Lancashire & Yorkshire Railway Co. in 1902, who in turn were taken over by the British & Irish Steam Packet Co. (B & I).

The census of 1901 recorded nine schooners/steamers on Steam Packet Quay, the largest being 440 tons: *Jessie, Kathleen Mavourneen, Tredagh, The Brothers, Givalia, Drogheda, Emerald Isle, Norah Creina, Porpoise*. Four schooners were moored at South Quay, all under 100 tons: *Elizabeth Conway, Cintra, Hope, Diudlm*.

In the 1911 census, only four small ships were docked: *Elizabeth Worthington, Downshire, Mary, Jubilee*.

In 1997, the Drogheda Harbour Commissioners were replaced by the Drogheda Port Co., a semi-State company.

BOYNE VIADUCT

In 1844, the railway service between Dublin and Drogheda opened, terminating at a station on the south bank of the River Boyne. The service from Belfast commenced in 1849, and the train terminated on the north bank at Newfoundwell. This meant that connecting passengers had to walk or take a cab between the two stations. The present station building is not on the original site, and dates from the mid-1870s.

The 1,760 foot long viaduct, linking the two railway stations, was completed in 1855. It was conceived by Irish engineer Sir John McNeill, but actually designed and built by James Barton, the Company Engineer for the Great Northern Railway Co. In 1932 the Motherwell Co. of Glasgow replaced the central wrought-iron lattice girders with a segmental profile for the middle one, and reduced it to single-line traffic. The bridge is 90 feet above high tide, with a centre span of 267 feet, and two side spans of 141 feet each. There are twelve semi-circular limestone arches on the south side, and three arches on the north side, each with a 60 feet span. All the piers are built of limestone.

BRIDGES

St Mary's Bridge was first built, in 1722, with three arches, but was then rebuilt in 1867 with only two stone arches. The present reinforced-concrete bridge dates from 1984. St Dominic's Bridge dates from 1863, but was closed to vehicles in 1872. The Boyne Bridge (by-pass) opened in 1976, and is also known as the Bridge of Peace. The enormous cable-stayed bridge on the new M1 motorway opened in 2003. The newest bridge in Drogheda is the De Lacy pedestrian bridge from North Quay to the South Quay, which opened in 2005.

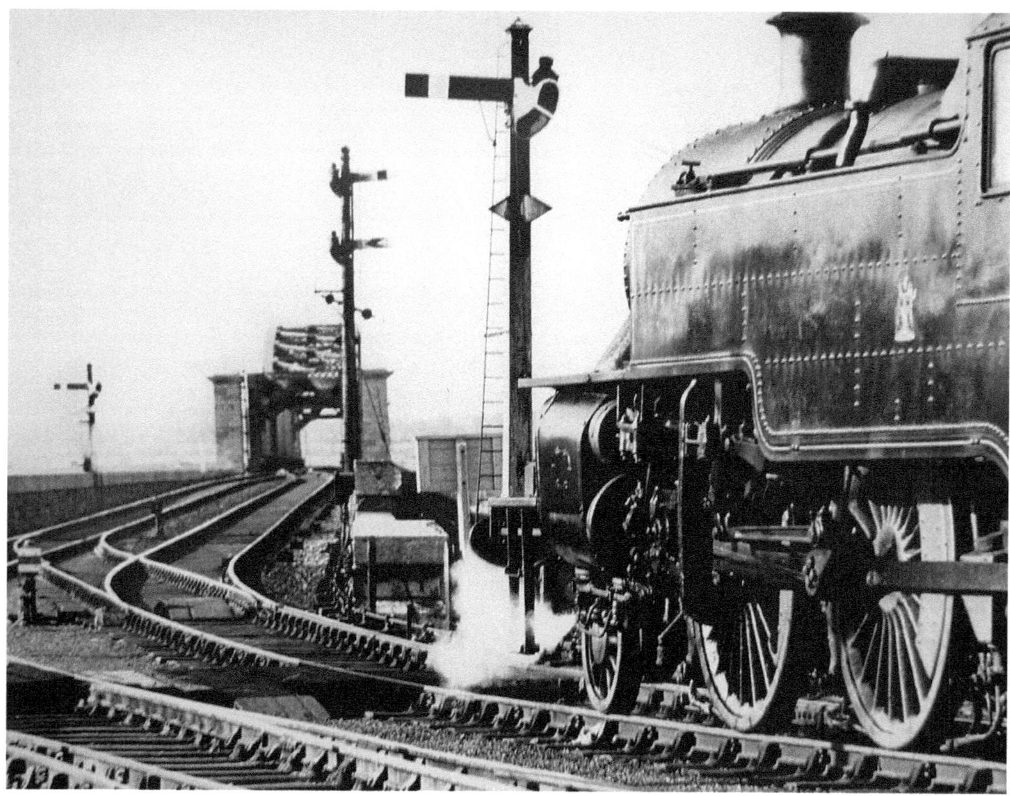

NCC Tank locomotive with the Boyne Viaduct in the background, in 1963. (Courtesy of Irish Rail)

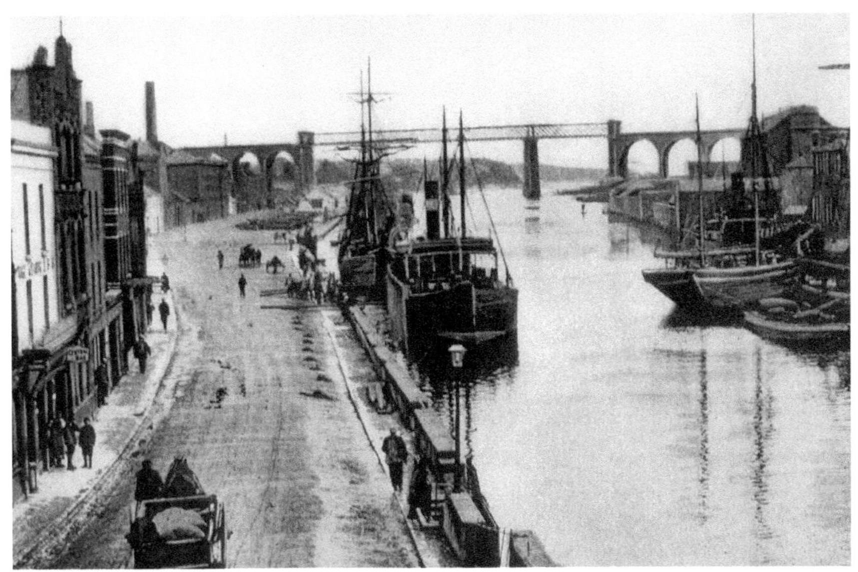

A postcard of the River Boyne from early 1900s. (Courtesy of Drogheda Port Co.)

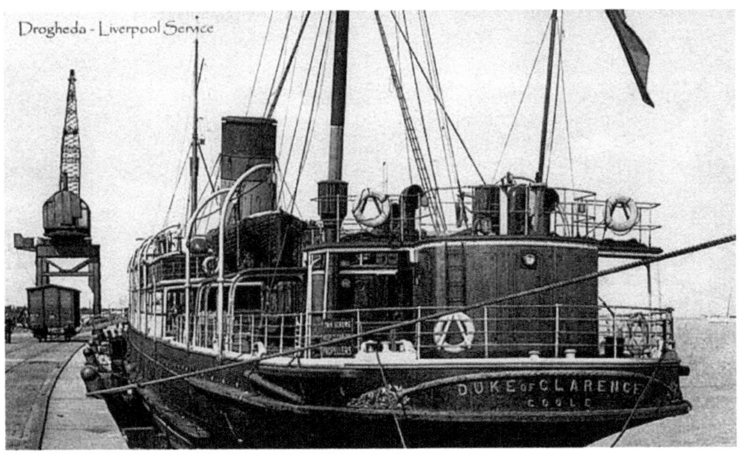

Duke of Clarence, probably in the mid-twentieth century. (Postcard courtesy of Drogheda Port Co.)

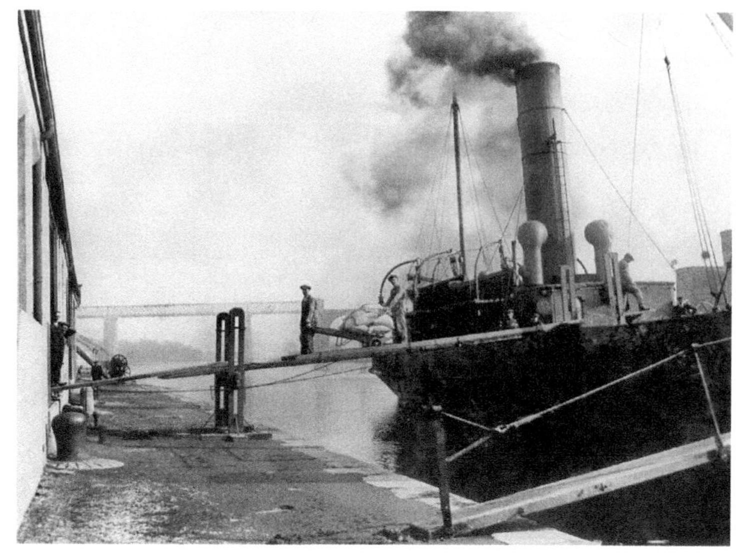

Outside McGettricks' warehouse on the North Quays in the 1920s. (Courtesy of Drogheda Port Co./Ester McDonell)

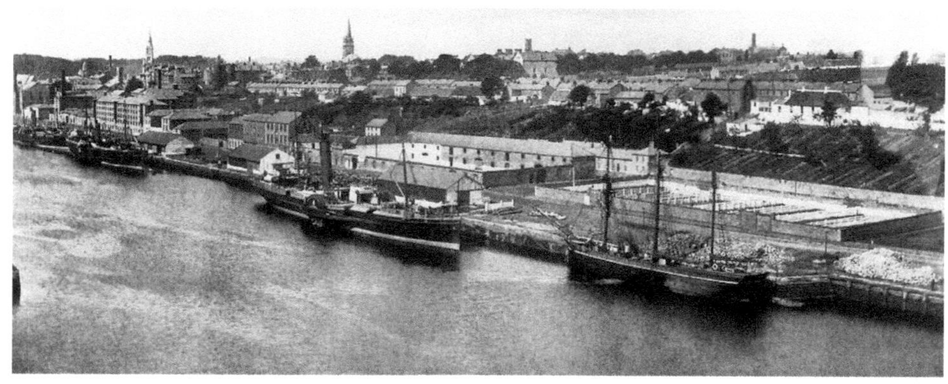

Paddle steamers and sailing ships at Steam Packet Quay. (Courtesy of Drogheda Port Co.)

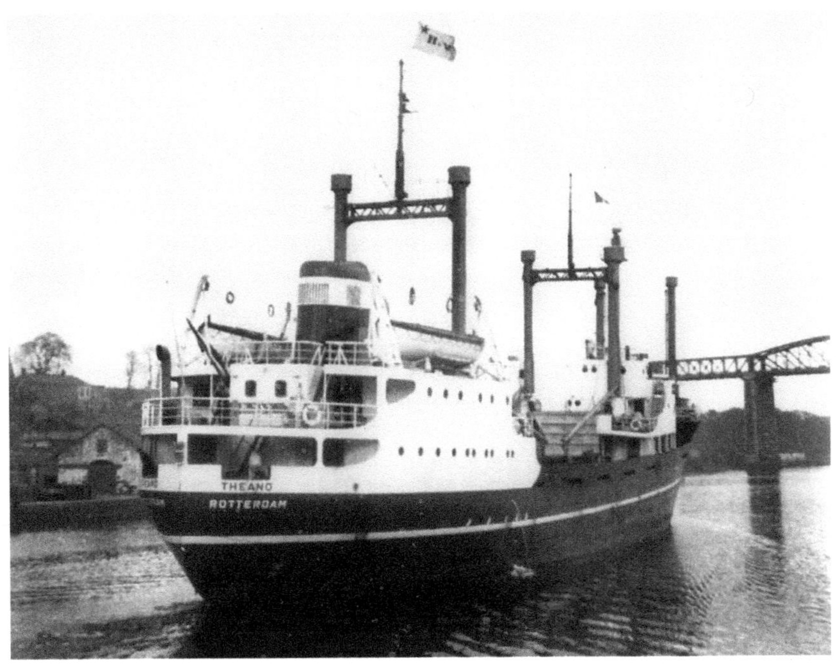

MV *Theano* leaving for Rotterdam. (Courtesy of Drogheda Port Co.)

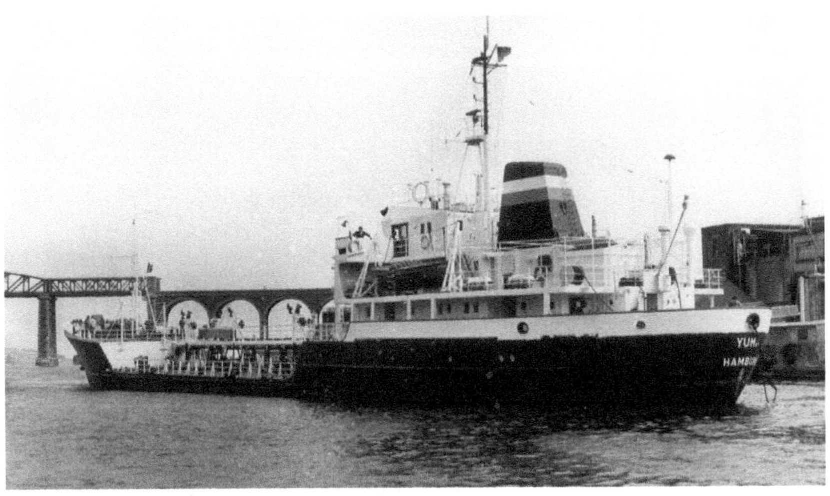

MV *Yuma* leaving Knaggs Head in the 1970s. (Courtesy of Drogheda Port Co.)

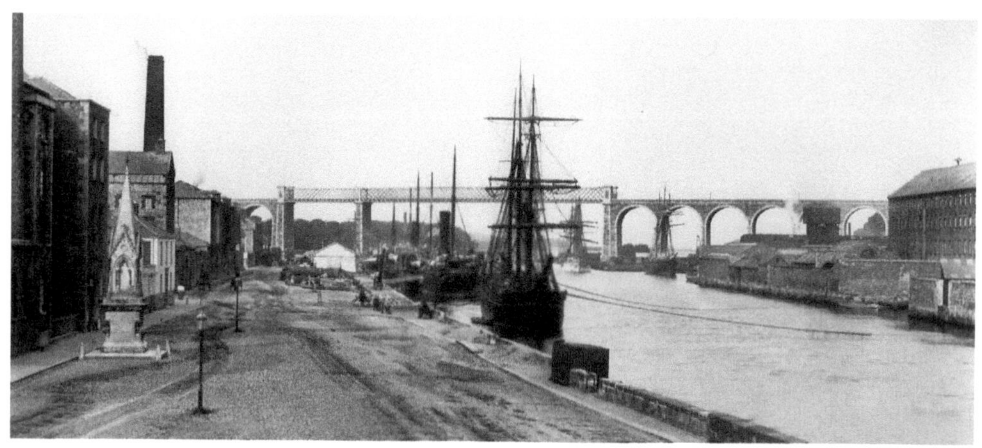

An early twentieth-century view of the Boyne Viaduct. Note the Whitworth Fountain on left. (Courtesy of Drogheda Port Co.)

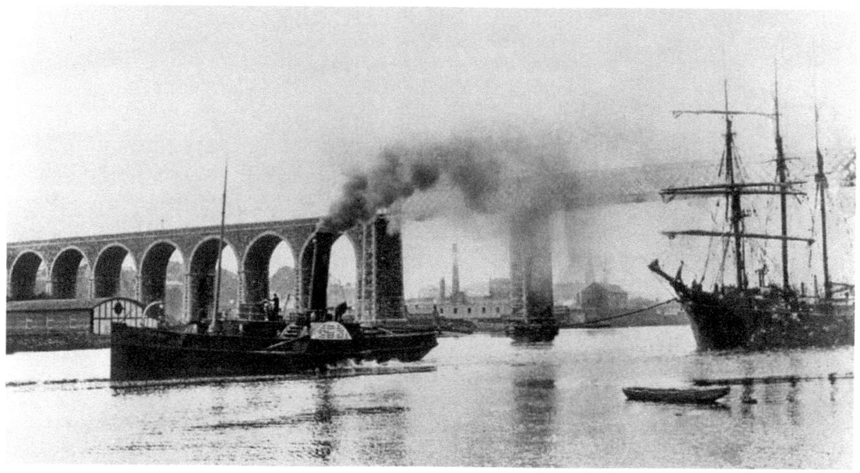

Tug boat *Drogheda* pulling a sailing ship. (Courtesy of Drogheda Port Co.)

3

RELIGION

ST PETER'S RC CHURCH, WEST STREET

St Peter's dates from 1791, and was designed by the famous architect Francis Johnston. Major alterations and additions were carried out by architects O'Neill & Byrne in the 1880s – the south part in 1884, the north part in 1891 – although most of the nave was retained. The 222 foot tower and spire contains a set of ten bells, sadly never rung nowadays.

Oliver Plunkett, Archbishop of Armagh, was executed at Tyburn in London in 1681. After the hanging, his head was smuggled to Rome, and the rest of his body was smuggled to Lamspringe in Lower Saxony, Germany, and then back to the Benedictine abbey at Downside, Somerset, in 1881, where it rests today. The head stayed in Rome for about fifty years, before being moved to the Siena Convent in Dyer Street, Drogheda, in the 1730s, and then to the new convent in Cord Road. On the instructions of Cardinal Logue, the head was given by the nuns to St Peter's church in 1920, in exchange for one of Oliver Plunkett's ribs, which the nuns still possess to this day. Oliver was canonised a saint in 1975, and his head was positioned on the altar in Killineer in 1979, during the Pope's visit to Drogheda. A new free-standing shrine of St Oliver Plunkett's head in St Peter's was opened in 1995.

ST MARY'S RC CHURCH

The original church was built in 1820 on the site of the former gaol, and set well back from the road. The present church, designed by local architect P.J. Dodd, was consecrated in 1884, with the tower and spire added in 1892, and finally completed inside in the 1890s. It contains a lot of stained glass by Meyer of Munich, and Lobin of Tours (France). The 1911 apse mosaics are the work of Oppenheimer of Dublin.

The lovely presbytery on the hill above the church was bought in 1889, and uses the same yellow Glasgow brick as nearby St Mary's Convent Boys National School (Mercy nuns).

ST MAGDALEN'S PRIORY, DOMINICK STREET

This small and cosy church, with a nice apse and stained-glass windows, dates from 1882, and was designed by George Coleman Ashlin. Prior to that, the Dominican friar's chapel was roughly on the site of the present monastery, but hidden behind street properties. The Dominicans also built the fourteenth-century Magdalene tower and belfry, still standing on Upper Magdalene Street. This latter structure is also called Sunday Steeple, because of the nearby town gate, which was free of levies or taxes on Sundays.

ST AUGUSTINE'S, SHOP STREET

This attractive Dominican church, designed by Michael Moran, was dedicated in 1866. The spire originally intended for the south-west tower was omitted because of concerns about the foundations. The north-west stained-glass window is the work of Harry Clarke, although not one of his finest. The famous 'Penny Bank' was run by the clergy here from 1975 to 2012. The old Abbey of St Mary, in Narrow West Street, was built by the Augustinians in 1206, and some remains are still visible today.

ST FRANCIS' FRIARY, LAURENCE STREET

The monastery and church, designed by J. Butterly, were built on a steeply sloping site in 1830. After being donated to the town in 2000, the public Highlanes Art Gallery opened here in 2006, retaining most of the original building.

OUR LADY OF LOURDES

A chapel-of-ease was built in 1939 at the corner of Hardmans Gardens and Bothar Brugha. The new, bigger church opened nearby in 1959, and the former chapel was demolished in 1962, to make way for a Nurses' Home for the new General Hospital. The stained-glass windows in the new church were donated by parishioners, including two from the workers in the Boyne Mills (Blessed Oliver Plunkett and St Joseph), two from the Presentation Sisters (St Patrick and St Brigid), and one from the workers in Cement Ltd (St Columba).

ST PETER'S C OF I CHURCH

This famous church was built in 1752, to a design by Hugh Darley. In the 1780s, the steeple was replaced by one designed by Francis Johnston. In the tower, there are eight 1791 bells by John Rudhall of Gloucester, England, ranging in weight from 6 to 22 cwt (20 cwt is a ton). The tenor (heaviest) bell was recast in 1889 by Taylor of Loughborough, England, and the other bells were rehung at the same time. The bells were used for 'change ringing' (mathematical patterns) in the past, but not so much nowadays.

Internally, the box pews, which were owned by different families, were replaced by benches in 1865. Besides the beautiful ornate plasterwork around the east chancel, other attractions include the carved stone medieval baptismal font at the rear, and the old 1770 Snetzler organ on the west gallery (although rebuilt to a different design in 1934, with around 1,000 pipes).

After a small fire in 1999, the entire church was restored inside and outside, including a new roof, at a cost of €1m.

The graveyard is famous for two cadaver headstones, which date from 1520, of Sir Edmond Goldyng and his wife Elizabeth Fleming, from Piercetown, Co. Meath. The cemetery is also the burial place of the Moore family (Marquis of Drogheda), and also Lord Chief Justice Singleton, who lived in Laurence Street. A booklet produced in 1913 records that there were five stone slabs built into the cemetery wall, which originally comprised an altar tomb inside the former church on this site.

To the east of Church Lane there are The Alleys, comprising sixteen almshouses built in the early eighteenth century for widows of Protestant clergymen. St John's Home, built in 1816 for the poor, is still outside the church gates.

Nowadays, the church is also used by the St Peter & St Paul Indian Orthodox congregation, for 1.30 p.m. mass on Sundays.

The parish had a chapel-of-ease in Fair Street, called St Mark's, which was built in 1828. Around 1870, it became the Oliver Plunkett Temperance Hall, and later it was converted into the Boyne Cinema (now gone).

ST MARY'S C OF I CHURCH

South of the River Boyne, St Mary's was built in 1807, with the vestry added in 1909. Adjoining the south wall of the church is the Henry Duff headstone from 1610. The church closed in 1998 and became a heritage centre (now also closed). The large surrounding cemetery contains the partial ruins of a Carmelite Monastery, and the south boundary wall of the cemetery is part of the original town wall.

METHODIST CHURCH, ST LAURENCE STREET

This attractive small church was built in 1811 and renovated in 1911. It comprises two storeys, and originally housed a school on the lower floor. Following closure, the building was used in recent years by C. Wilde & Sons, house furnishers. It is now owned by the new shopping centre, but not yet in alternative use.

PRESBYTERIAN CHURCH, PALACE STREET

The Presbyterians arrived with Cromwell in the 1650s. When King James occupied the town, the Presbyterians departed and only a few returned. The present church was built in 1827, to a design by Austin Nicholls. In 2012, the parishioners moved to a brand new church in Colpe Road, and the old church has been acquired by another Christian congregation.

QUAKERS

The Religious Society of Friends (Quakers) are Christians, but do not go in for formal religious services. Many of the businesses in Drogheda have Quaker connections (such as the Allens in Ushers Towel factory). The Drogheda Grammar School is partly run by Quakers, and hence the congregation hold their fortnightly meetings in the new (1976) school in Mornington Road.

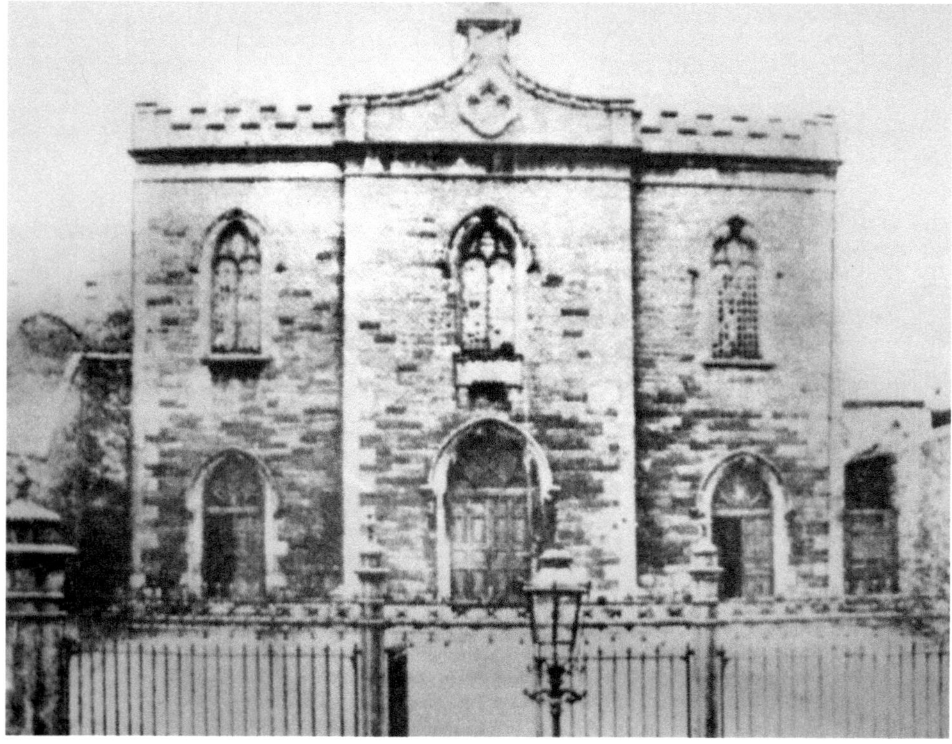

The original St Peter's Catholic church, which was built in 1793. (Courtesy of St Peter's Parish)

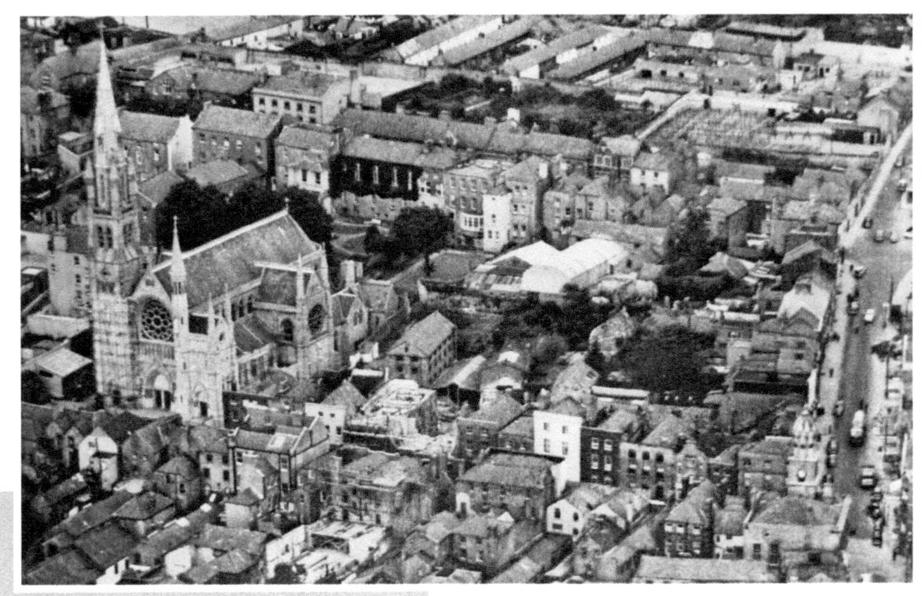

Above An aerial view of St Peter's, West Street, with the Presentation Convent behind. (Courtesy of the Medical Missionaries of Mary)

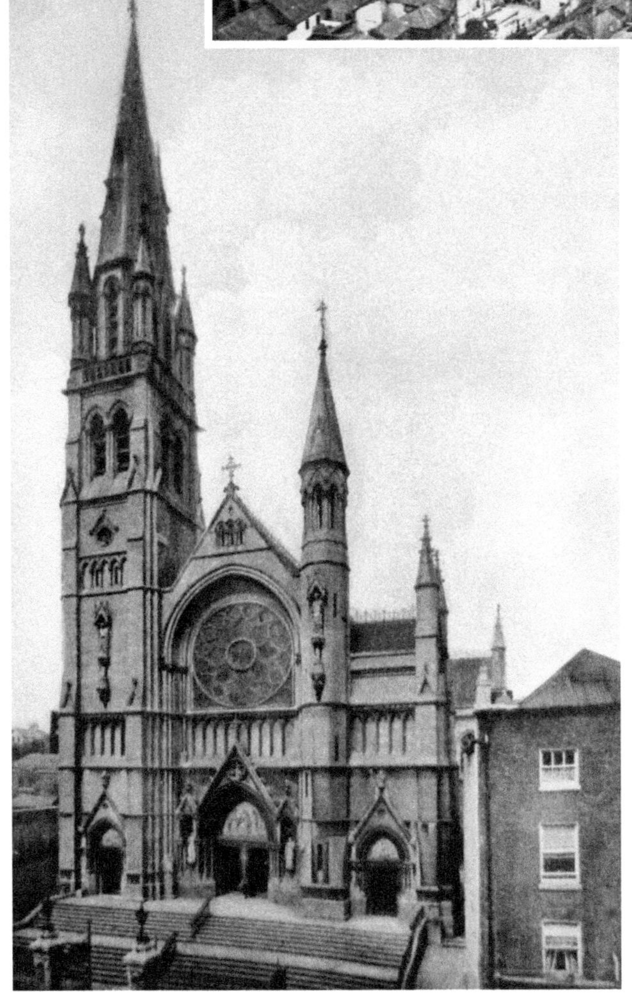

Left St Peter's, West Street. (Courtesy of the Medical Missionaries of Mary)

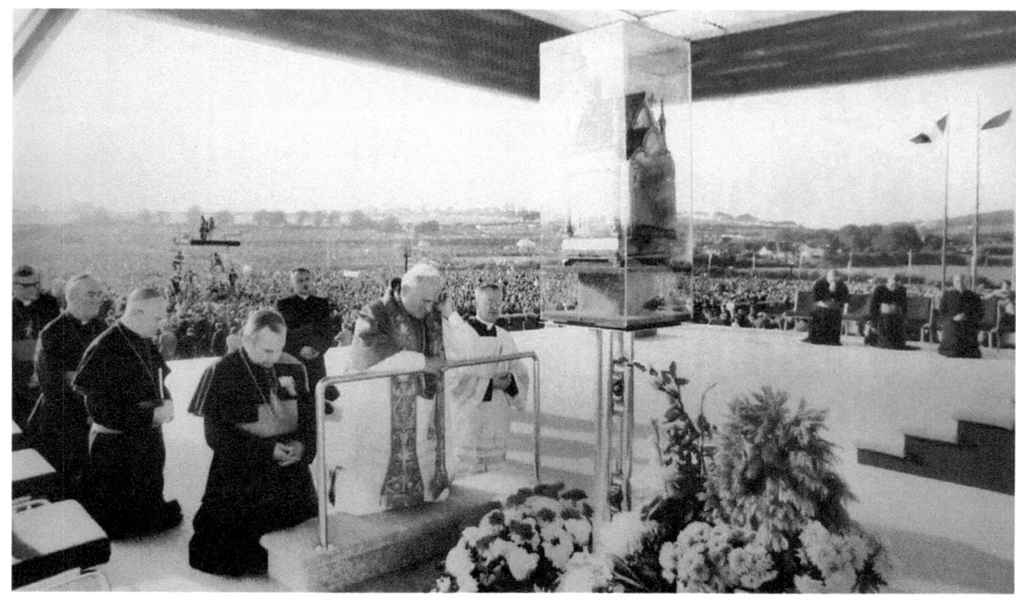

Pope John Paul II in Killineer, Drogheda, 1979. Here he prays at the reliquary of St Oliver Plunkett. (Courtesy of St Peter's Parish)

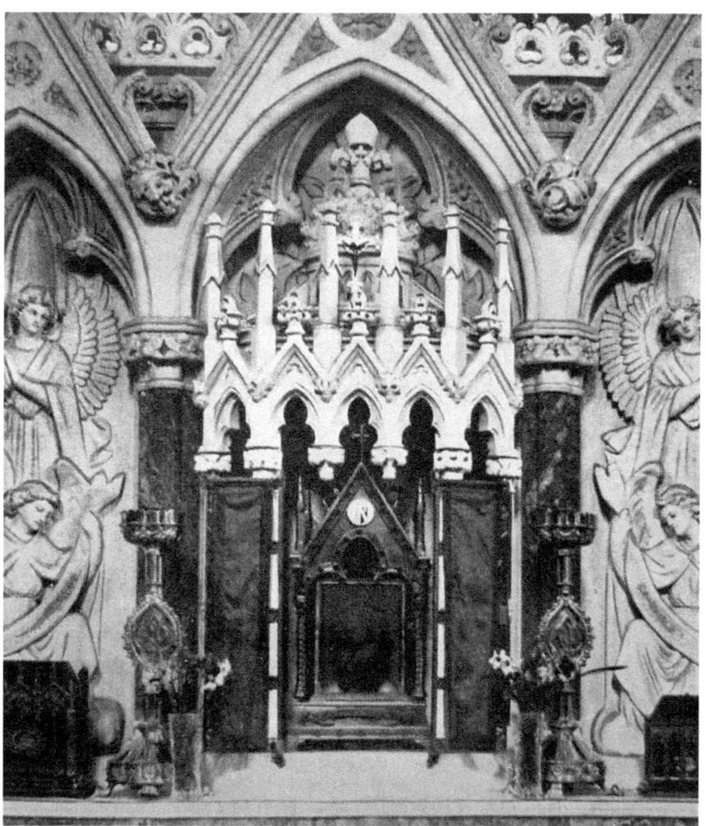

The head of Blessed Oliver Plunkett was originally displayed in the open tabernacle of the side altar in St Peter's church. (Courtesy of the Medical Missionaries of Mary)

Right St Mary's Catholic church.

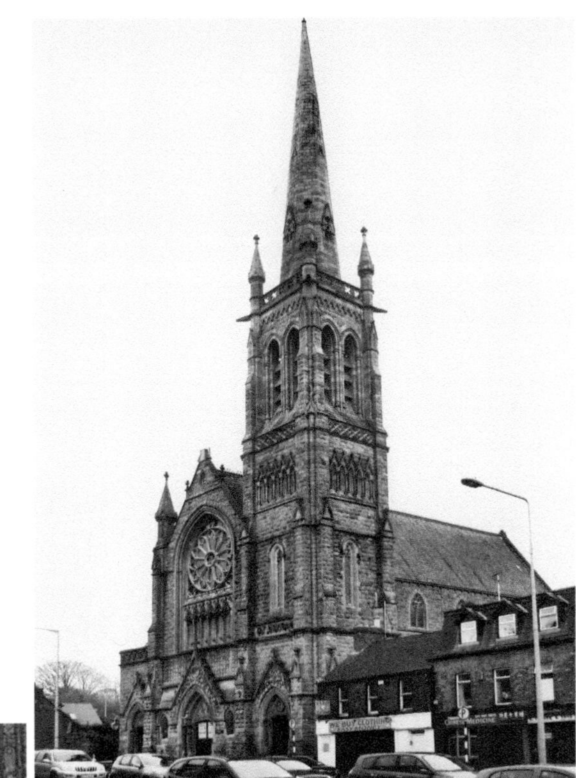

Below St Mary's Catholic church in 1934. (Courtesy of John McCullen)

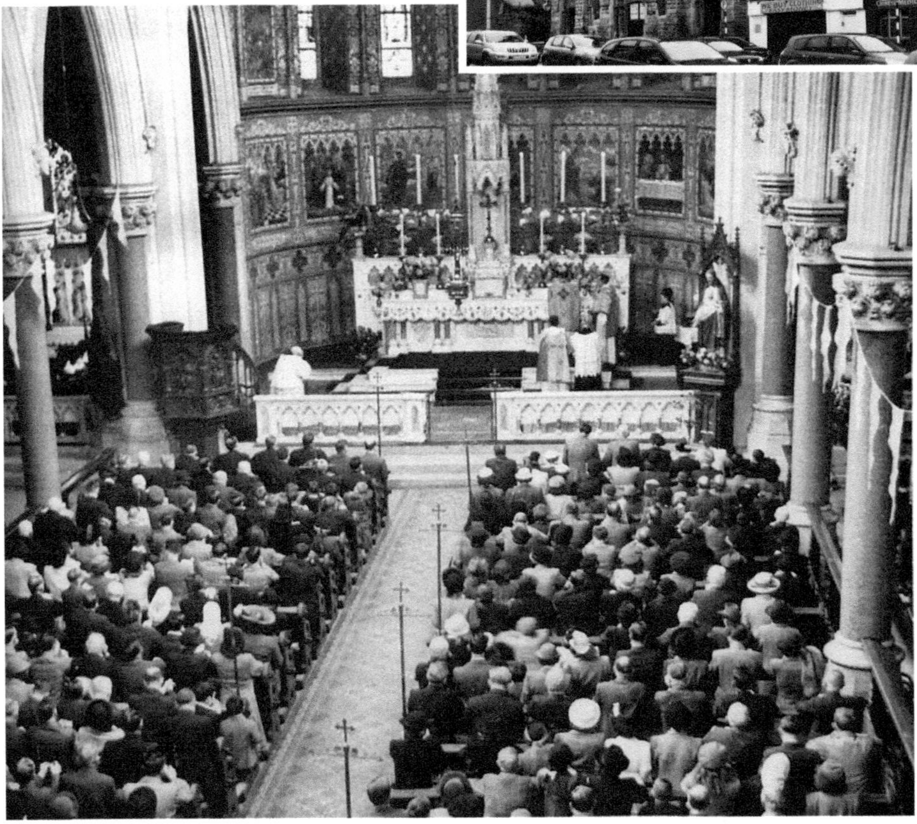

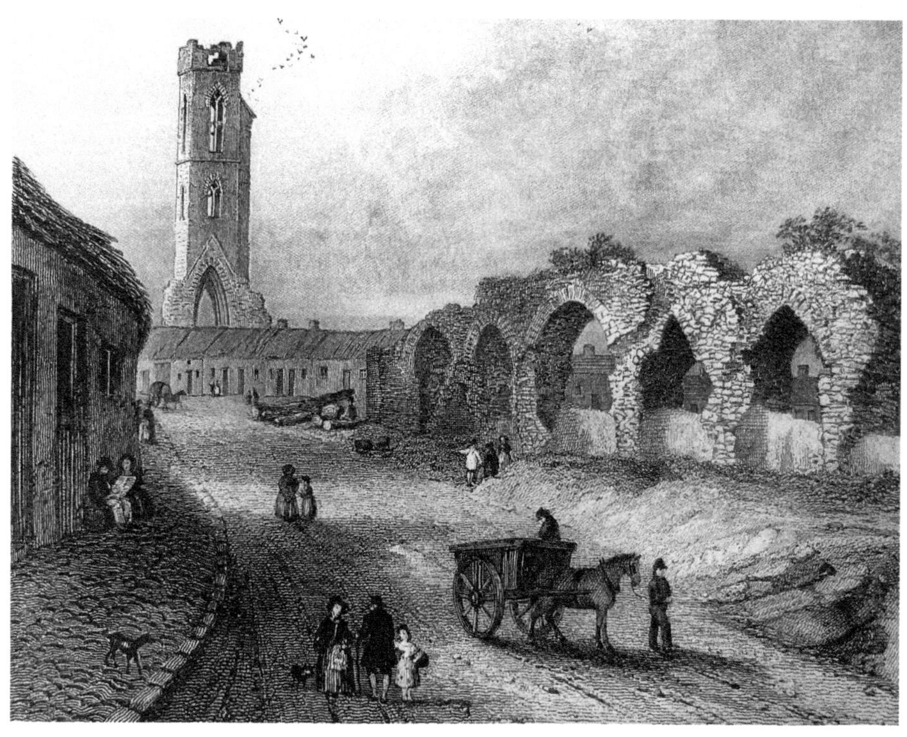

Magdalene Tower at Sundays Gate. (From Dalton's *History of Drogheda*, 1844)

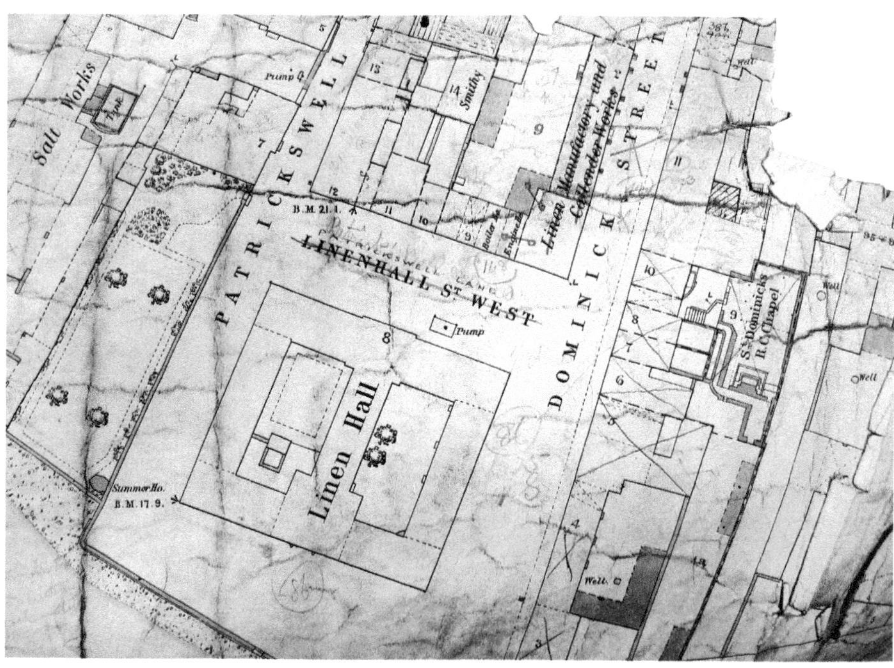

The Dominican chapel was originally hidden behind the shops. (Courtesy of Valuation Office)

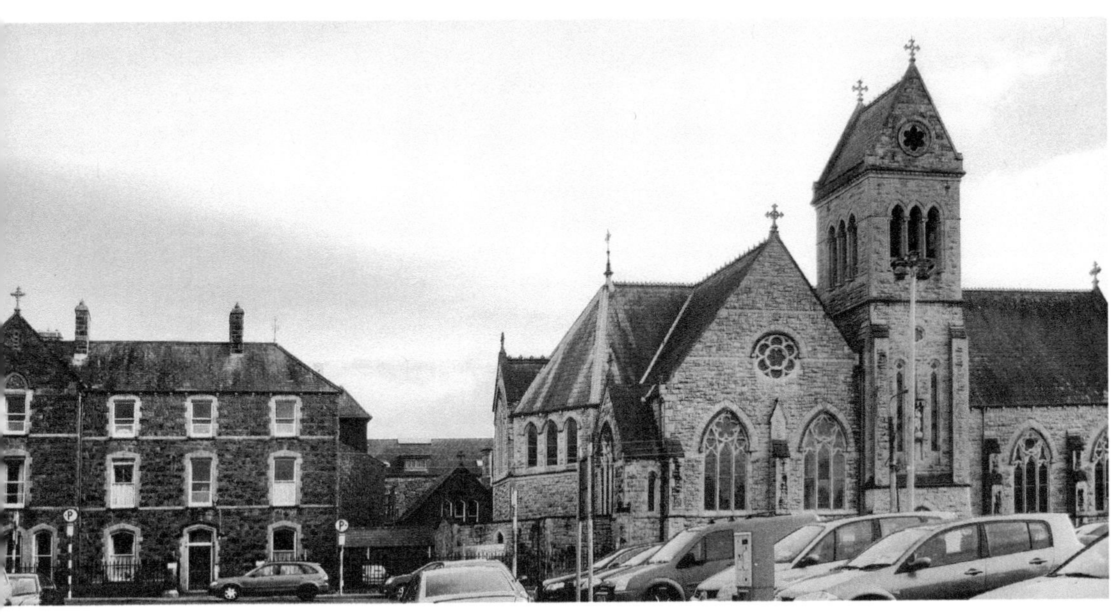

The present-day Dominican church and monastery, both built in 1882.

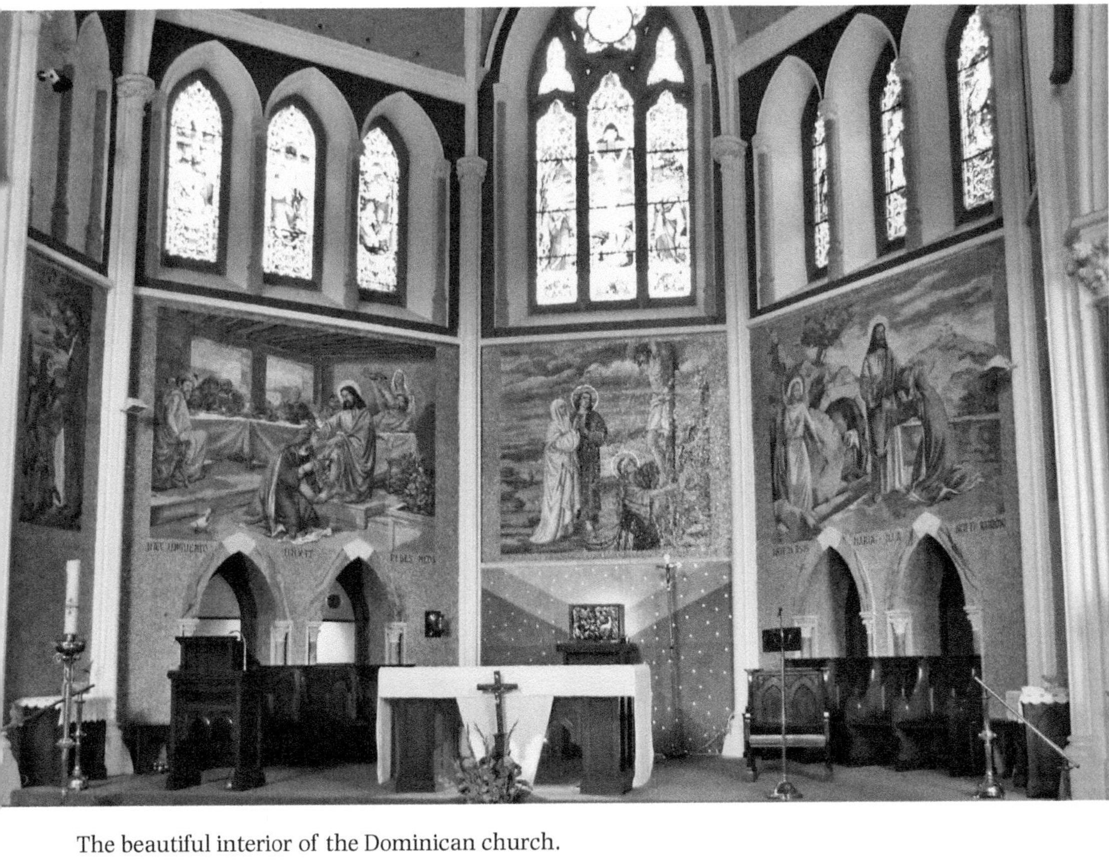

The beautiful interior of the Dominican church.

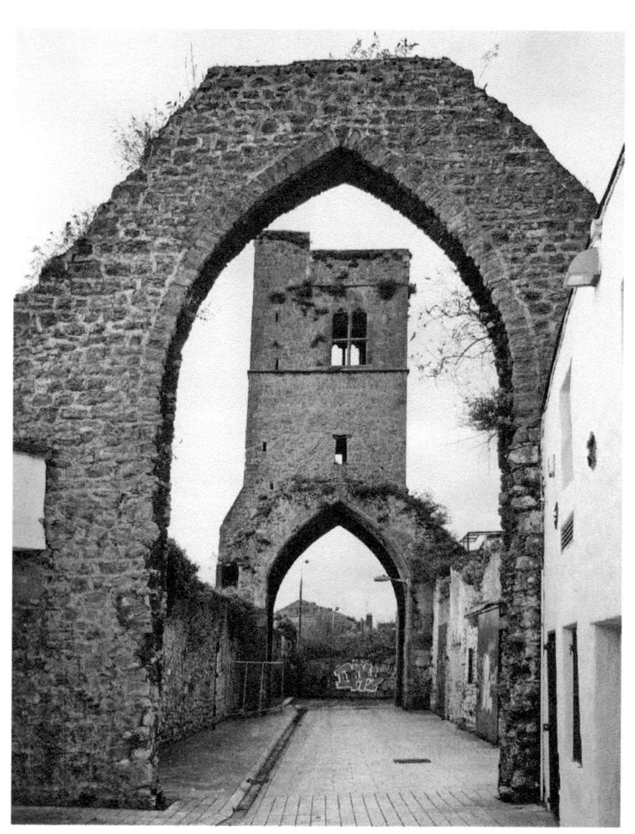

Left The ruins of the thirteenth-century St Mary's Abbey (Augustinians) in Narrow West Street.

Below The Augustinian church in Shop Street, built in 1866. On the lower left is the Harry Clarke stained-glass window. The right tower was never finished.

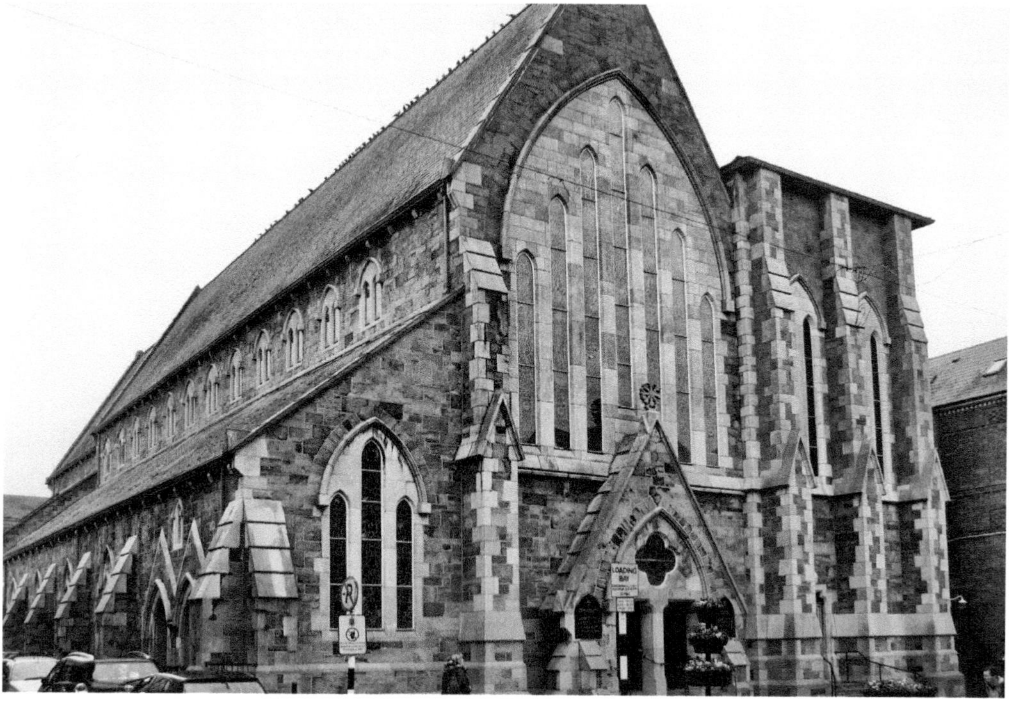

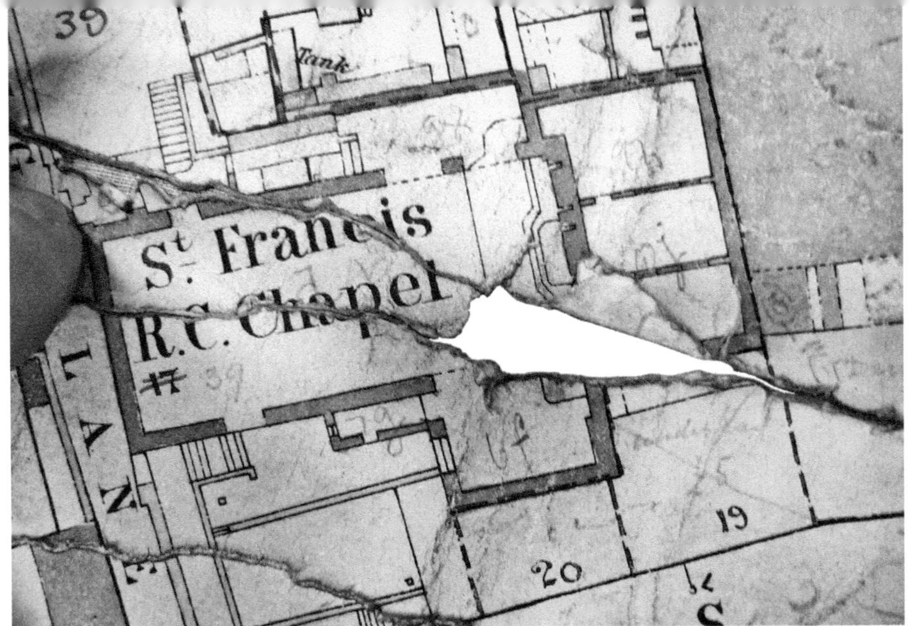

A plan of Franciscan church, St Laurence Street. (Courtesy of the Valuation Office)

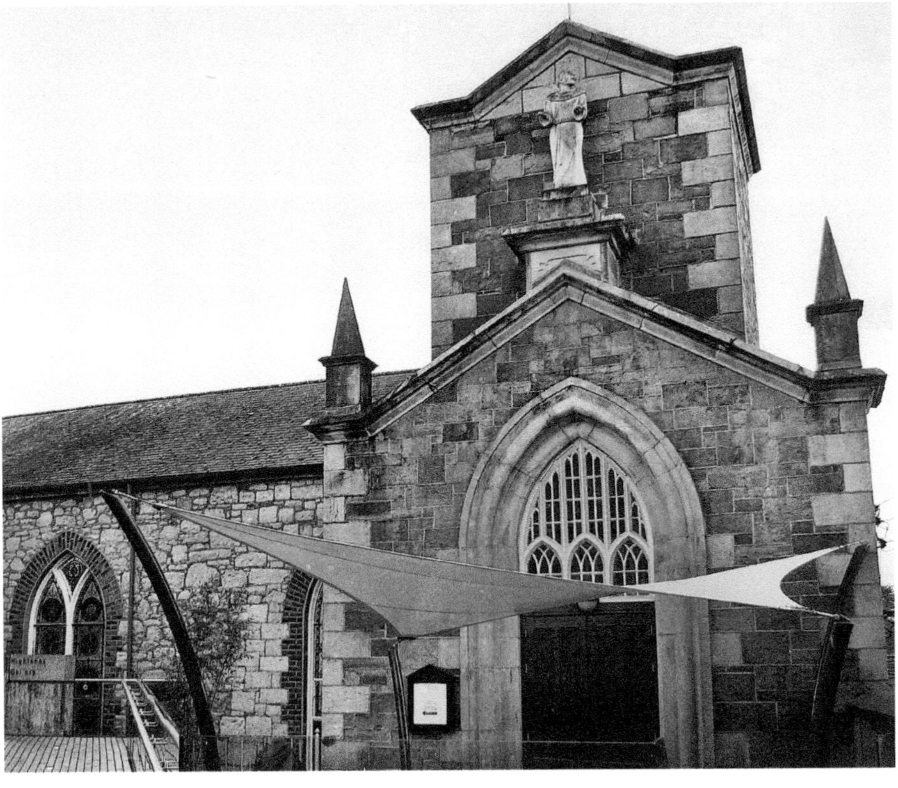

The Highlanes Art Gallery now occupies the former Franciscan church in St Laurence Street. There was a Calvary grotto to the left of the door, and this entrance led directly into the rear gallery.

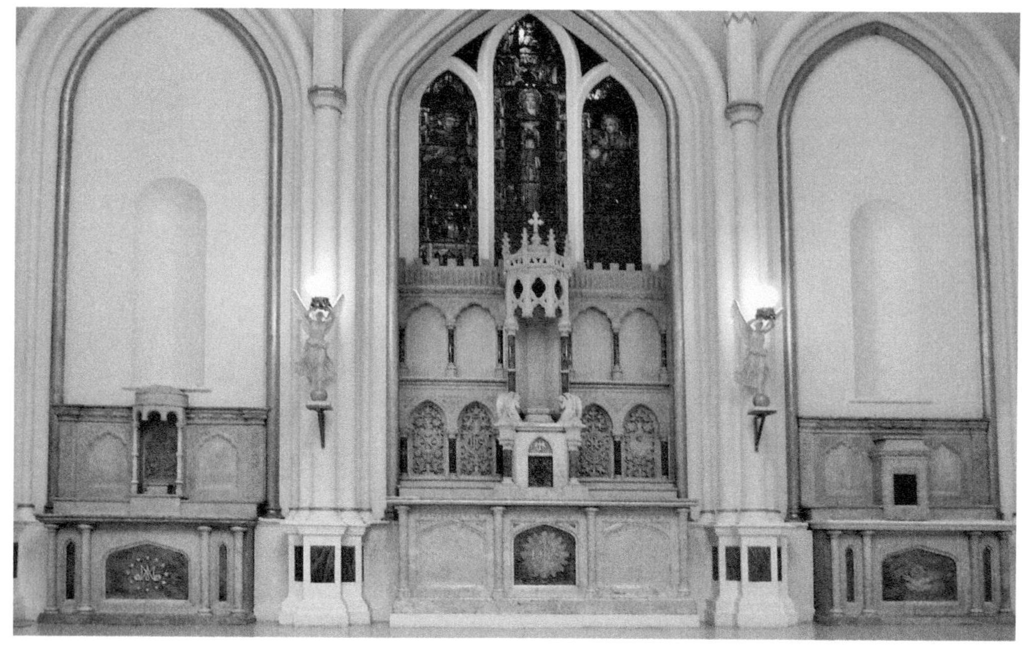

Most of the 1857 Franciscan marble altar has been retained in Highlanes Gallery.

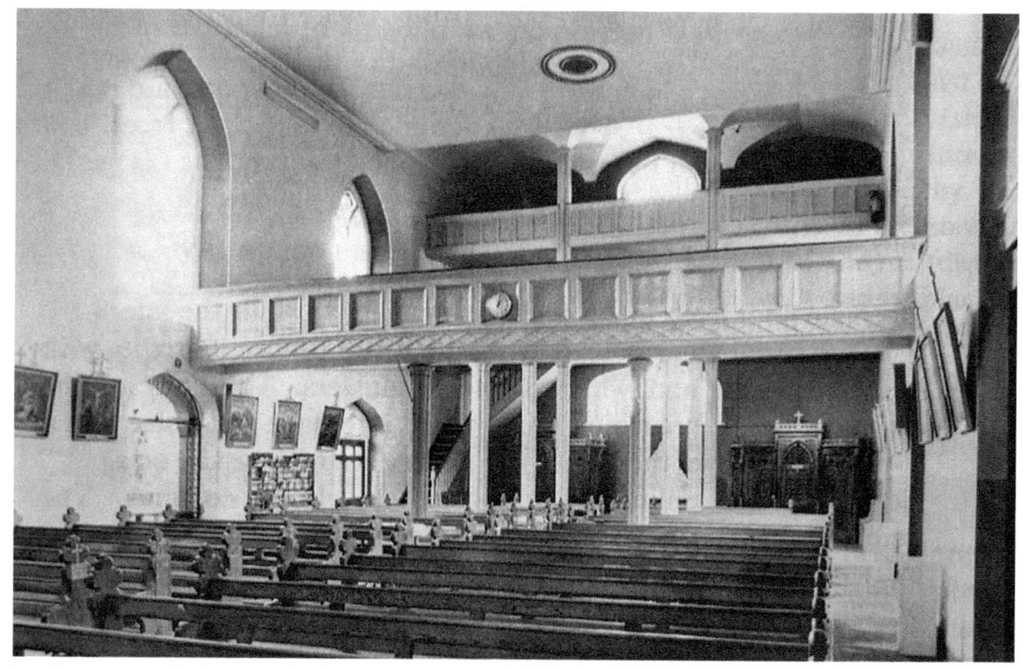

The Franciscan church in the mid-1980s, with double-tier gallery. (Courtesy of An Foras Forbartha)

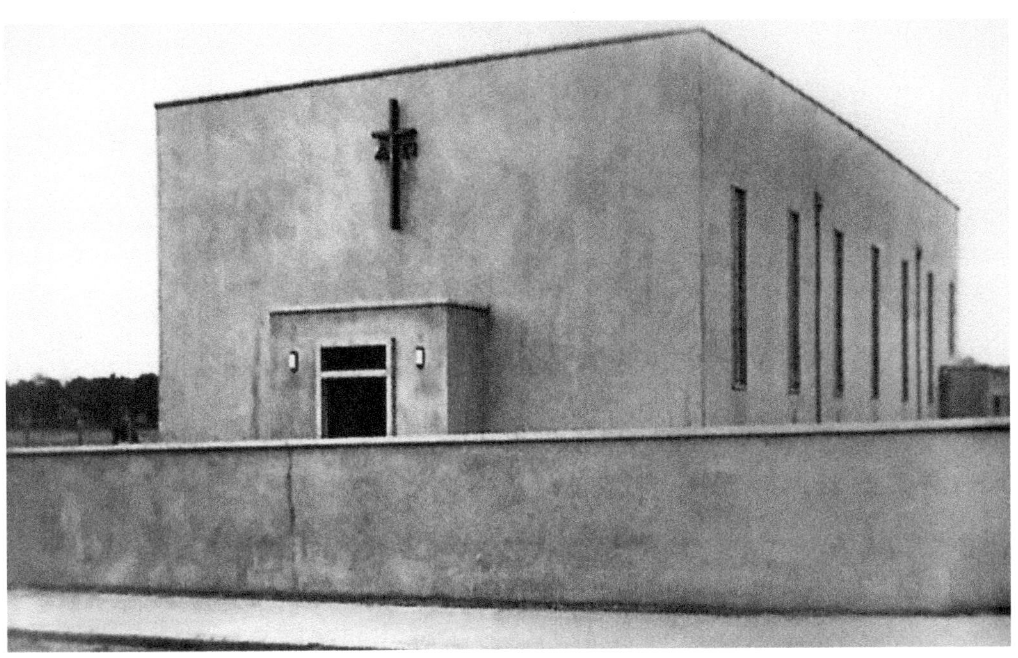

The Lourdes chapel-of-ease in Hardmans Gardens had a charming simplicity. (Courtesy of the Medical Missionaries of Mary)

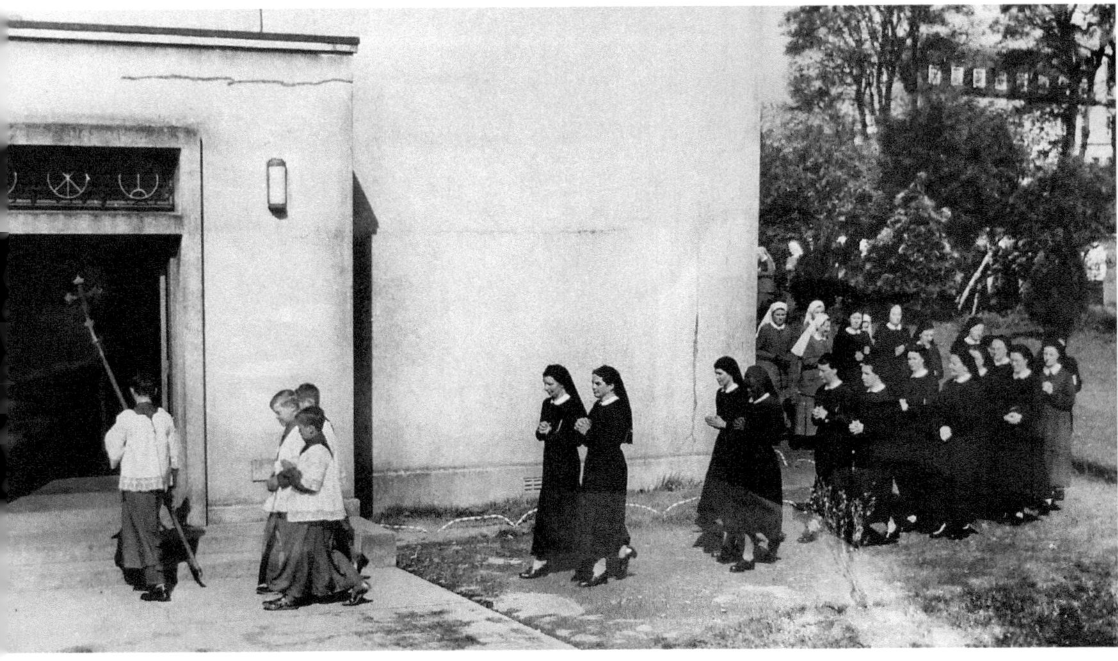

Nuns processing into Lourdes chapel-of-ease. (Courtesy of the Medical Missionaries of Mary)

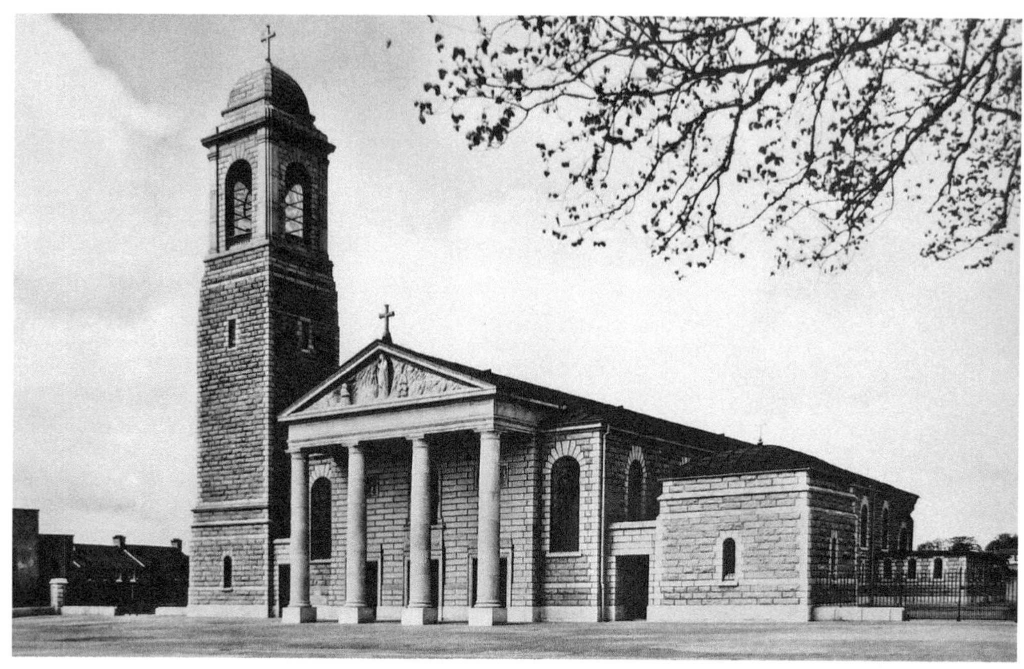

Our Lady of Lourdes' church was built in 1959. (Courtesy of the Medical Missionaries of Mary)

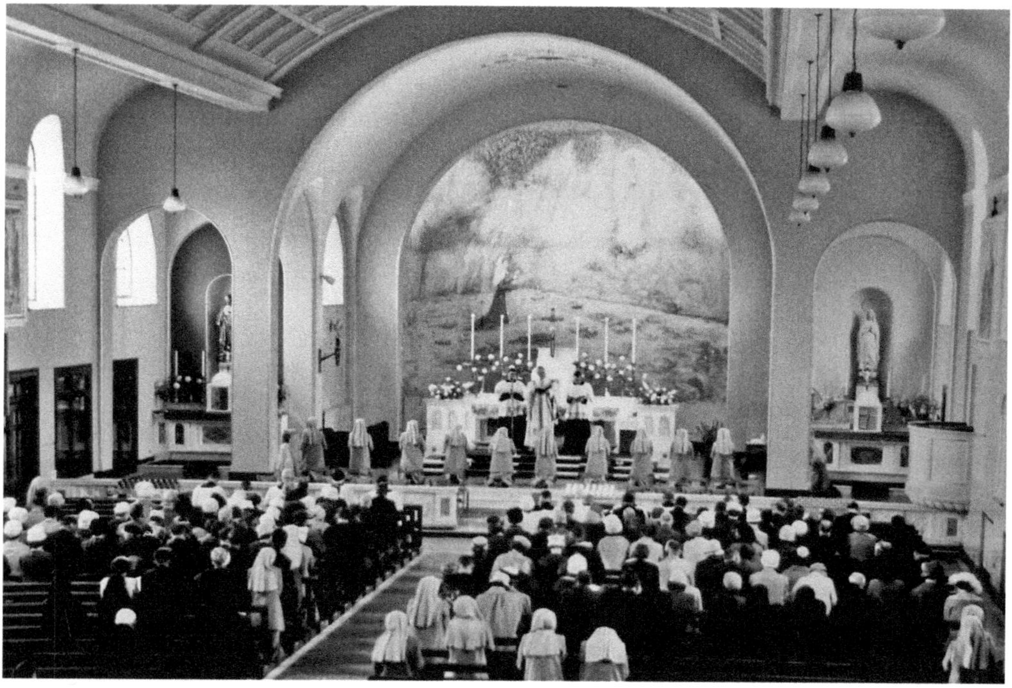

Nuns being 'professed' in Our Lady of Lourdes' church. (Courtesy of the Medical Missionaries of Mary)

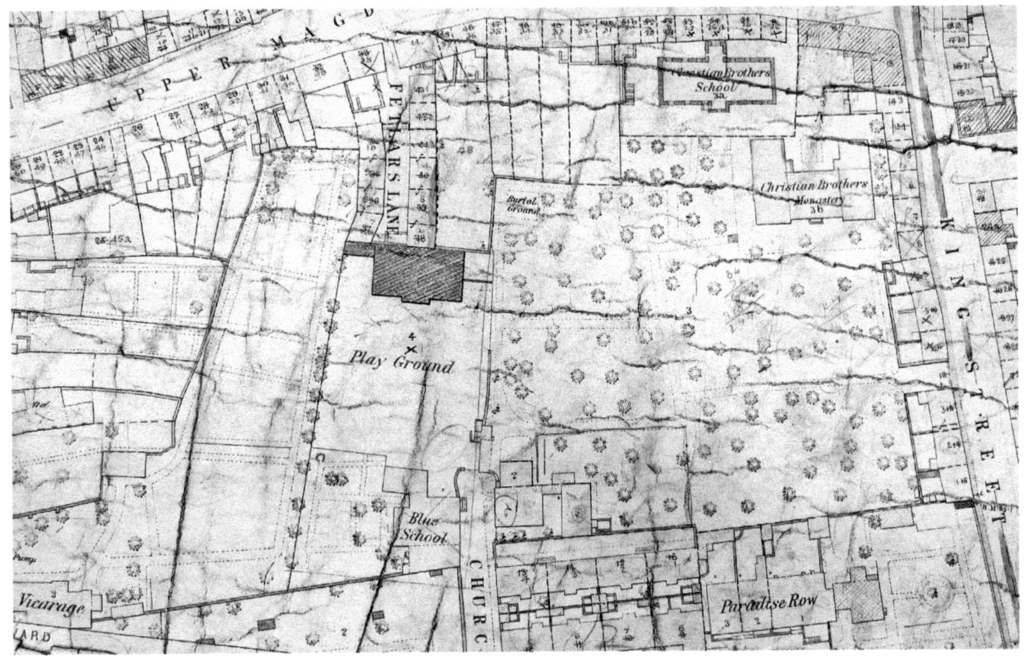

The original Blue School was exactly at the north end of Church Lane. The darker building further north is the newly built Blue School. (Courtesy of the Valuation Office)

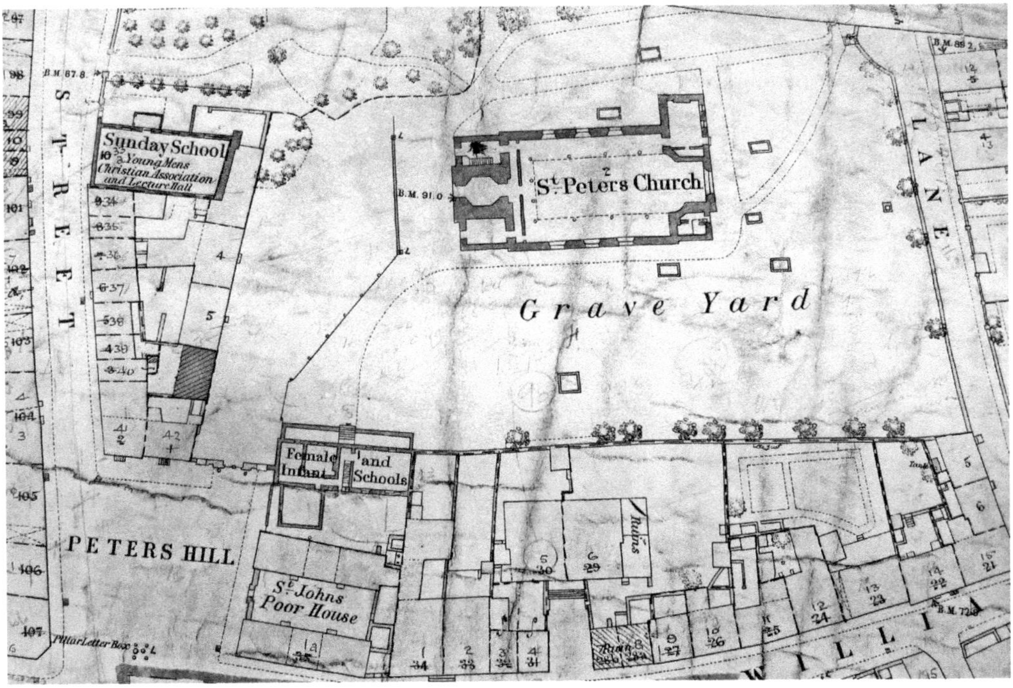

A plan of St Peter's church. The Alleys/Almshouses can be seen top right. (Courtesy of the Valuation Office)

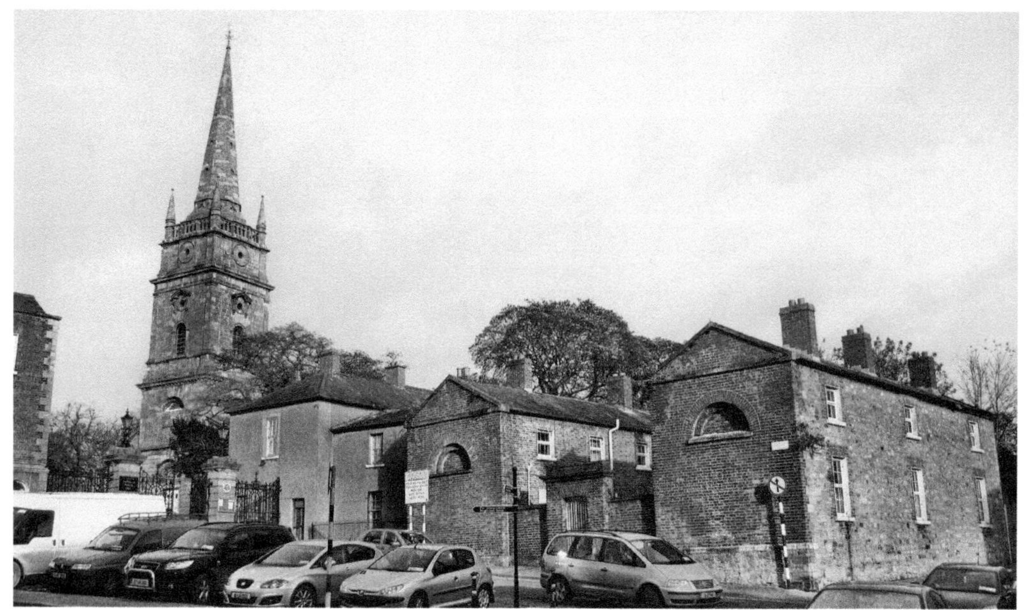

St John's Poor House, with its twelve apartments, is still at the entrance to St Peter's church.

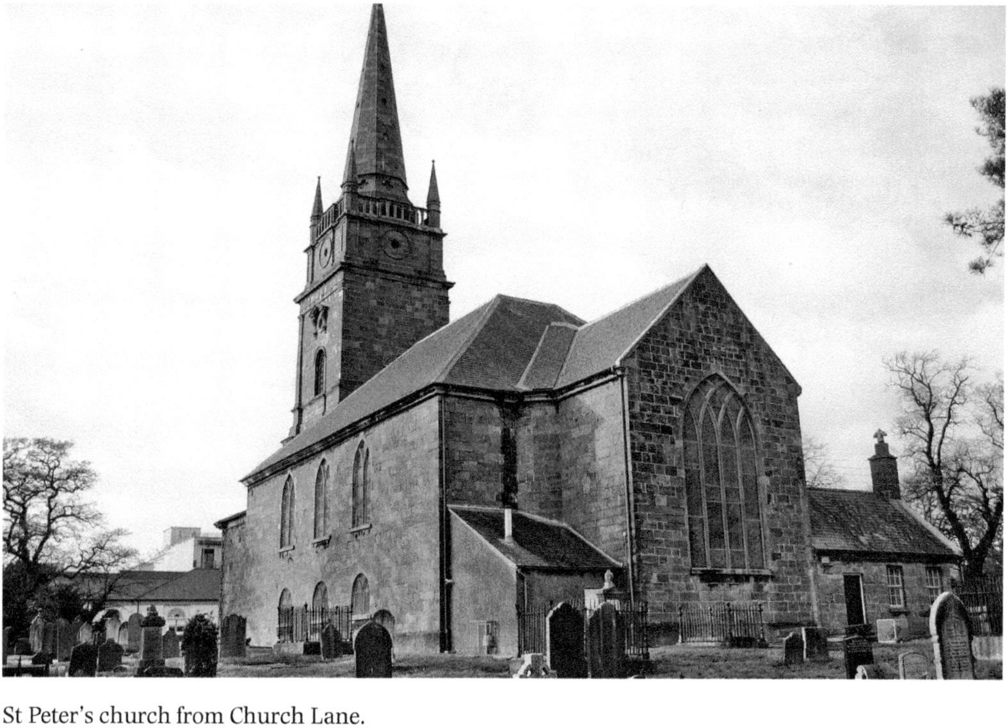

St Peter's church from Church Lane.

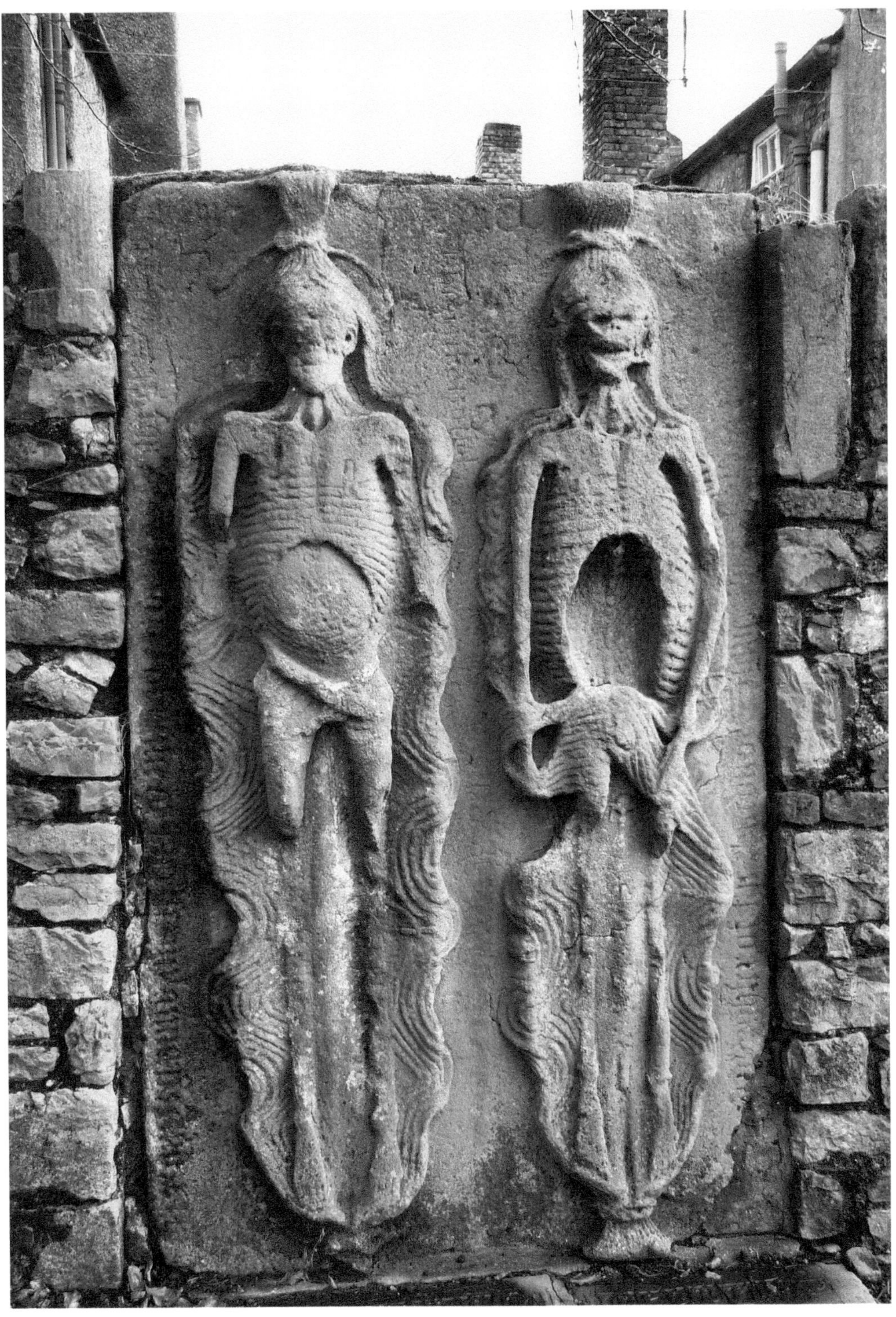

The cadavers at the east boundary of St Peter's church. The Alms Houses are behind.

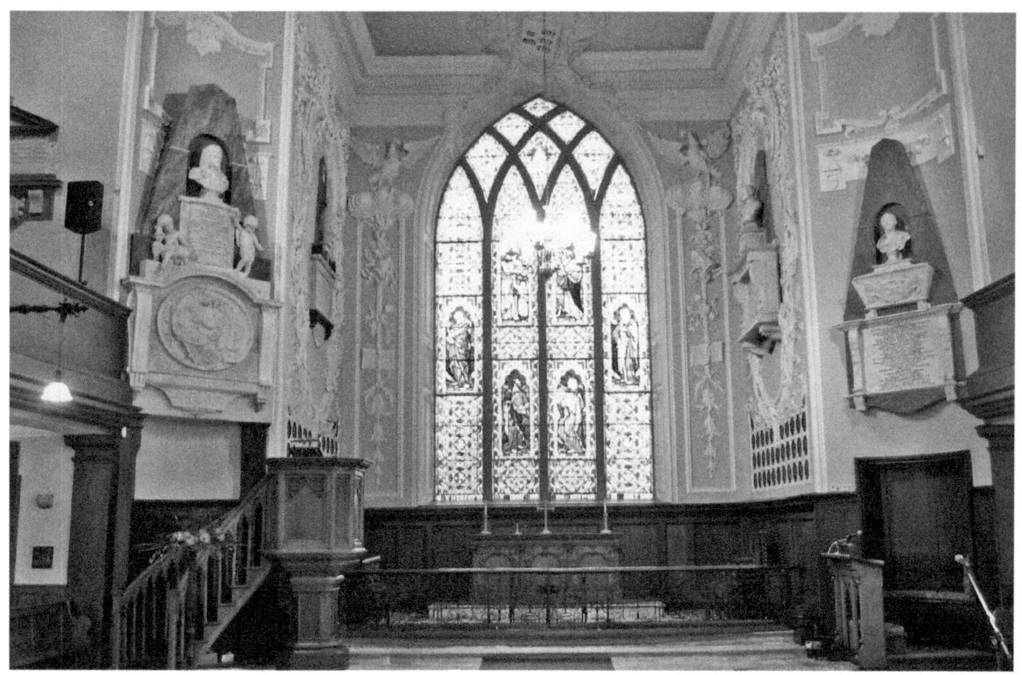

The fabulous interior of St Peter's church.

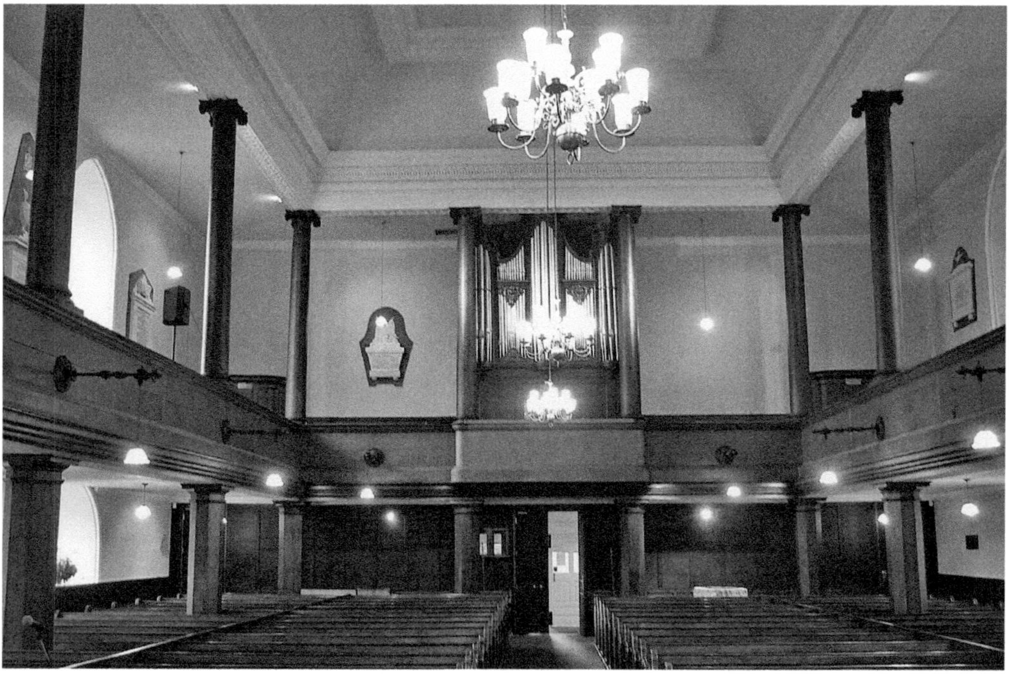

St Peter's church has galleries on three sides and a famous Snetzler organ at the rear.

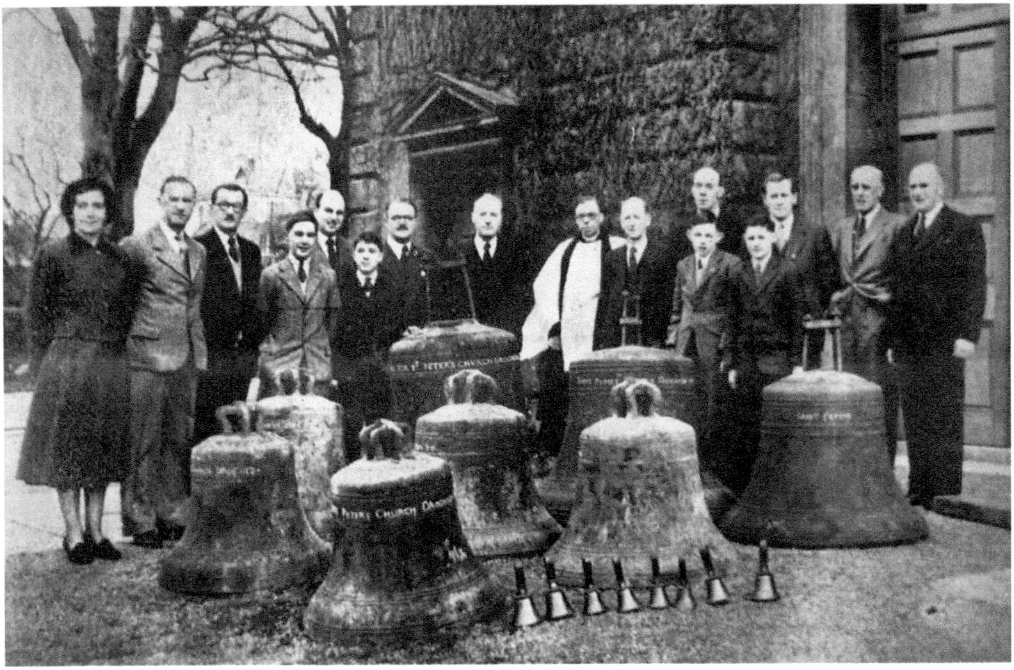

St Peter's bells were overhauled in 1952 and the canons (top hooks) removed. (Courtesy of St Peter's Parish)

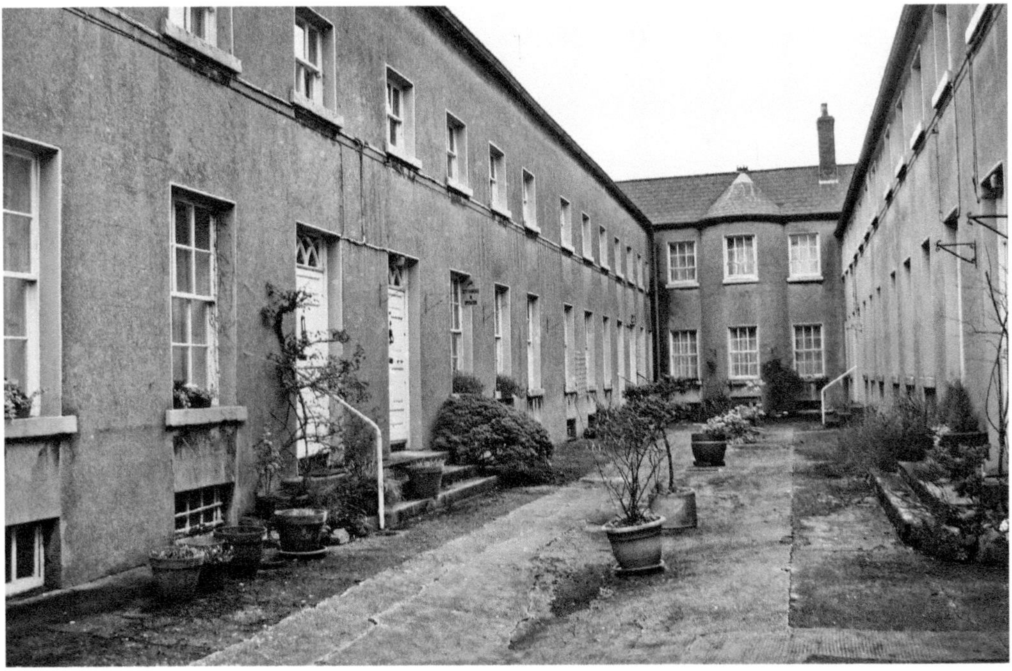

The 1706 Alleys are still a charming oasis on the east side of St Peter's church.

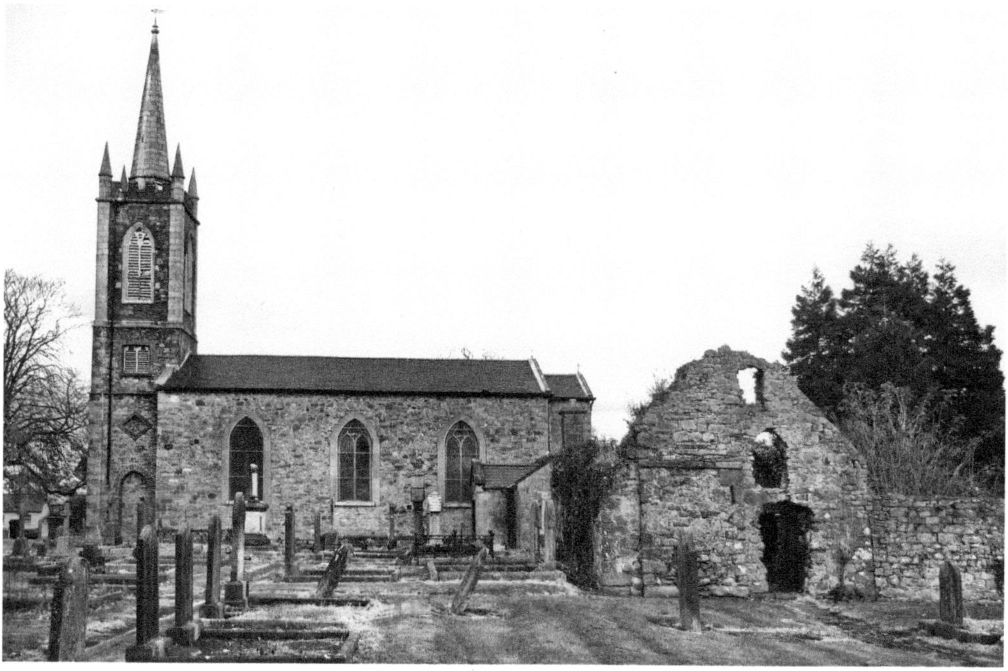

St Mary's church now lies vacant.

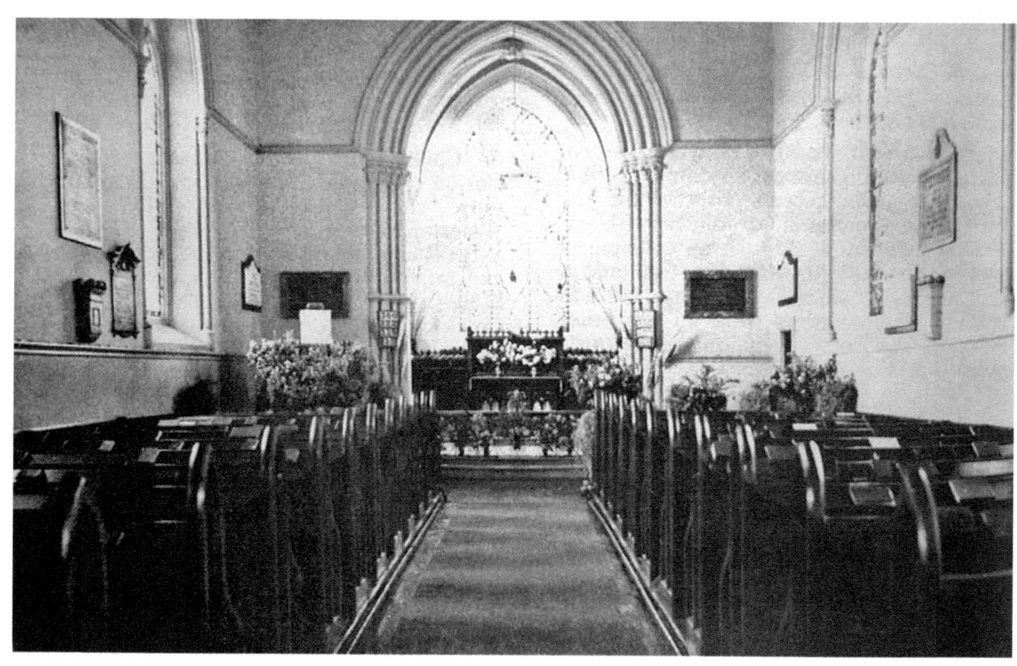

The interior of St Mary's church in bygone days. (Courtesy of John McCullen)

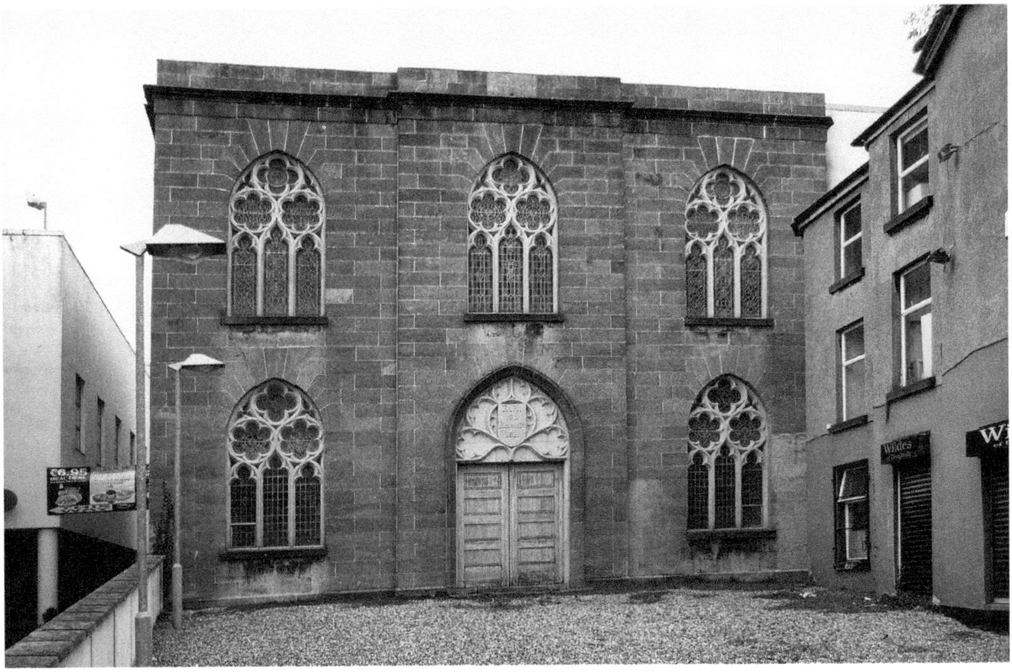

Above The former two-storey
Methodist church has been
preserved, although the interior has
been removed.

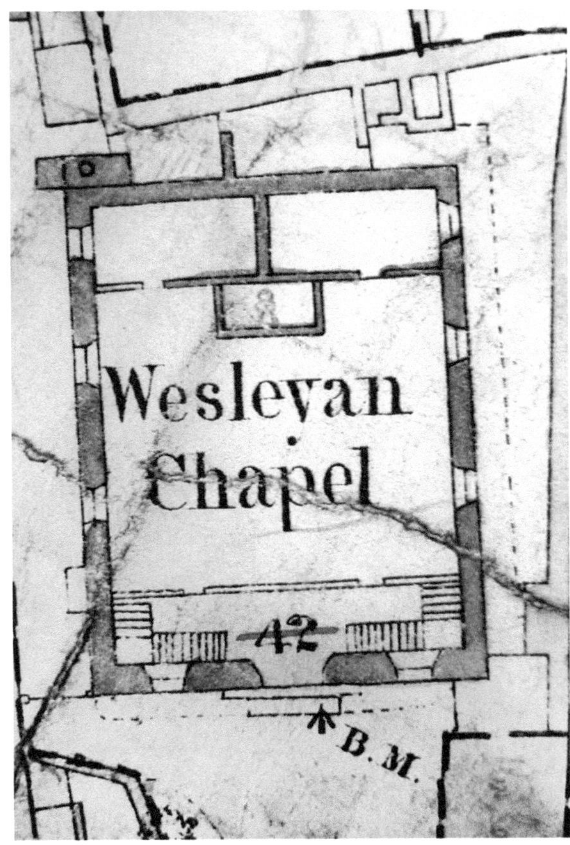

Right The original plan of the
Methodist church. (Courtesy of the
Valuation Office)

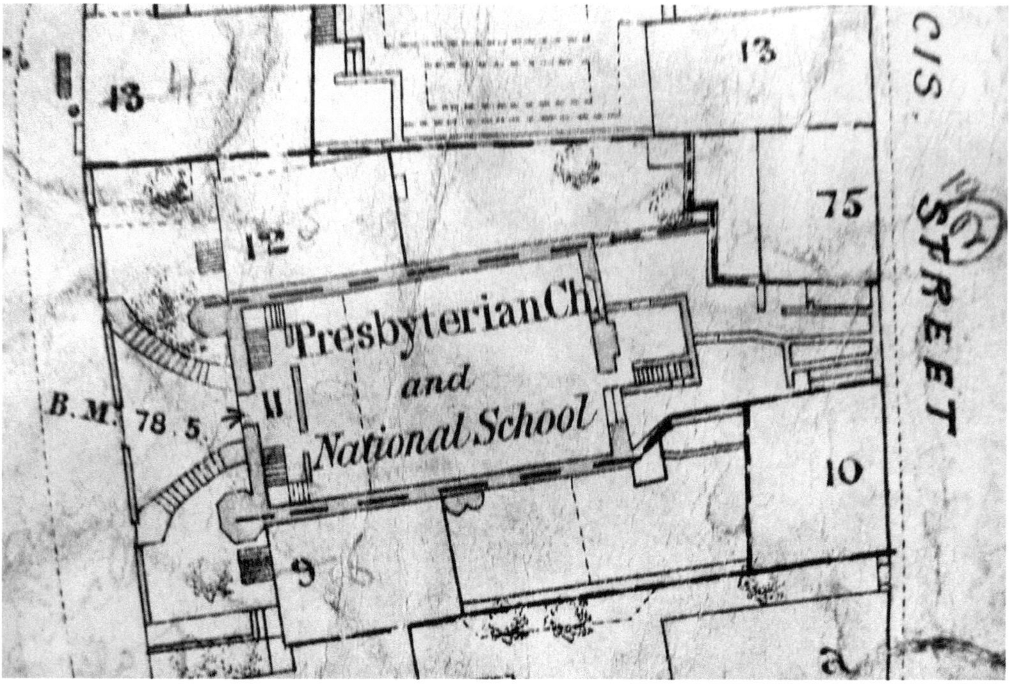

Above The original plan of the Presbyterian church. The school was in the basement. (Courtesy of the Valuation Office)

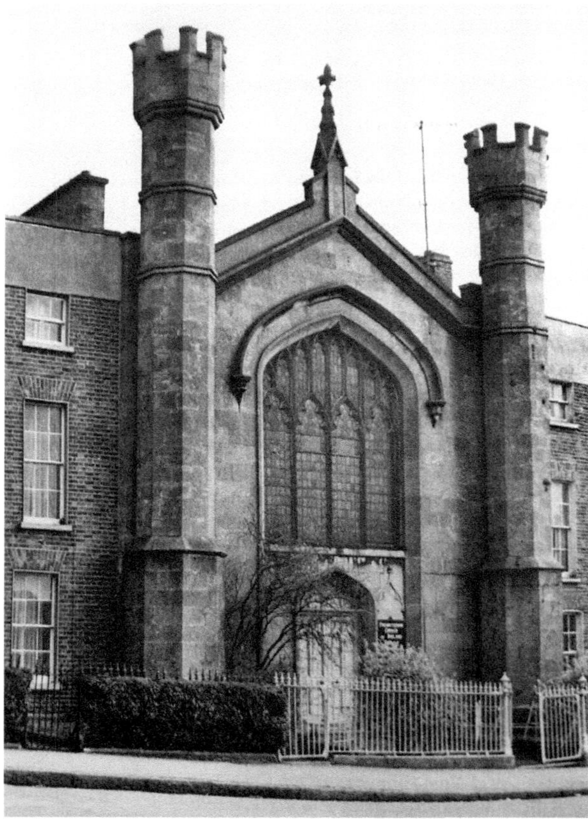

Left The imposing Presbyterian church in the mid-1980s. The houses on each side are privately owned. (Courtesy of An Foras Forbartha)

4

EDUCATION

PRESENTATION SISTERS, FAIR STREET, AND DUKE STREET

Nano Nagle founded the Presentation order in 1775. In 1813 a few sisters came to Drogheda and opened schools for boys and girls in a basement in Fair Street. In 1858 a new mixed school was built on a nearby site. The boys school closed soon after the Daughters of Charity began educating boys in a new school directly opposite the Presentation convent in 1870.

In 1922 the nuns opened St Philomena's Secondary School in Duke Street at the back of Fair Street, after the Dominican nuns in the Siena Convent in Cord Road withdrew from education in 1921.

In 1923, the nuns, who were still an enclosed order, bought the late eighteenth-century Greenhills, on 13 acres, from the Smith family, for use as a summer home and for retreats, and changed its name to Our Lady's. A detached chapel was built shortly afterwards.

In 1940, the nuns opened a boarding school for forty girls in Our Lady's. In 1951, St Philomena's in Duke Street joined with Our Lady's. The increased pupil numbers meant that Nissen army huts had to be used until 1963, when a new secondary school opened. The old building in Duke Street became St Philomena's Private Junior School. Boarders were phased out by 1978 and in 1988 Padraig Byrne became the first lay principal.

The 1901 census recorded eighteen nuns, three postulants, and two servants, led by Sr Margaret Markey. The Catholic Directory for 1957 recorded forty nuns.

SISTERS OF MERCY

In 1854 a small group of nuns moved into No 2 Dublin Road. By 1858, St Mary's Girl's NS (with a plastered finish) had been built on the adjoining site. The top floor was used as a private senior school, called a 'Pension School'. The buildings are now empty.

In 1879 St Mary's Boys NS opened next door. This is the lovely T-shaped yellow-brick building, designed by local architect P.J. Dodd. The boys only occupied the ground floor, as the upper floors comprised the convent and chapel. In 1900 the boys were moved out, to make way for a lace and hosiery factory, which lasted until

1941, when the building reverted to private school use. The building was sold by the nuns in 1994 for an apartment development, called Priory Hall.

From 1906 to 1947, the nuns operated the Mercy Electric Laundry, or St Mary's Laundry, on the site immediately to the west of the yellow-bricked building. Then, in 1952, Scoil Naisiunta Muire Fatima was built on the laundry site, a NS for girls. Nowadays this building also lies empty.

The 1901 census recorded eighteen Mercy nuns led by Mother Gilmore, plus two servants. About half of the nuns were aged around twenty years. By the 1911 census the number of nuns had dropped to twelve.

SISTERS OF CHARITY, FAIR STREET (DAUGHTERS OF CHARITY OF ST VINCENT DE PAUL)

This order was founded in Paris in 1633, and their habit was distinguished by the white cornettes on their heads. Four nuns (two French, one Welsh, and one Irish) arrived in Drogheda in 1855 and moved into Harpur House, William Street, which was donated by Francis Chadwick. Here they started a night school for factory girls.

The parish priest exchanged his Parochial House in Fair Street, which had land attached (it was previously an army barracks), for Harpur House, and the nuns built a red-brick Industrial School (St Vincent's orphanage) there, which opened in 1870, for girls of all ages and boys under 9 years. Initially there were ninety-two children. When the boys reached 9 years of age, they were transferred to the Christian Brothers Industrial Schools in various locations, such as Artane in Dublin, and Letterfrack in Galway. This policy was stopped in 1970. In 1876 the girls were transferred to Birr, leaving only boys in the hands of the nuns. In 1885, a rear extension was added to the Industrial school.

In 1894, the nuns built a separate NS for Drogheda boys (the two-storey red-brick building nearest the present Council offices), but this was not open to orphans until 1939. This school closed in the early 1970s and was converted to orphanage use, but is now empty.

In 1900, the nuns opened St Vincent's Girls Orphanage to the east of their convent. By the time the red-brick Carnegie Library was built around 1906, the nuns occupied all the buildings between the former Court House and the library.

The 1901 census recorded 114 boys in the orphanage, mostly under 10 years of age, and two young female teachers. There were eleven nuns and four servants in the convent, under Sr Anne Clare Redman.

In the 1911 census, there were 132 young boys, and twenty-two girls, aged 6-18, with the same number of nuns as 1901.

In 1934, the nuns opened a private summer holiday camp for the orphans at Termonfeckin, including a little chapel for the nuns. Since 1975, only nuns use this holiday home.

A report in 1974 records that a new home had just been built at No 4 Magdalene Street, beside the laundry, for adolescent boys, with men in charge. Some of the boys went outside to work. The report also noted that the two orphanages now had thirty-seven boys and fifteen girls, and the nuns received £12.50 per week per child from the government. At this stage, the children went to different schools around Drogheda.

In the 1970s, the nuns donated their red-brick buildings for a community centre, and sold off most of the other buildings, which were converted to apartments.

SIENNA DOMINICAN CONVENT, CORD ROAD

The Dominicans arrived in Drogheda in 1722, and established their convent in a cottage on the south side of the Boyne, led by Catherine Plunkett, a grand-niece of St Oliver Plunkett. In 1725, they rented a big three-storey house in Dyer Street, and opened an exclusive girls boarding school. They also opened a Poor School.

The nuns moved to Cord Road in 1796, with eleven boarders, into a newly built house. The house was designed by Francis Johnston and was four storeys high and seven bays wide. A chapel was built in 1834 on the east side of the convent/school, but later demolished to make way for extensions to the original building. A new chapel was built on the west side of the building in the 1870s, to a design by G.C. Ashlin. The nuns also provided a Poor School on Scarlett Street, on the north edge of their estate.

The nuns ran a secondary boarding school for girls until 1920. The 1901 census recorded twenty-two boarders, mostly teenage girls, and forty-five nuns of all ages.

After 1930, the nuns resumed their enclosed and contemplative life, selling altar breads, religious icons, and church vestments, for a livelihood.

The convent caught fire in 1994. Twenty-nine nuns escaped with only minor injuries, but one nun died of smoke inhalation in her sleep. As a result, the nuns moved to a brand new monastery in The Twenties in 1997 (north side of Drogheda), and the Cord Road buildings were sold for a housing and apartments development. However, their cemetery is still in Cord Road. In 1972, Mother M. Catherine Plunkett, who had died in 1757, aged 67, was moved from the Cord cemetery to the Siena cemetery (along with other nuns who died before 1818).

CHRISTIAN BROTHERS, KING STREET

The brothers opened two single-storey schools in 1859, one at Trinity Street, Westgate, backing on to the former Infirmary, and St Aonghusa at Sundays Gate. A second storey was added to Sundays Gate in 1866. The school at Westgate closed in 1955, and is now the Planet Pub.

The brothers built their lovely monastery in King Street in 1868, designed by the famous architects, Pugin & Ashlin, and the red bricks came from Belfast. This building is now the very cosy Scholars Hotel.

DROGHEDA GRAMMAR SCHOOL

This boarding school was founded in 1669 by Erasmus Smith, a Drogheda merchant, whose trust set up a few other schools around Ireland.

Revd F.S. Aldhouse and his wife were running the school in the 1901 census, which comprised a matron, five servants, two young teachers, and nineteen boys, aged 11-18. In the 1911 census, there were four young teachers, and twenty teenage pupils.

Sport was an important feature of the curriculum, and in the 1940s, Bertram Allen paid for an outdoor swimming pool in the garden behind the school. The school sports grounds were originally on the Ballymakenny Road, now occupied by the Boyne Rugby Club.

The Quakers have run the school since the mid-1950s, and committee members have included such names as Bewley, Allen, Jacob, Douglas, all well known in Quaker circles. Arnold Marsh, the ex-headmaster of Newtown School in Waterford (another famous Quaker school), was the driving force in the setting up of Drogheda Grammar School Ltd in 1956, when the original school was in danger of closure. These days, the school is non-denominational.

Until 1976 the co-educational school was in St Laurence Street, occupying Mr Clarke's Free School (built in 1728) and the Lord Chief Justice Singleton's house (built in 1740). In 1976, they moved to Eden View House, on a 22-acre site on Mornington Road, bringing the Bole stained-glass window with them (created by the Harry Clarke Studios in the 1940s). Following various extensions over the years, and the opening of a major new building in 2012, the Drogheda Grammar School is now a first-class secondary school.

The St Laurence Street buildings were demolished in 1989 by a developer to make way for a new shopping centre.

BLUE SCHOOL

This small school was founded in 1730, to cater for poor Protestant boys, and was located in the grounds of St Peter's church. On the 1868 Ordnance Survey map, the small school abuts the north-east boundary of the church graveyard. However, on the 1909 map, the school is bigger and re-located closer to Upper Magdalene Street. The 1901 census recorded eleven boys (boarders), aged 9-15.

The detached building is now a private house.

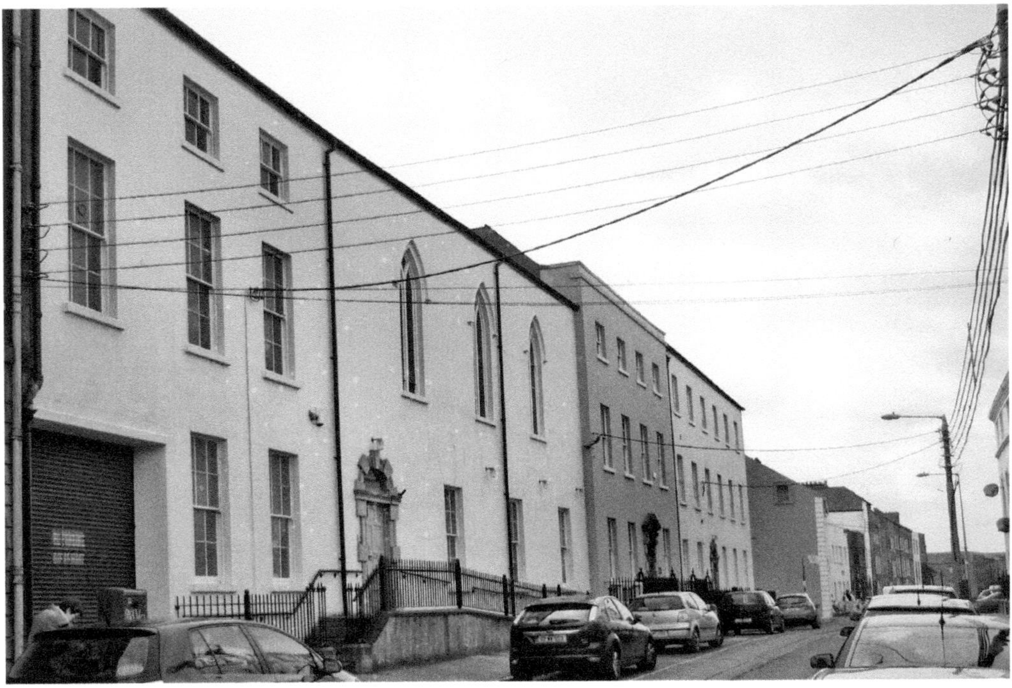

A current view of the former Presentation Convent and school, looking west up Fair Street. The lancet first-floor windows of the former chapel are obvious.

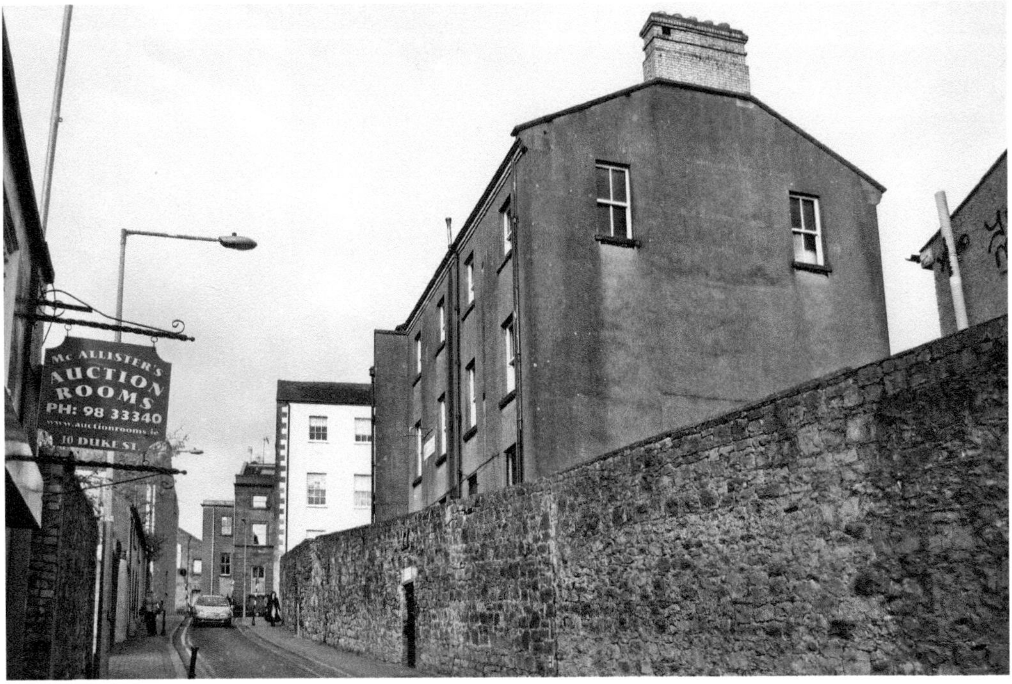

A current view looking north up Duke Street, with Presentation Schools on right.

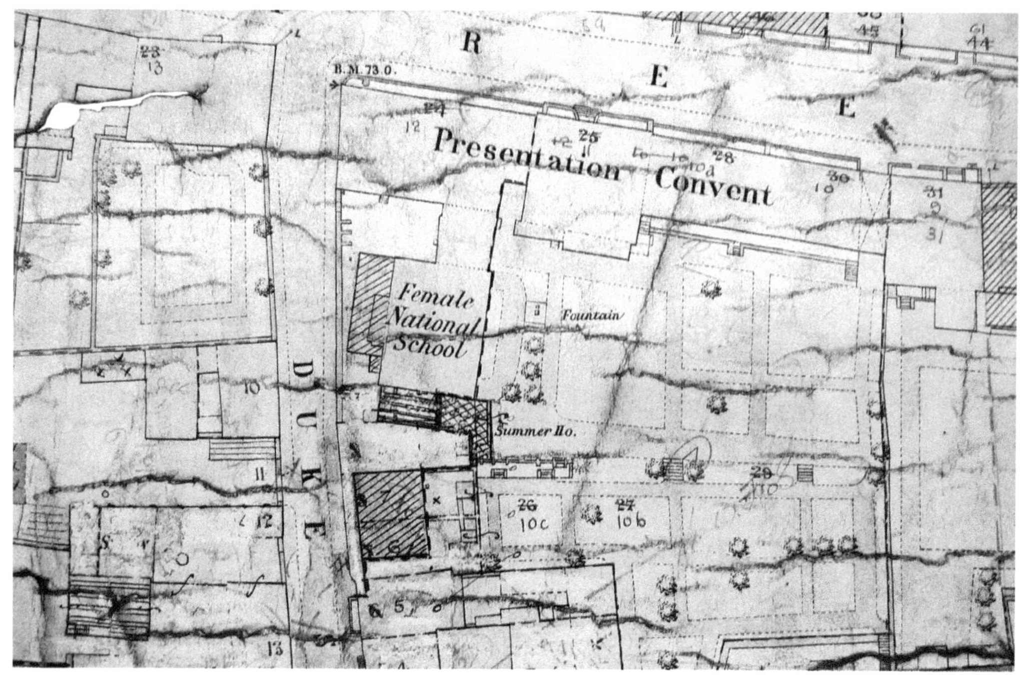

A map of the former Presentation Convent in Fair Street/Duke Street. (Courtesy of the Valuation Office)

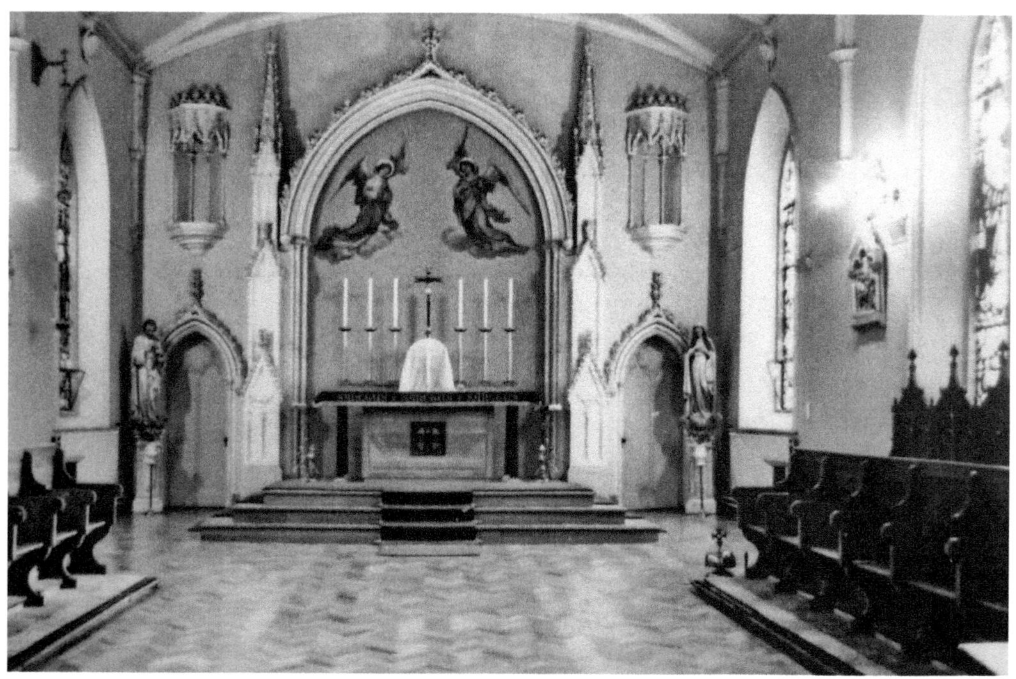

The lovely chapel in the former Presentation Convent in Fair Street/Duke Street. The priest had his back to the nuns in the days of the Latin Mass. (Courtesy of the Presentation Sisters)

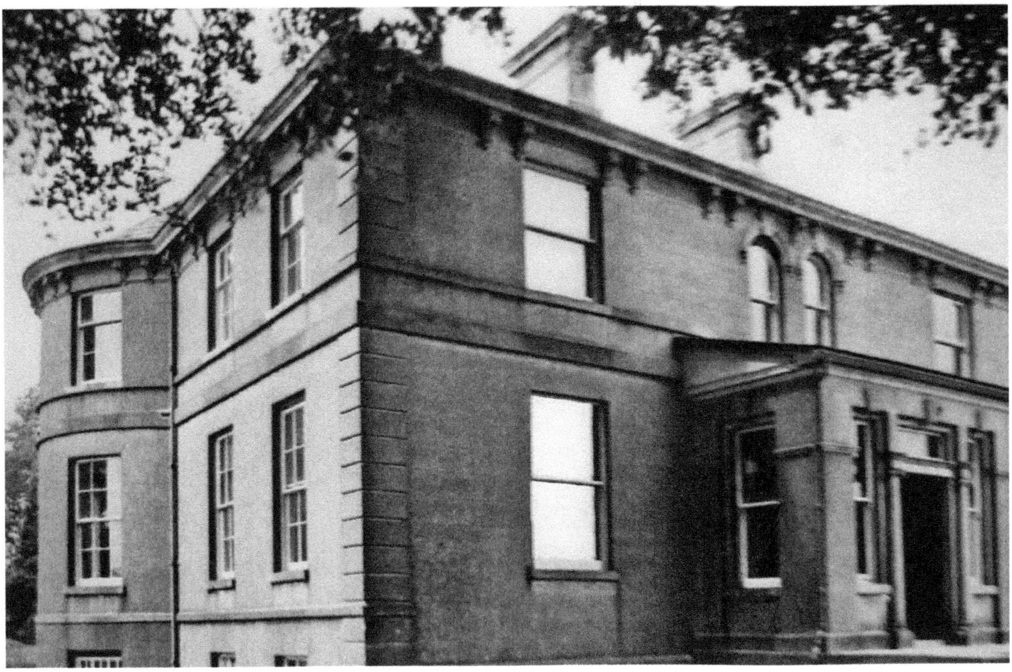

The two-storey over-basement Greenhills House, which the Presentation nuns bought from the Misses Smith. It is now part of Our Lady's Schools. (Courtesy of the Presentation Sisters)

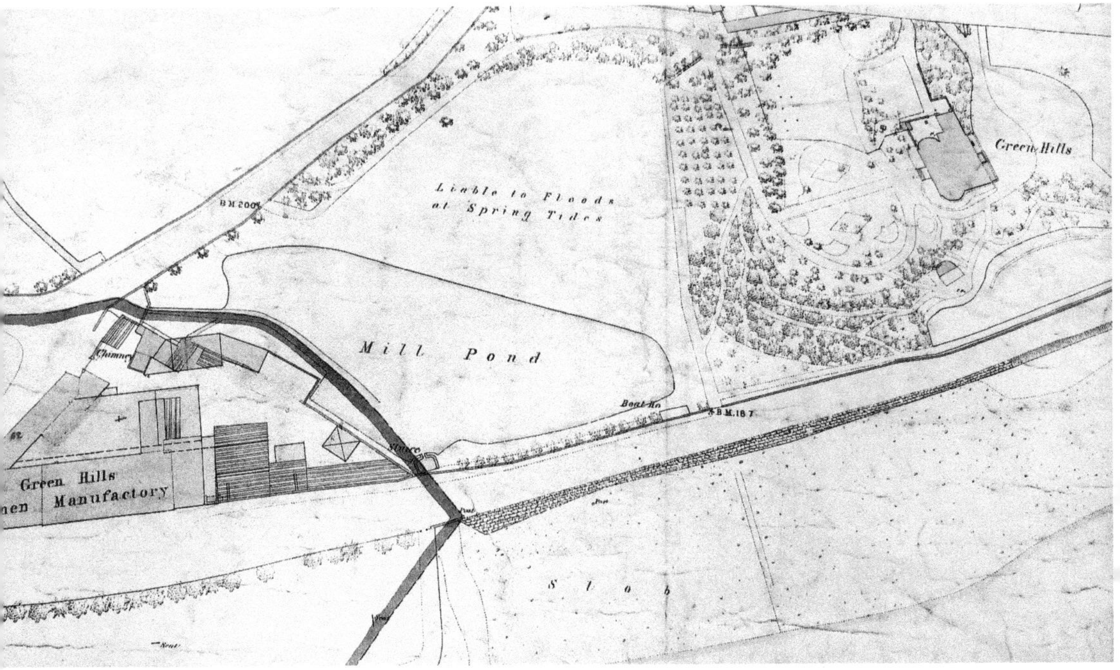

An old map showing Greenhills House on right and the Usher mills on left. (Courtesy of the National Archives)

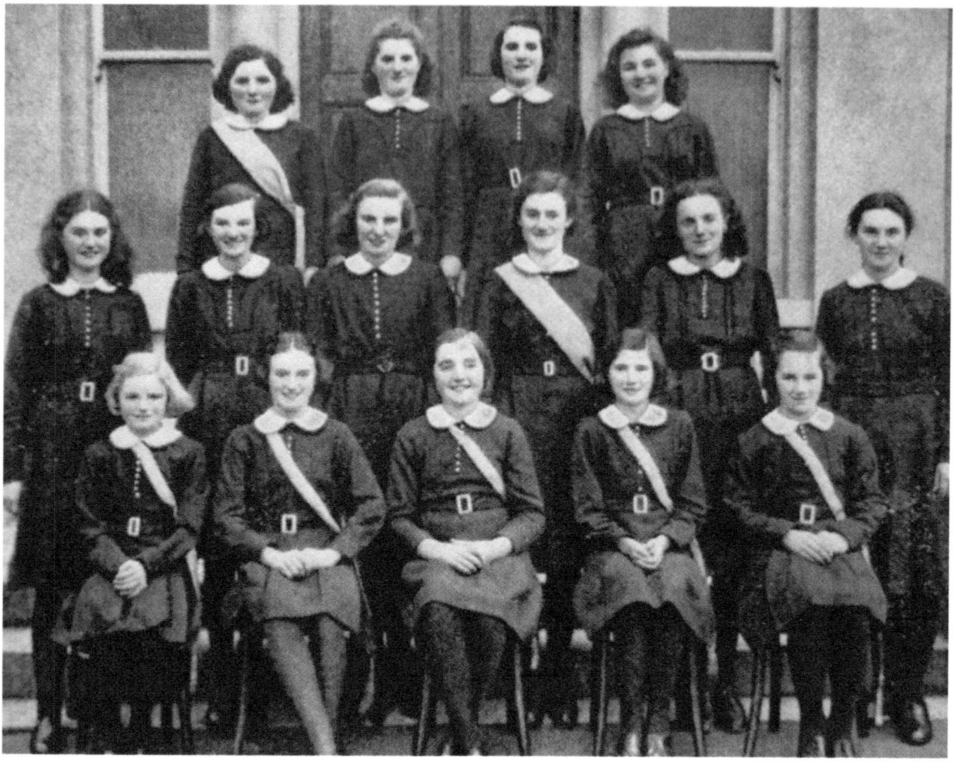

Some of the first boarders in Greenhills/Our Lady's in 1940. From left to right, back row: Maureen Martin, Molly Finegan, Maeve Carr, Philomena Carr. Middle row: Helen McEnteggart, Nan Rogers, Kitty McEnteggart, Peggy Moran, Nancy Crilly, Noelle Gibney. Front row: Moya Connor, Bernadette Hughes, Kitty Osbourne, Annette Gibney, Joyce Carey. (Courtesy of the Presentation Sisters)

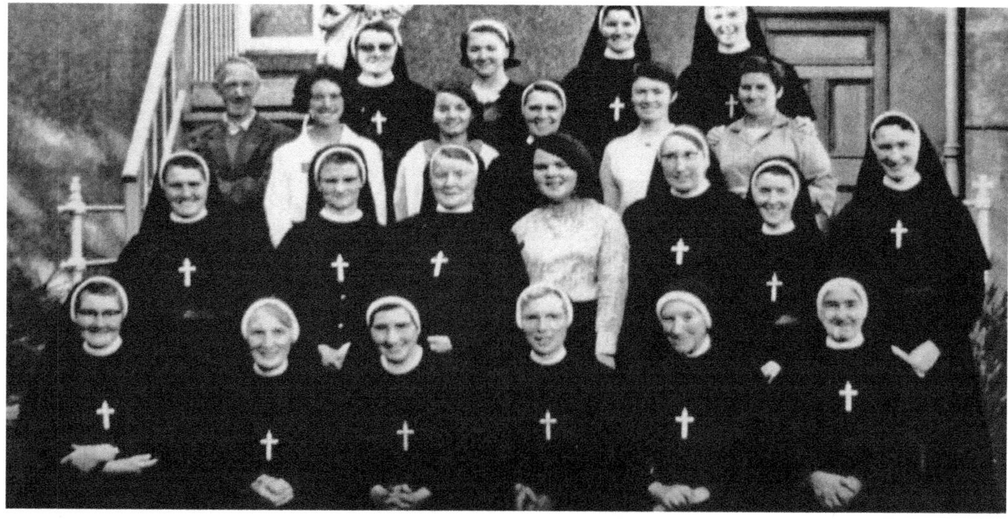

The nuns of the Presentation Convent, 1990. (Courtesy of the Presentation Sisters)

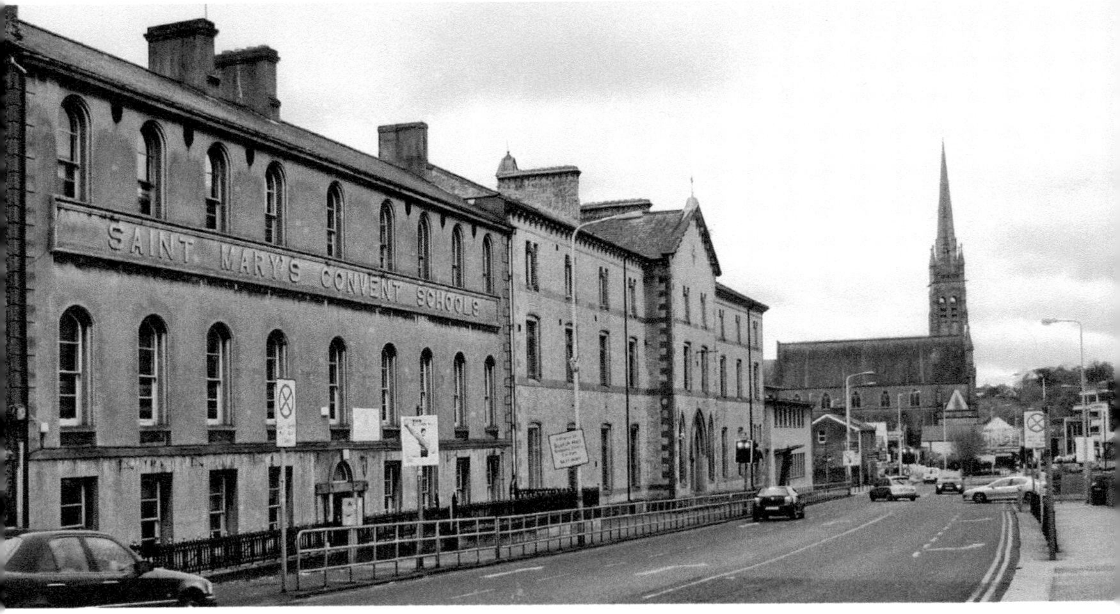

The 1858 former Mercy School (left) and the 1879 yellow-bricked convent (right). The latter is now Priory Hall apartments. St Mary's church can be seen in the background.

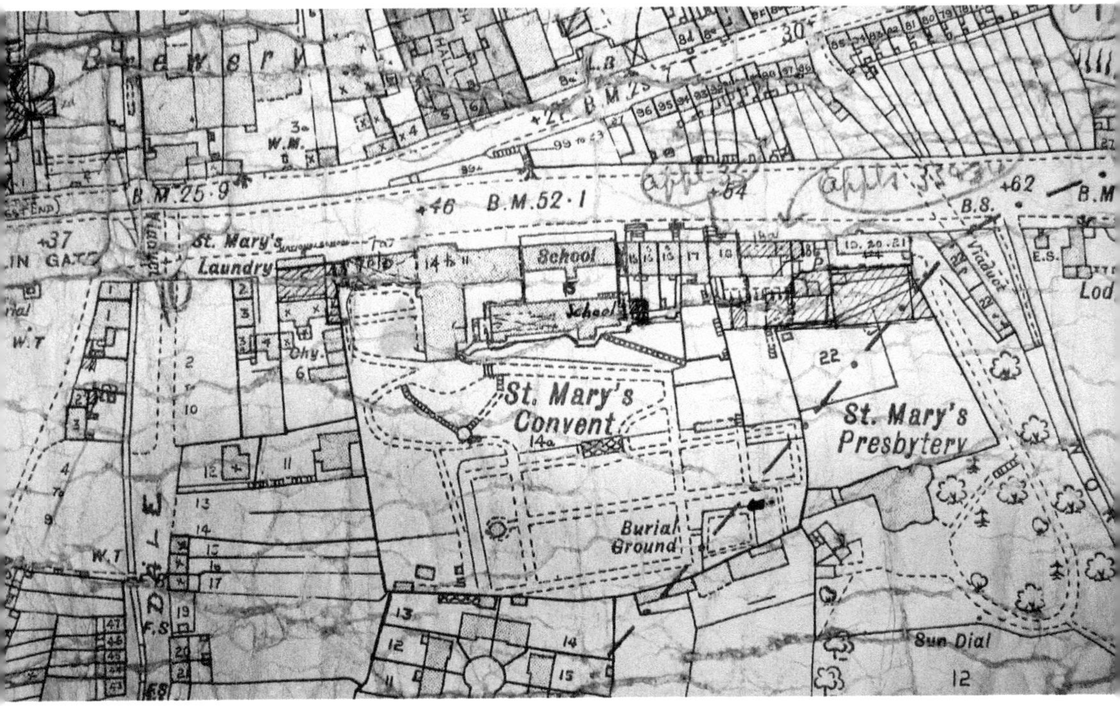

An old map of the Mercy Schools and convent on the Dublin Road. Note St Mary's Laundry on the left, which was replaced in 1952 by the flat-roofed Scoil Fatima. (Courtesy of the Valuation Office)

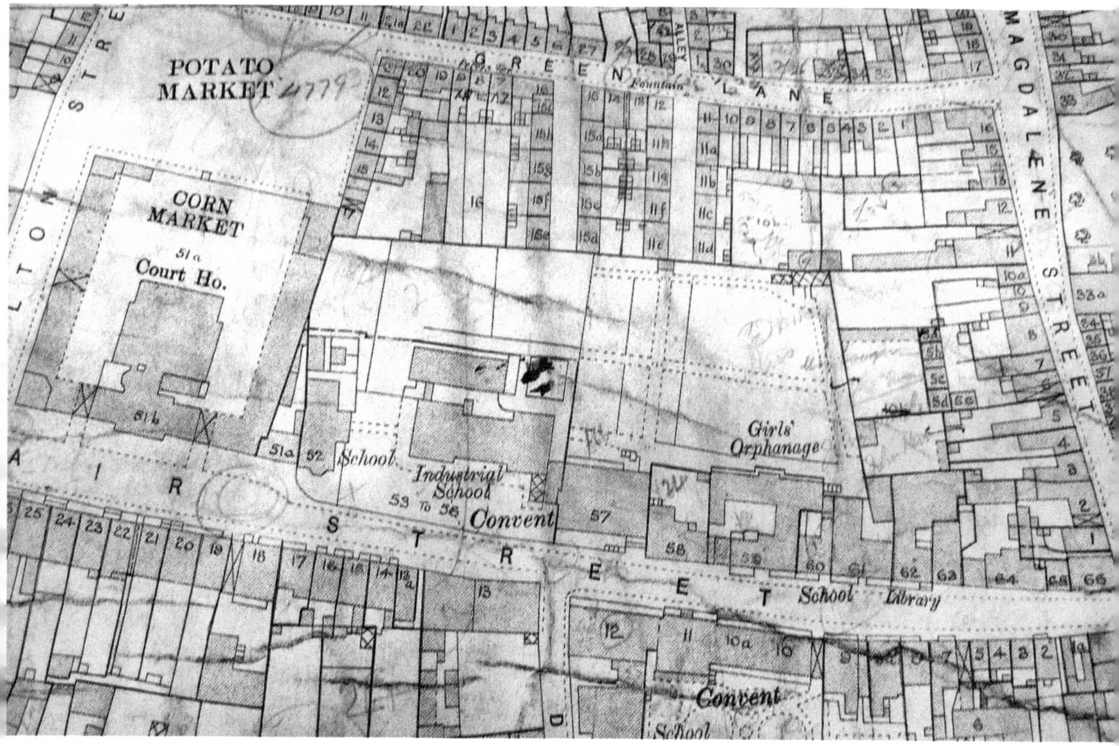

Fair Street, with the Sisters of Charity's two orphanages and schools stretching from the former Courthouse to the 1906 red-brick Carnegie Library. No 57 was the actual convent and the Presentation Convent was located opposite. (Courtesy of the Valuation Office)

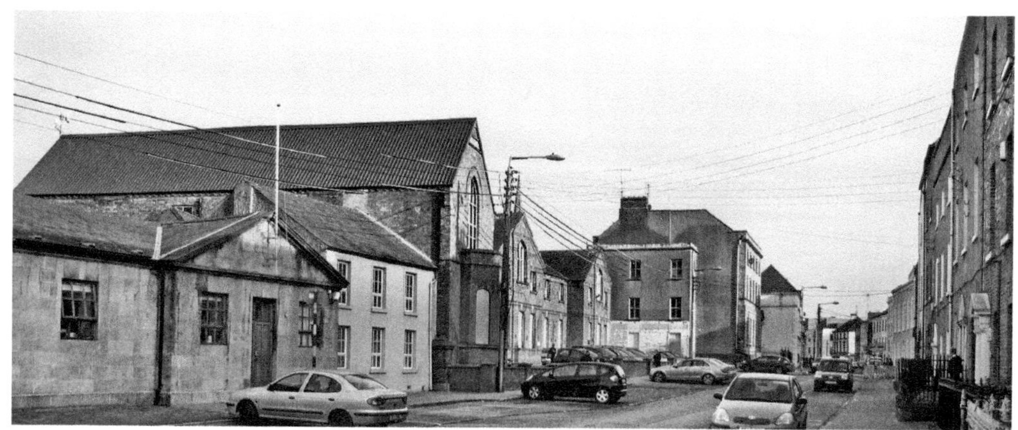

Fair Street today, looking east, with the former Sisters of Charity orphanages. On the left is the former Court House/Corn Market, which is now the Council offices.

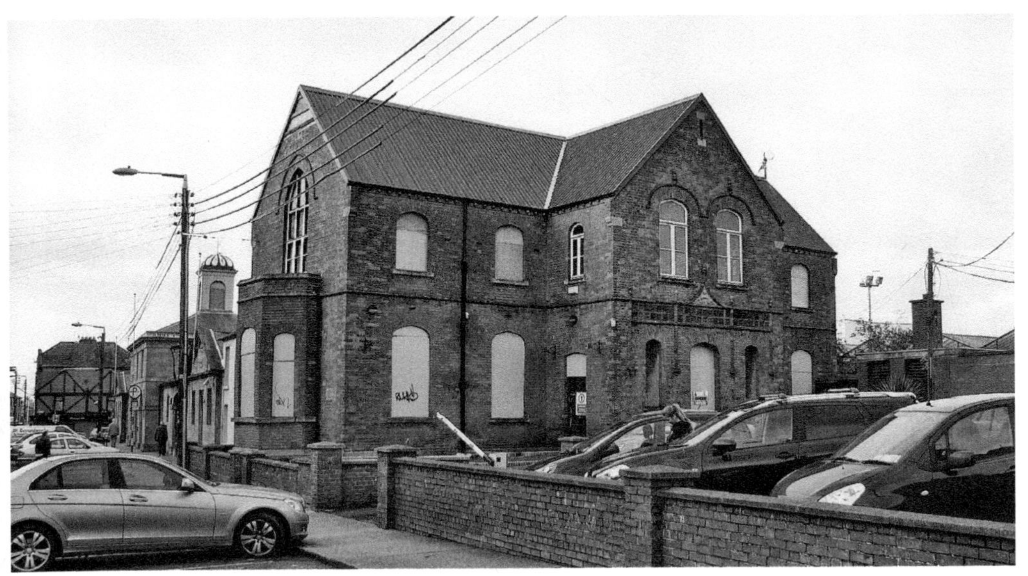

This was a boys National School in Fair Street, built in 1894 by the Sisters of Charity, and now vacant. The troughed metal roof replaces a slated roof following a recent fire.

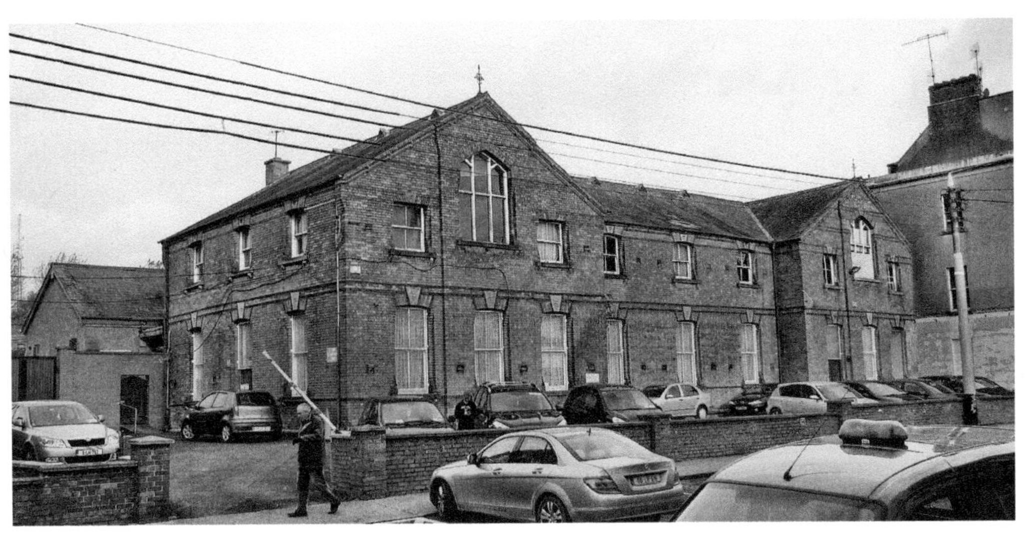

This was the Industrial School/Orphanage, built in 1870 by the Sisters of Charity. It is now a community centre.

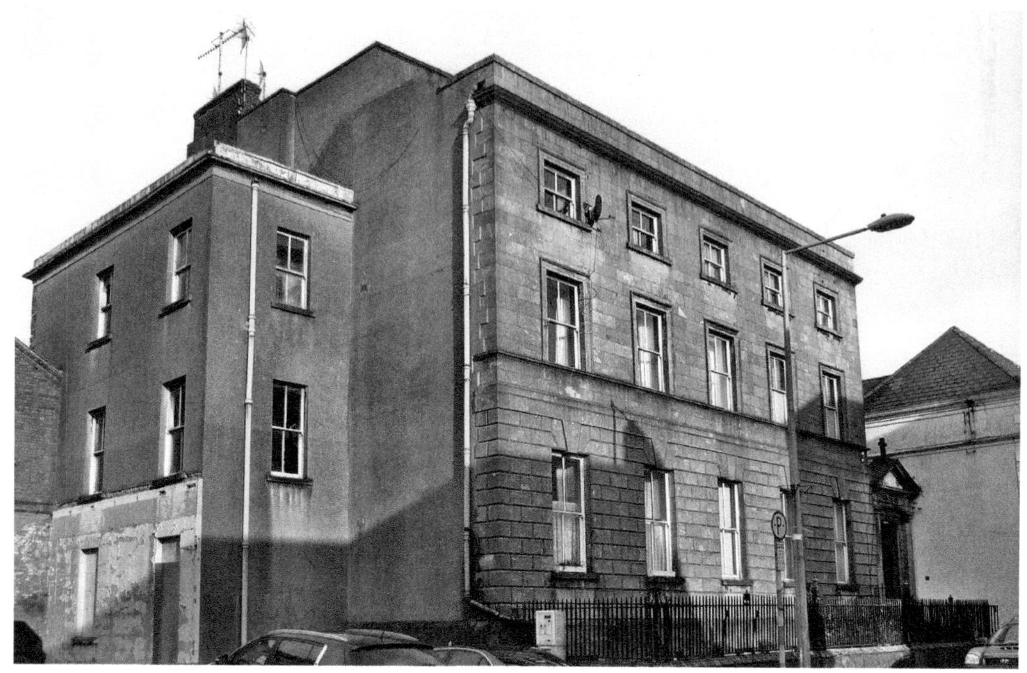

This was the Sisters of Charity Convent on Fair Street, with its imposing limestone front facade, and red-brick rear elevation. The Georgian building was an army barracks prior to 1870, and probably Alderman Henry Ogles' house before that. The entrance door was originally in the centre, but is now on the east side.

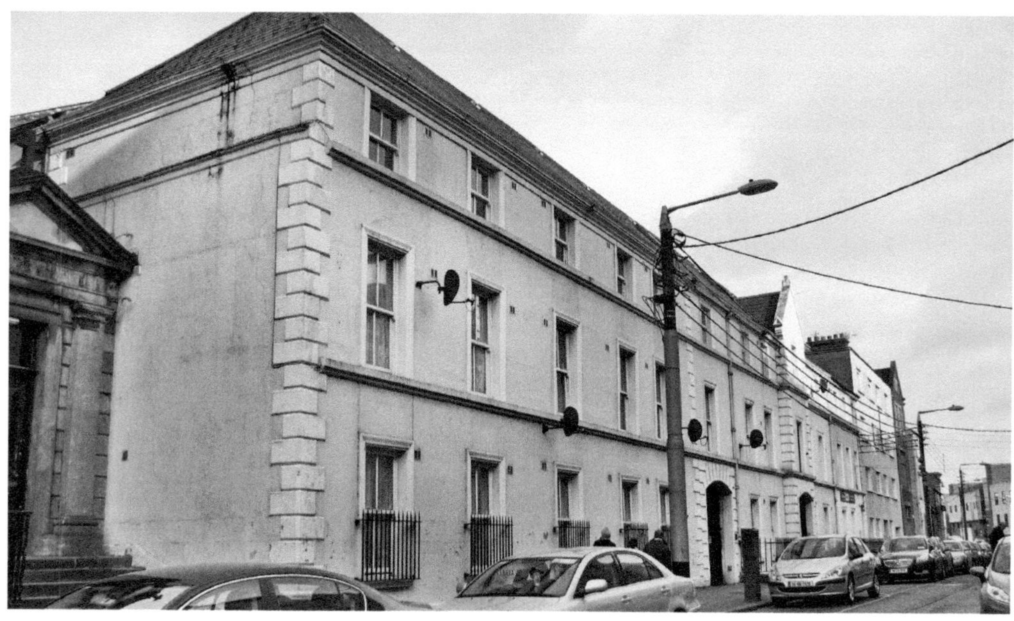

This was the Sisters of Charity girls orphanage and school in Fair Street. Until recent decades it was two-storey.

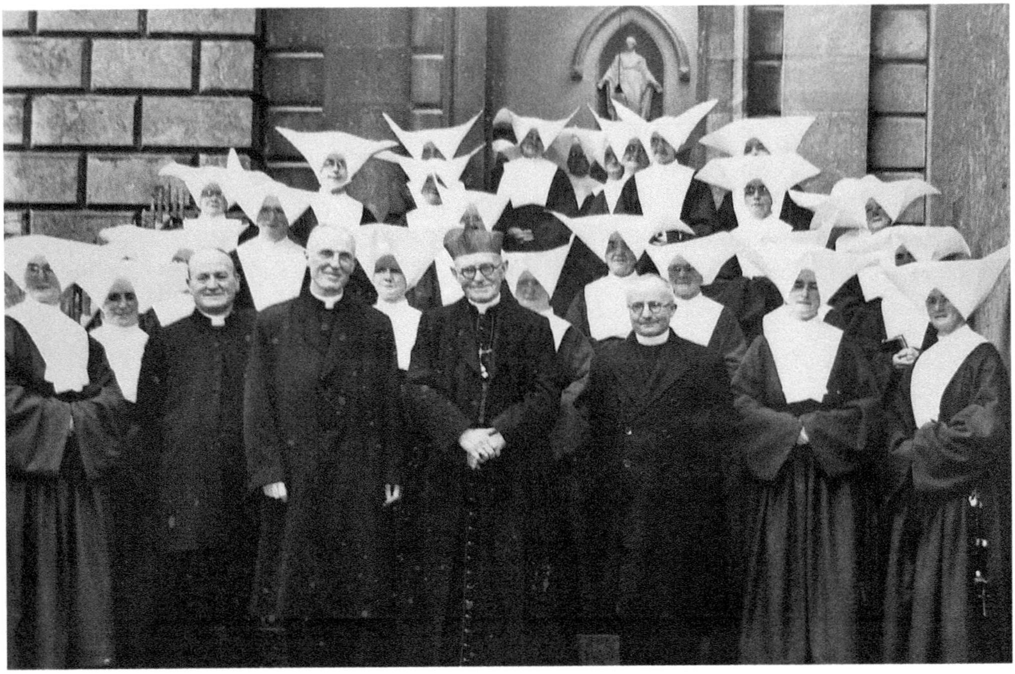

1955 group of Sisters of Charity in Drogheda, with Cardinal D'alton. (Courtesy of the Daughters of Charity)

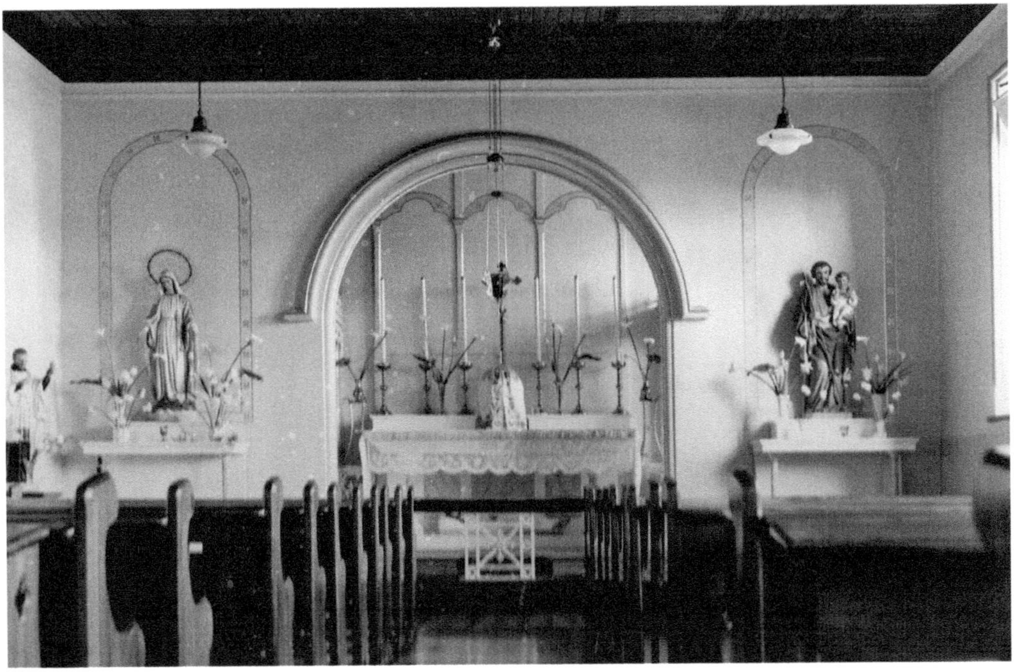

The former Sisters of Charity in Fair Street had a lovely chapel in their convent. (Courtesy of the Daughters of Charity)

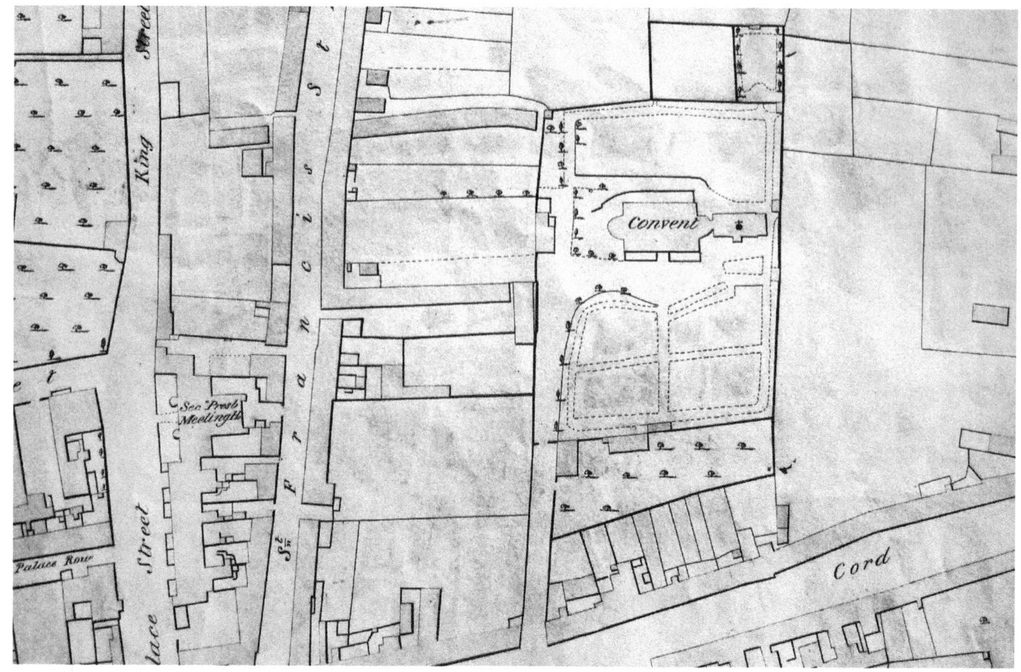

Siena Convent in Cord Road in the mid-nineteenth century. The chapel on the right was later demolished to make way for major extensions at both ends of the original Georgian house. (Courtesy of the National Archives)

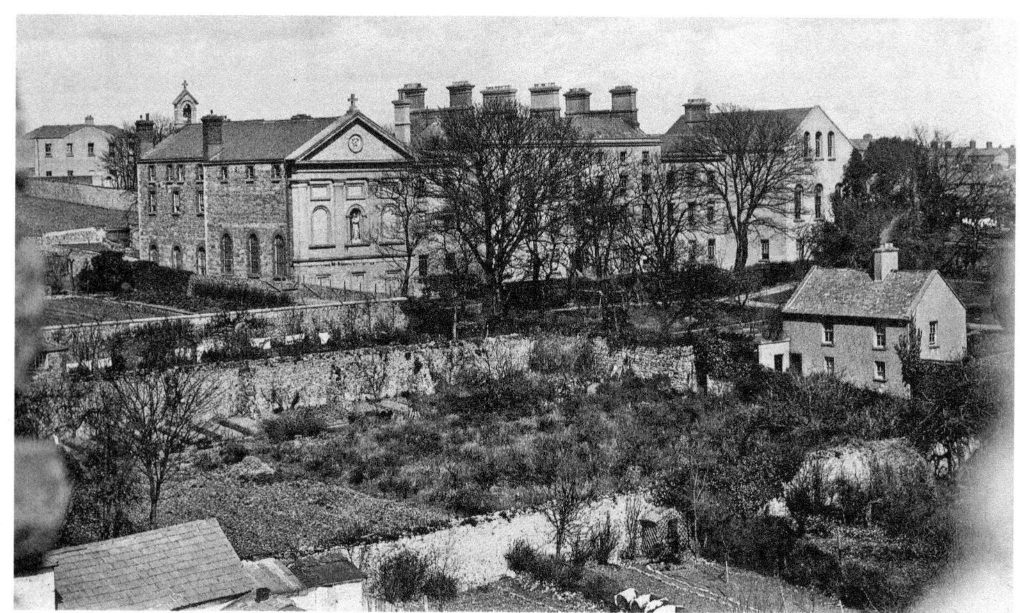

The former Siena Convent on Cord Road. The original house now has large wings at both ends, and the left one included a chapel. Note the two-storey Poor School in the left background, fronting onto Scarlett Street. (Courtesy of the Siena Convent)

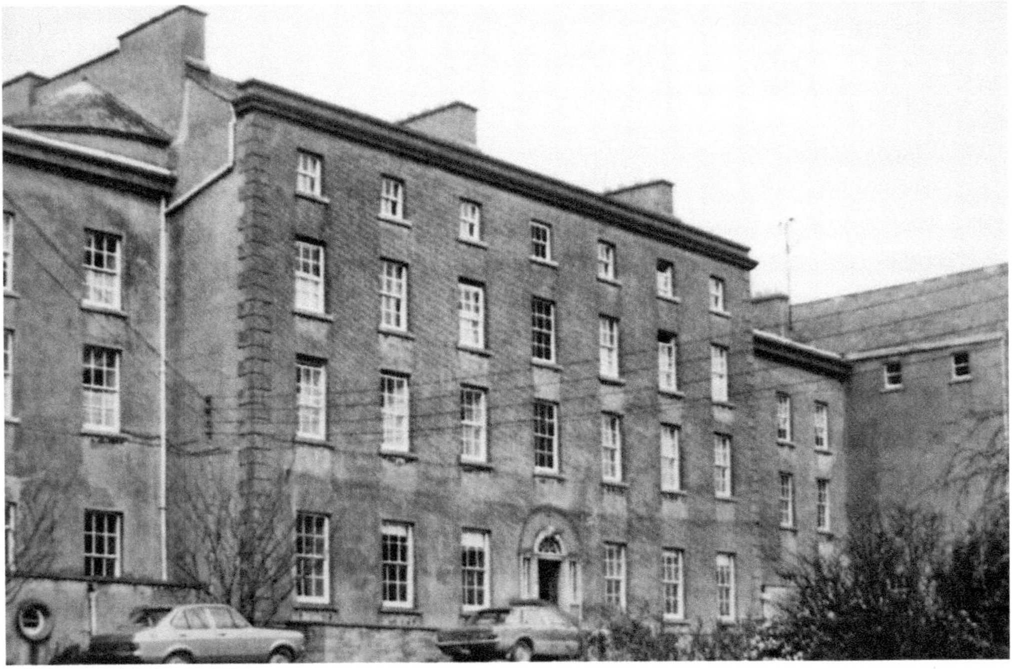

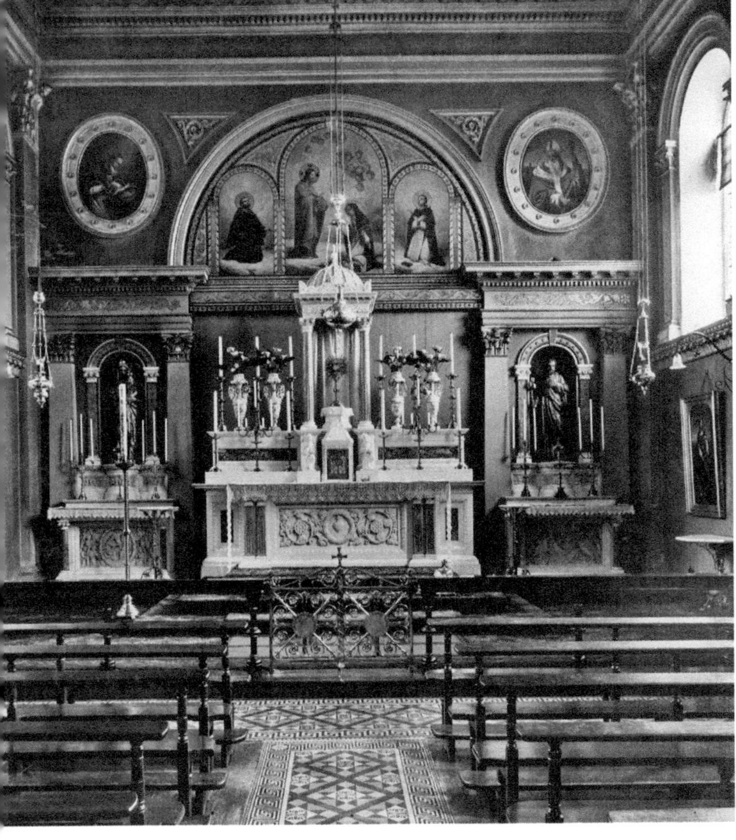

Above The former
Siena Convent in the
mid-1980s. (Courtesy of
An Foras Forbartha)

Left The former Siena
Convent chapel. (Courtesy
of Siena Convent)

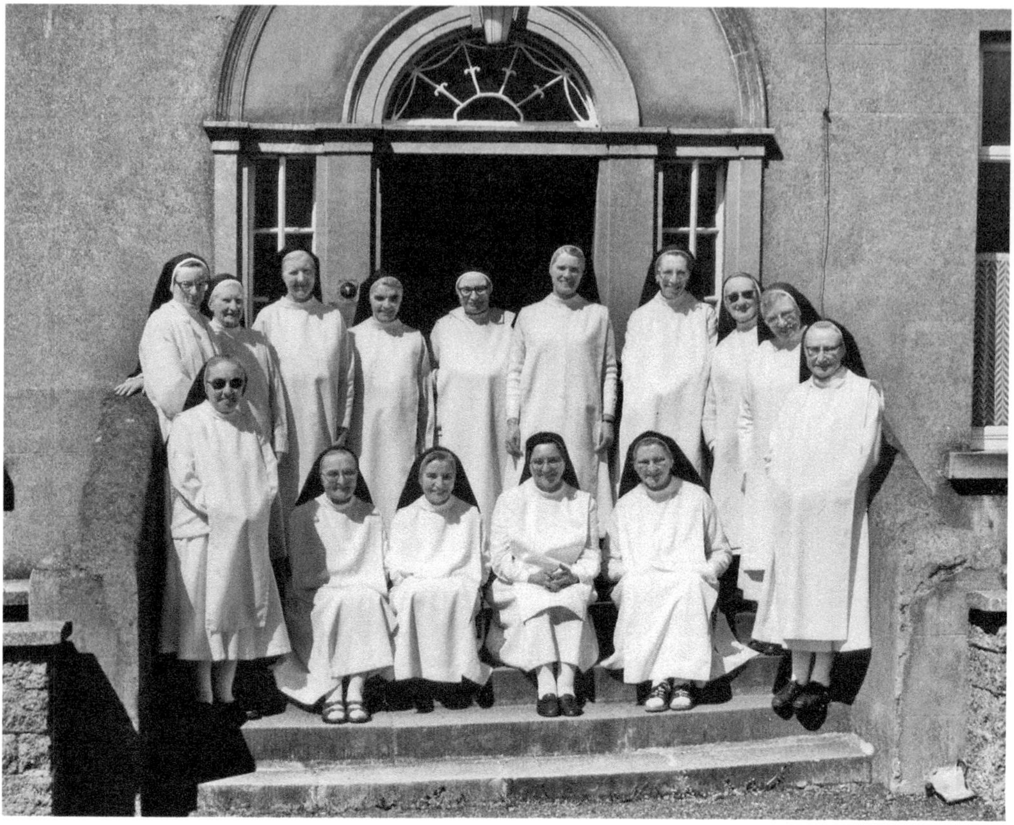

Above The final farewell to the Siena Convent in Cord Road in the 1990s. Note the white habit and dark veil. (Courtesy of Siena Convent)

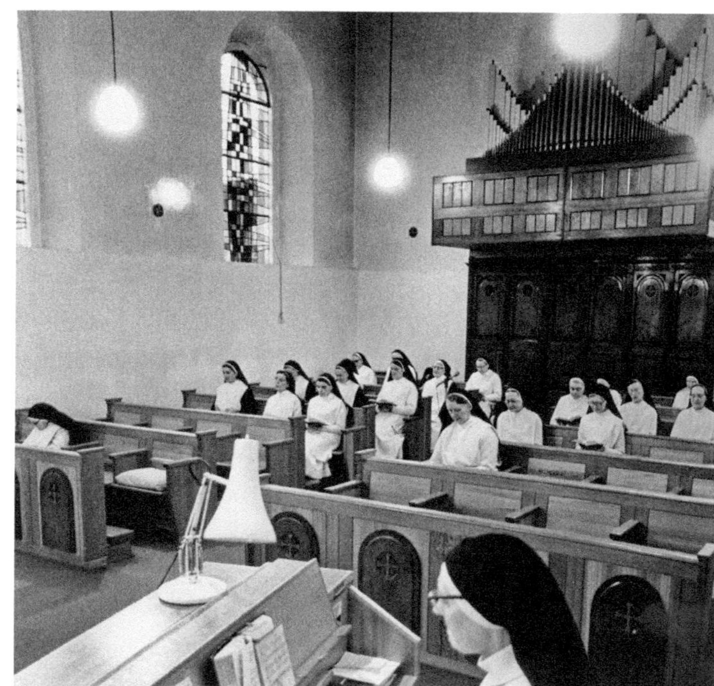

Right The choir in the Siena Convent, Cord Road, with the organ at the rear. (Courtesy of Siena Convent)

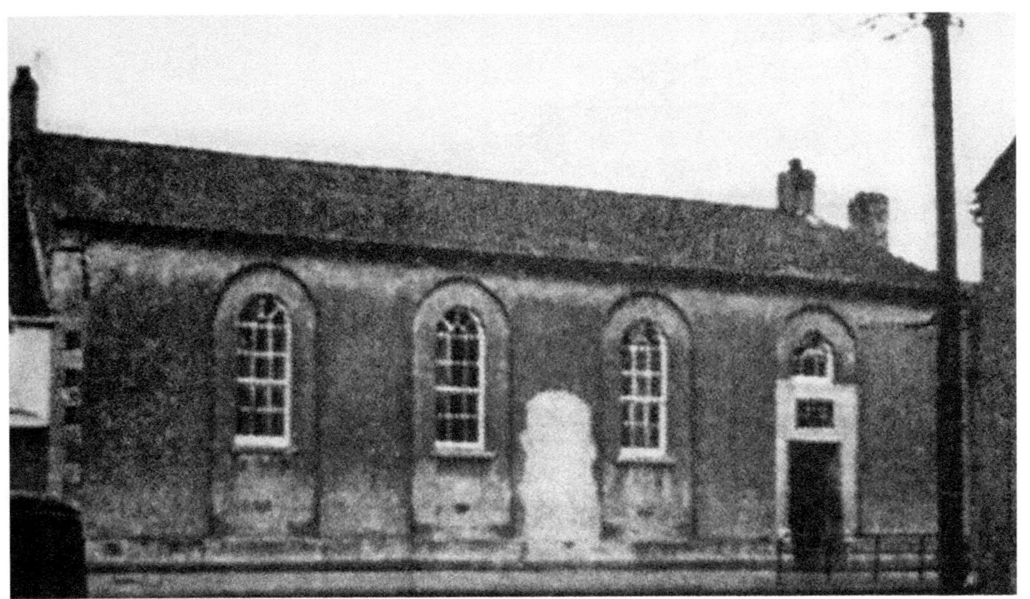

The Christian Brothers School in Trinity Street lasted from 1859 to 1955. It is now the site of the Planet Pub. (Courtesy of the Christian Brothers)

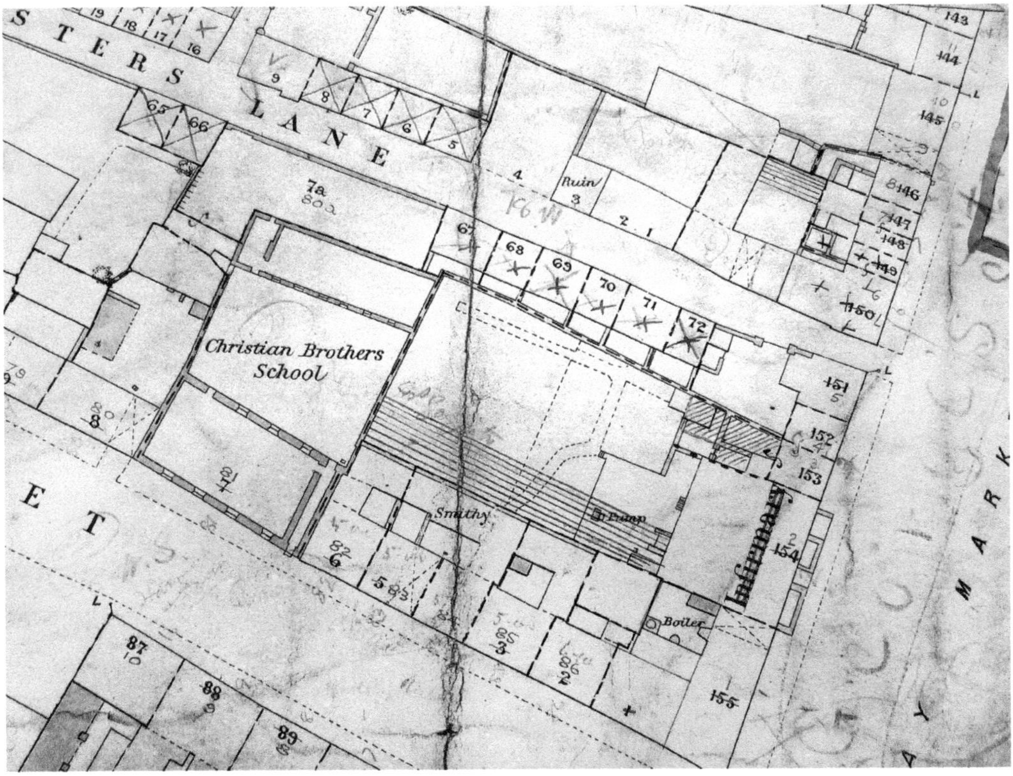

A plan of the former Christian Brothers school in Trinity Street. (Courtesy of the Valuation Office)

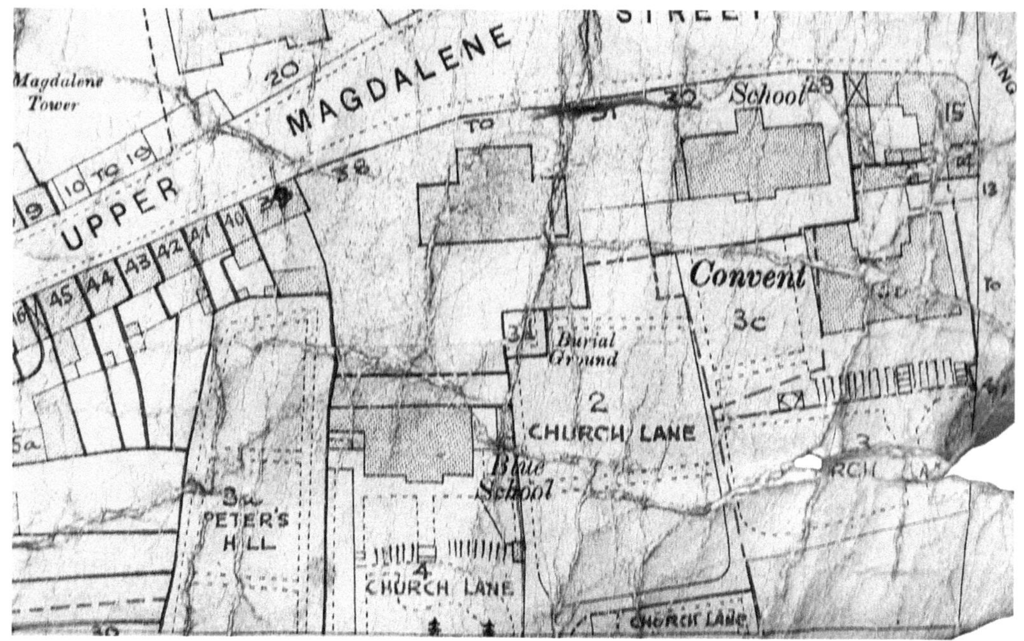

A plan of the Christian Brothers school at Sundays Gate. The brothers' monastery is also called a convent. (Courtesy of the Valuation Office)

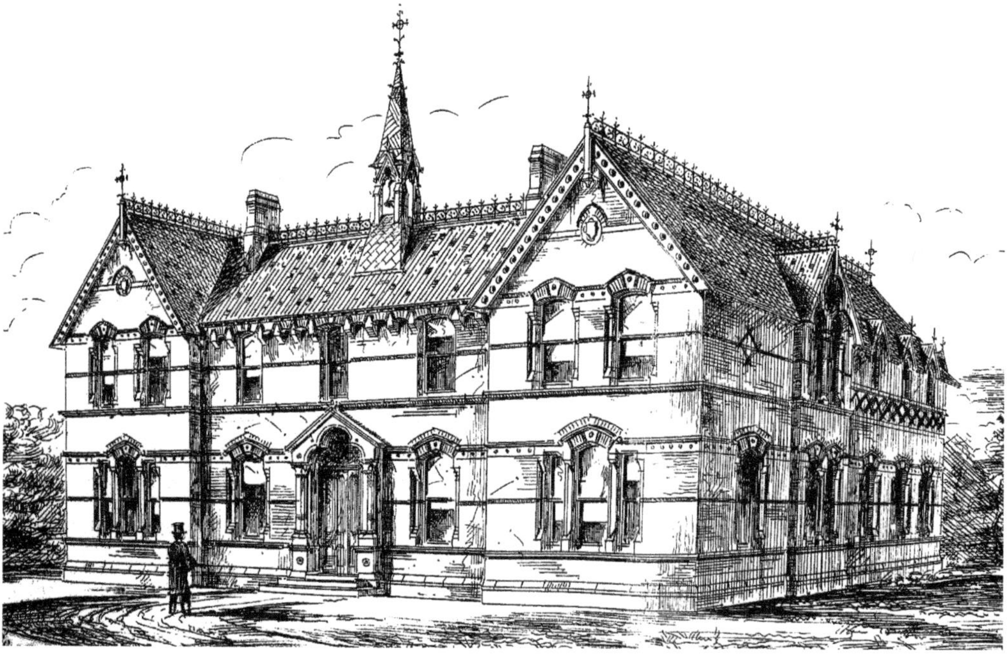

An architect's sketch of the proposed 1868 Christian Brothers monastery in King Street. (From the *Irish Builder*, courtesy of the Irish Architectural Archive)

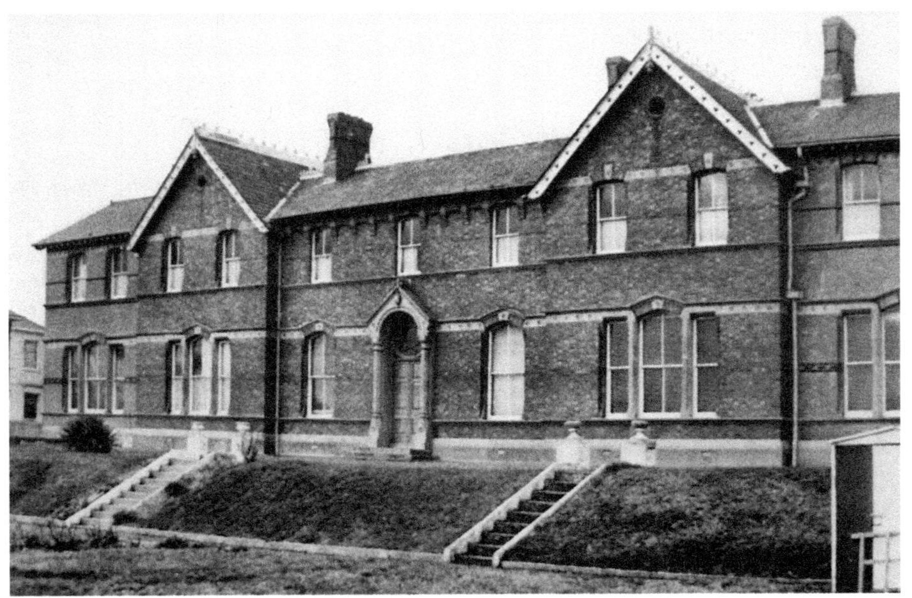

The Christian Brother's monastery in King Street in 1986. (Courtesy of An Foras Forbartha)

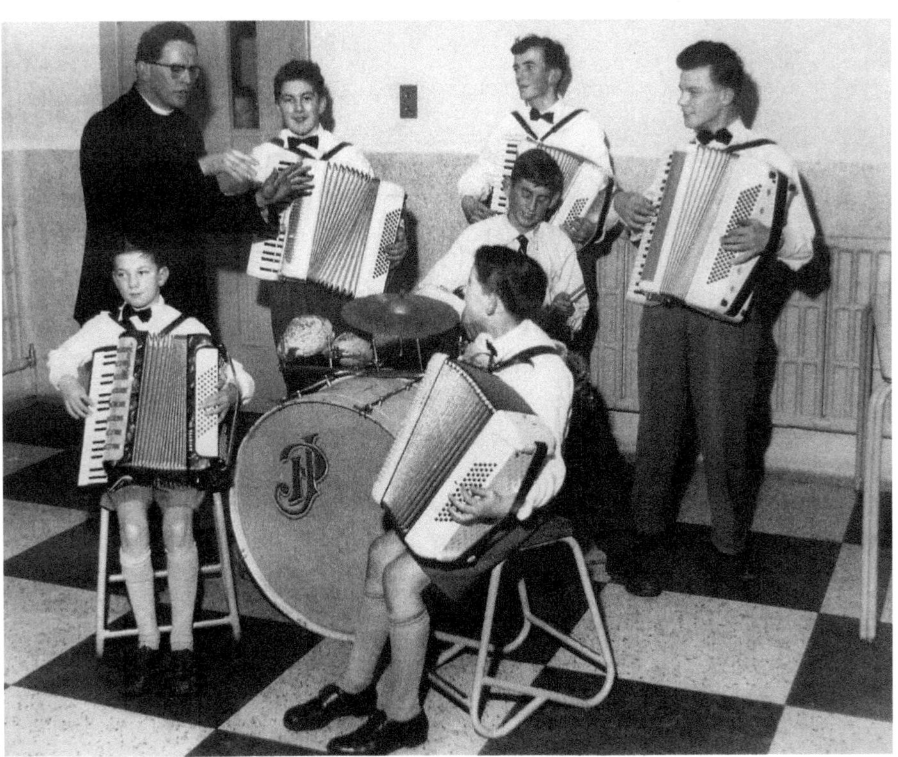

The Christian Brothers were famous for teaching the accordion. From left to right: Brother O'Donnell, Paul Hamlett, Harry O'Reilly, Patrick Carton, Nicholas Smith, Jack O'Reilly, Paddy Farrell. (Courtesy of the Christian Brothers)

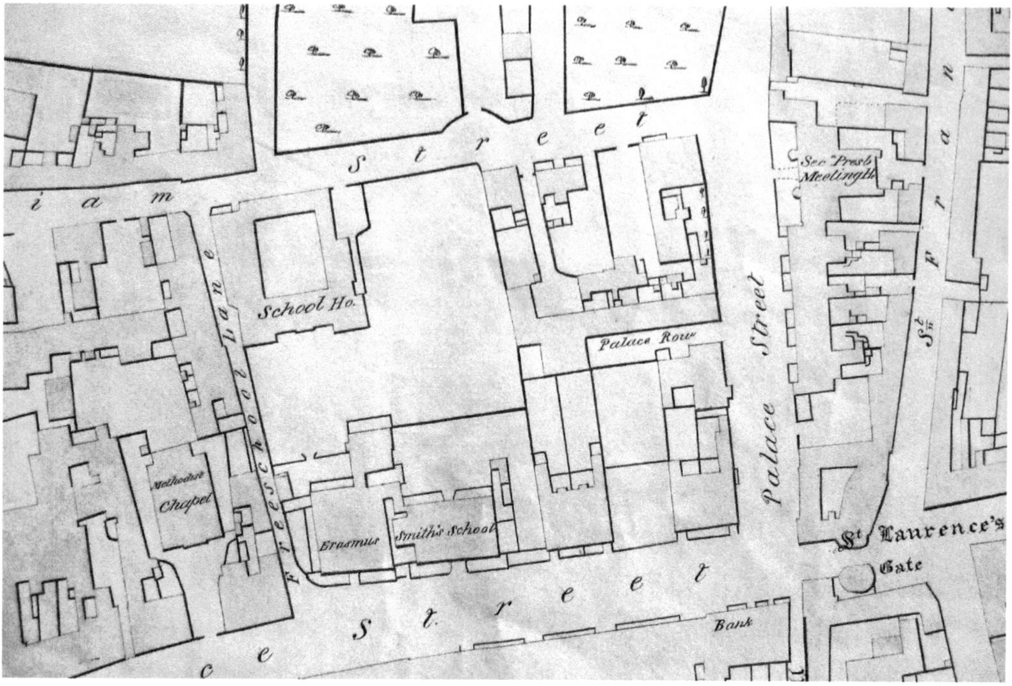

A plan of Erasmus Smith's School in the 1830s (later called Drogheda Grammar School) in St Laurence Street, backing on to William Street. Note that the towers of St Laurence Gate are joined with adjacent buildings. (Courtesy of the National Archives)

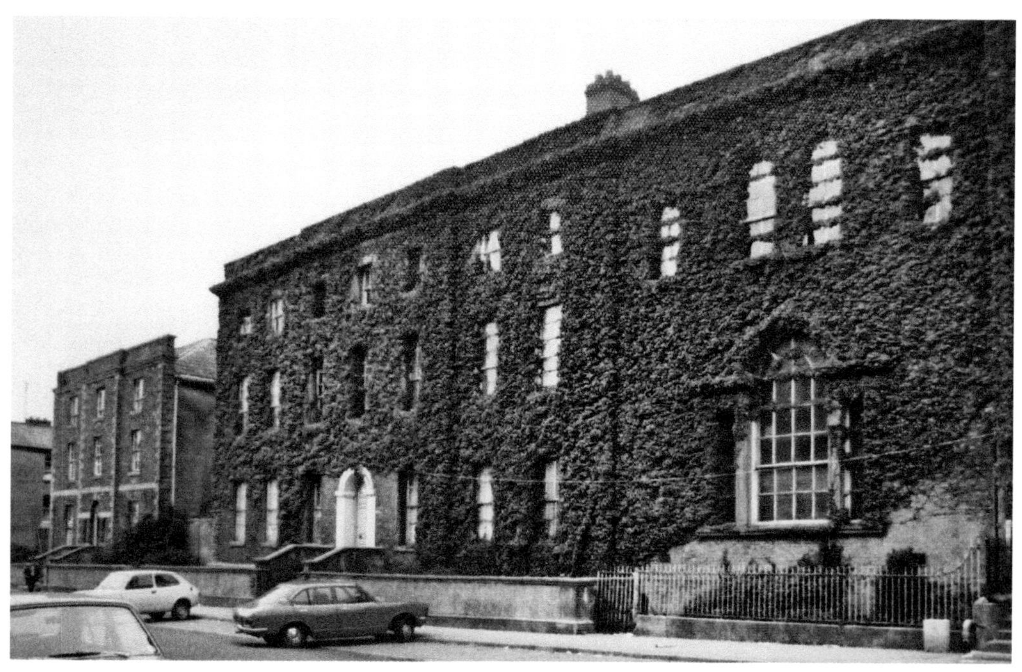

Drogheda Grammar School in recent decades. (Courtesy of the Irish Architectural Archive)

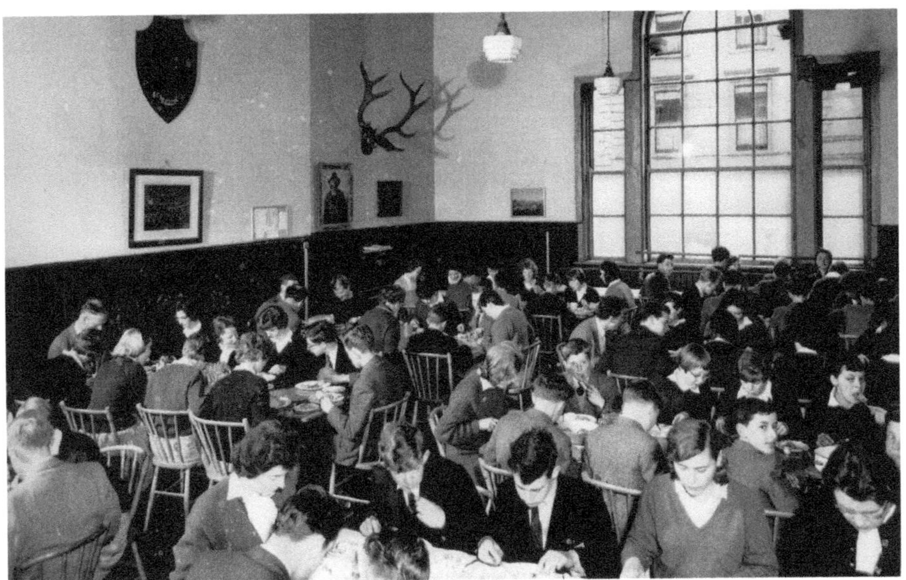

The dining room in Drogheda Grammar School was behind the iconic Venetian window facing St Laurence Street. (Courtesy of Drogheda Grammar School)

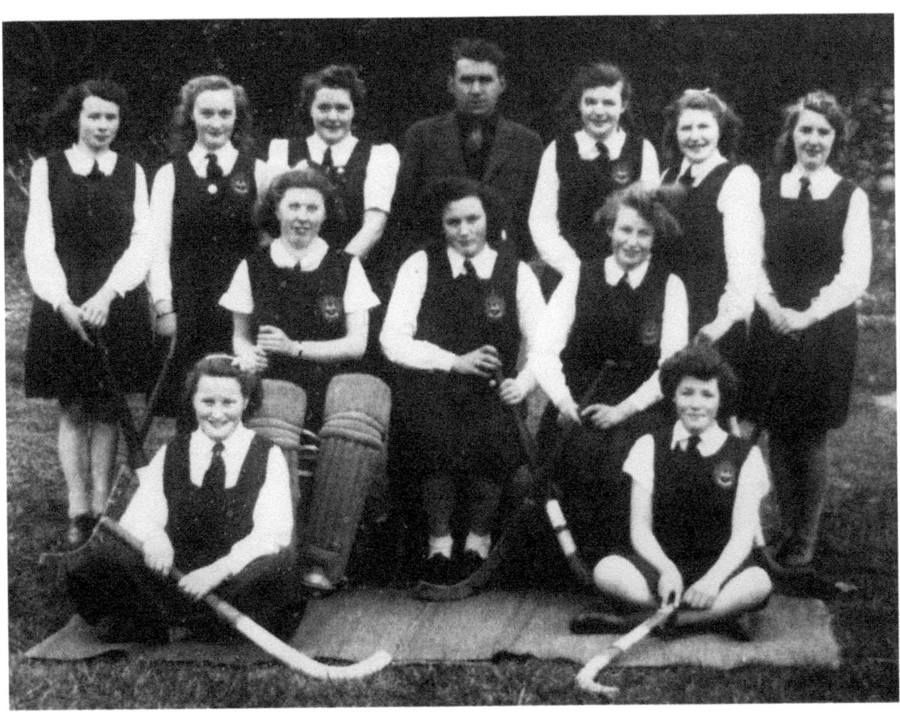

Drogheda Grammar School in 1946/47. From left to right, back row: S. Hatch, F. Watson, M. Robinson, G. Kells, D. Warren, A. Cochrane, P. Shaw-Hamilton. Middle row: V. Shekleton, E. Walker, C. Jordan. Front row: A. Mortier, G. Nichols. (Courtesy of Drogheda Grammar School)

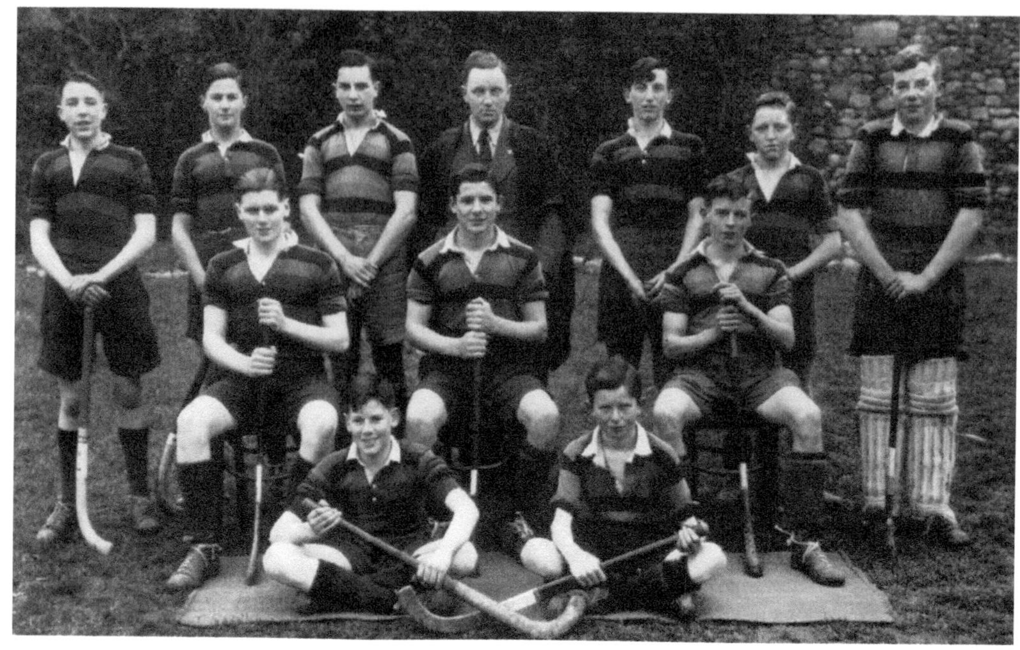

Drogheda Grammar School in the 1940/50s. From left to right, back row: A. Dunne, D. Epstein, D. Smith, -?- , R. Harris, R. King-Hall, J. Jordan. Middle row: R. Wright, J. Hatch, B. Athey. Front row: F. Ryan, C. Hatch. (Courtesy of Drogheda Grammar School)

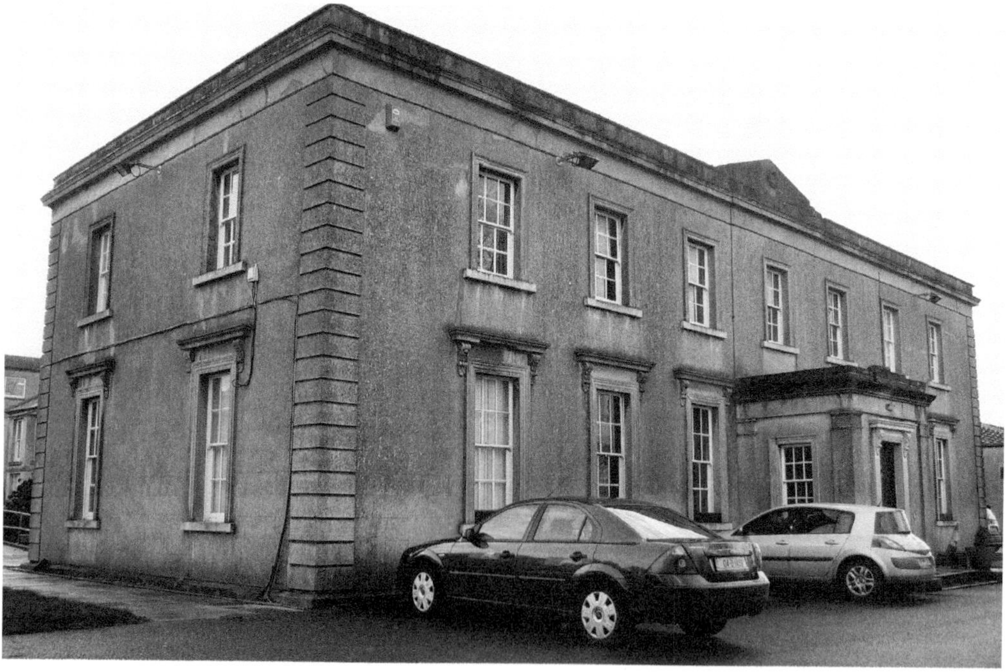

In 1976 Drogheda Grammar School moved to Eden View on the Mornington Road, a fine old house, which is still the centre of a very modern school campus.

5

HEALTH

MEDICAL MISSIONARIES OF MARY

Mother Mary Martin was one of twelve children, born in Glencar, No 20 Marlborough Road, Glenageary, County Dublin, in 1892, as Marie Helena Martin. They were a wealthy Catholic family, owning T. & C. Martin, builders providers in D'Olier Street, Dublin, and timber yards in the North Wall port area.

Marie was a Voluntary Aid Defence nurse during the First World War, serving in Malta and France, before training as a midwife in the National Maternity Hospital, Holles Street, Dublin.

Marie spent time as a lay missionary in Calabar, Nigeria, from 1921-23, before returning to Ireland, where she suffered poor health for about ten years.

In company with Mary Patrick Leydon, Mary Magdalen O'Rourke, and Mary Joseph Moynagh, Marie spent 1934-36 assisting and learning with the Benedictine monks in Glenstal Abbey, Limerick, before receiving permission from the Pope to start a medical nun's order to serve women and children in Nigeria, West Africa.

Marie set off for Calabar, Nigeria, early in 1937, with Mary Magdalen O'Rourke and Mary Joseph Moynagh, and started as novices of the Sisters of the Society of the Holy Child Jesus. But Marie became very ill, and was professed a nun in her sick bed in Port Harcourt, Nigeria, on 4 April 1937. Taking the religious name, Mary of the Incarnation, she was immediately shipped back to Ireland, leaving behind her two companions to continue their education.

Mother Mary soon regained her health, and settled into Rosemount, Booterstown, Co. Dublin, which her brother Desmond, an architect, bought for her as a gift in 1937. Rosemount was intended as a residence for student nurses and doctors.

In December 1938, at the instigation of the Primate of Armagh, Mother Mary rented Elm View, Main Street, Collon, near Drogheda, as a novitiate for religious training.

In the summer of 1939, the parish priest of Drogheda invited Mother Mary to run a new maternity hospital which he was building, by extending an old house called Beech Grove (previously called Mount Harmon), at the corner of Hardmans Gardens and Windmill Road. Our Lady of Lourdes Maternity Hospital opened in December 1939, and in 1940 the novitiate moved from Collon to a wing of the new hospital. In 1942 and 1946, extensions were added to the hospital, so that it could be used for training midwives.

By Christmas 1941, a new convent/novitiate was built, consisting of three storeys, including a mansard roof storey. However, on 13 February 1952, a fire destroyed the mansard storey, and this was not reinstated until around 1962.

Mother Mary started to build the east half of a general hospital in 1953, known as the International Missionary Training Hospital, for the express purpose of training nuns as nurses and doctors for mission work in Africa, and also sending back African students to Ireland to train in medicine. The boiler house and laundry were the first buildings to be completed, to cater for a commercial laundry for the businesses in and around Drogheda, and three delivery vans were constantly on the road. The Mercy Electric Laundry had been a similar operation from 1906 to 1947. In October 1956 the lower three storeys of the East Wing of the new hospital were officially opened, and in September 1957, the four upper storeys were completed. Part of the sixth floor was designated as the Tropical Diseases Department in 1960. In the early 1960s, the low level St Patrick's was built to link the convent with the hospital, comprising extra space for the novitiate, along with a concert hall. The west wing was added to the hospital in 1968. In 1956, a statue was placed on top of the full-height bow window linking the east and west wings. It is the work of Rome artist, Cecola Carmine, and called 'Our Lady of the Visitation'. In the 1960s, the hospital began training lay nurses, and a Nurses Home was built to accommodate them on the site of the former Lourdes chapel-of-ease, with a distinctive Edward Delaney bronze sculpture on the front facade.

Mother Mary Martin received the 'Freedom of Drogheda' in 1966. She died in 1975, and is buried in St Peter's cemetery behind the hospital.

The original Lourdes Maternity Hospital was demolished in 1994 to make way for Arus Mhuire, a nursing home for elderly nuns.

In 1997, the Health Services Executive acquired the main International Hospital from the nuns, although the nuns still live in the extended convent.

THE WORKHOUSE ('THE SPIKE'), DUBLIN ROAD

This historic complex opened on 16 December 1841, on an elevated 7½ acre site, at a total cost, including fit-out, of £9,320. It was designed for 800 'paupers', by English architect, George Wilkinson, using the same standard layout as the other workhouses throughout Ireland. A Fever Hospital was added at the very rear of the site around 1847, during the Famine years. The adjacent detached south-east former smallpox hospital dates from 1881.

The admissions front block was different from the standard Wilkinson design, and was very unusual and attractive. Another unusual feature is that the stand-alone chapel was parallel to the rear infirmary; it was more usual for the chapel to share the dining hall in the link building between the main block and the rear block.

The Mercy nuns got involved in nursing in the rear infirmary in the 1890s, and built the red-brick St Joseph's convent at the south-west corner of the campus in 1896. In 1903 it was recorded that two nuns were working as nurses in the infirmary, each earning a salary of £45 per annum.

In 1924 the County Health Board assumed responsibility for the workhouse, and called it the County Home. The main buildings were demolished in the late 1970s and replaced by Boyne View House, a public Nursing Home. The Upper Infirmary (old fever hospital – now called St Marys Hospital) is still in use by the HSE as a Nursing Home, but the Mercy nuns ended their involvement in 1988.

The 1901 census recorded eleven staff in the workhouse, including the master, Henry Duffy, and the matron, Agnes Levins. There were forty-eight 'paupers', twenty-nine 'lunatics and idiots', and twenty-nine patients in the hospital. There was one girl aged 10, and seven babies.

In the 1911 census there were sixteen 'paupers', and twenty-one 'lunatics', under the master, Mathew Langan, assisted by a labour master, an assistant matron, cook, porter, and six nurses. The Mercy Nuns convent housed the matron, two nurses, an assistant, and their 13-year-old servant girl.

Bully's Acre, opposite the Calvary cemetery, is the forlorn cemetery for the workhouse, and comprises a large overgrown field, filled with thousands of un-named and forgotten Christians, with a blank Celtic cross in the centre.

COTTAGE HOSPITAL, SCARLETT STREET

This red-brick two-storey hospital was founded in 1908 by Miss Sidney Smith and Miss Rosa Smith, who lived in Greenhills House (which was later bought by the Presentation Sisters). Sixteen patients were recorded in the 1911 census, mostly Catholic. It is now run by the HSE.

INFIRMARY, 2 GEORGES SQUARE (ALSO CALLED HAYMARKET)

This small two-storey hospital was built in 1809, to a design by the famous architect Francis Johnston, and appears to have lasted until the Cottage Hospital opened in 1908. It included a dispensary for giving out free medicine.

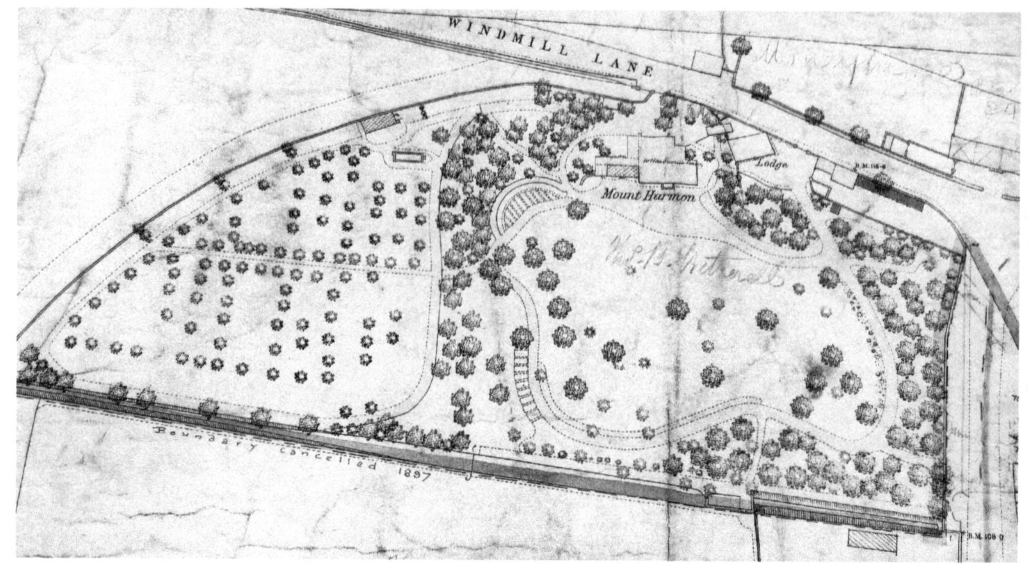

A nineteenth-century map of the estate purchased by the Medical Missionaries of Mary in the 1930s. It was called Mount Harmon at one stage, and also Mr Hardmans, before being renamed Beech Grove. In the eighteenth century, the road on the right from Sundays Gate was called Gallows Green. (Courtesy of the Valuation Office)

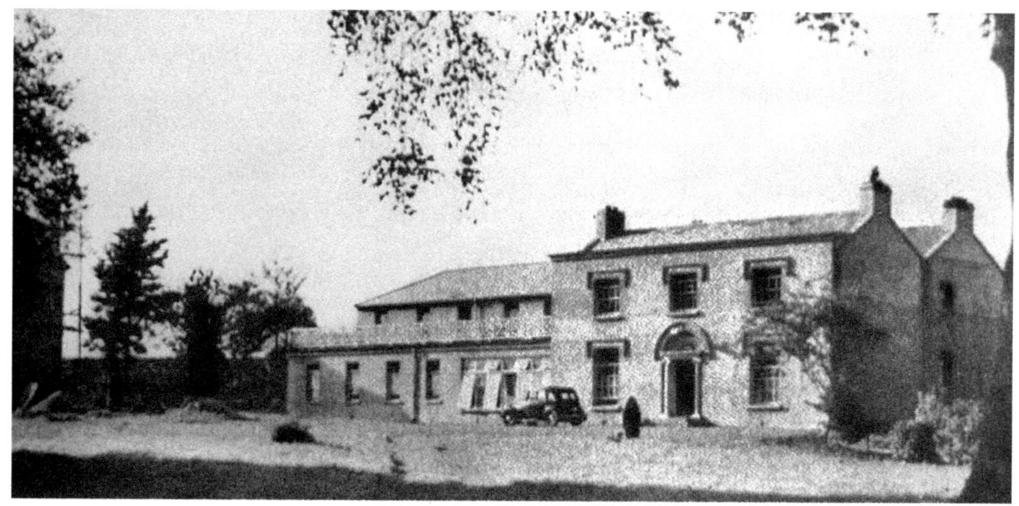

Beech Grove in 1938, with the new convent being built on extreme left. (Courtesy of the Medical Missionaries of Mary)

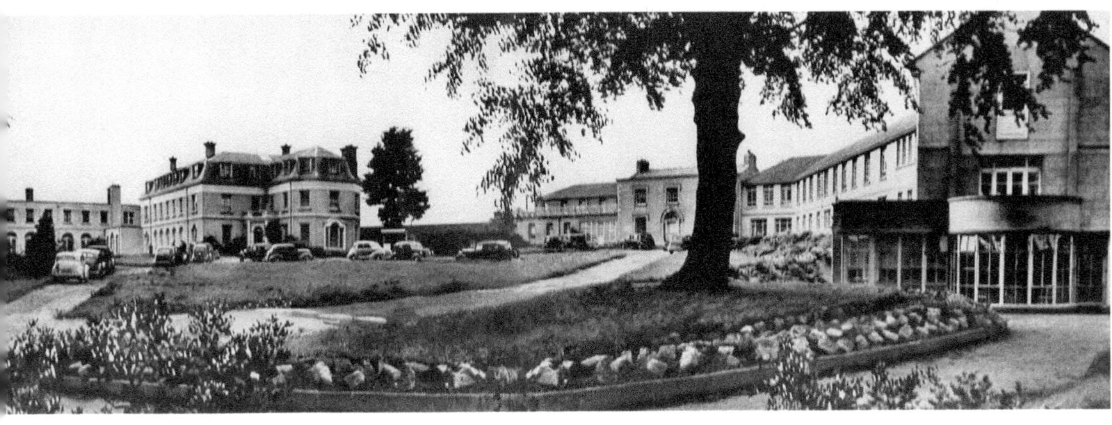

Beech Grove (behind the tree) with the Maternity Hospital on right, and the convent plus novitiate on left. (Courtesy of the Medical Missionaries of Mary)

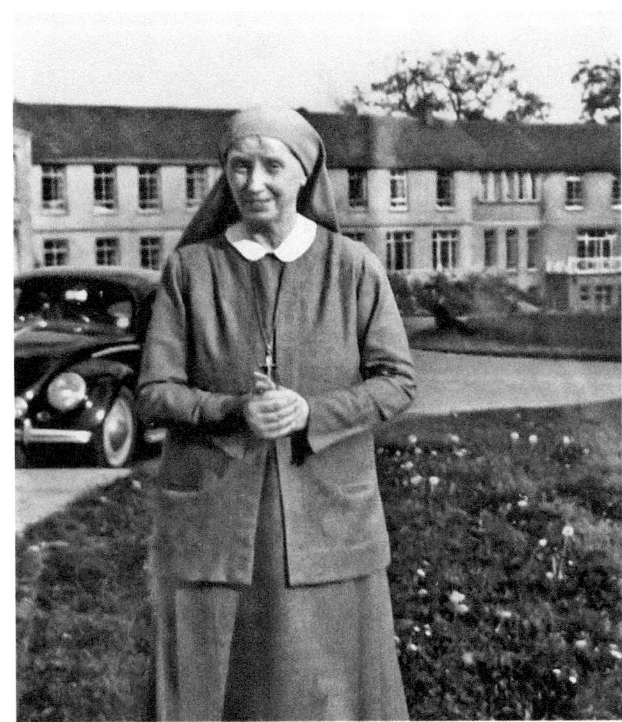

Mother Mary Martin outside the Maternity Hospital. (Courtesy of the Medical Missionaries of Mary)

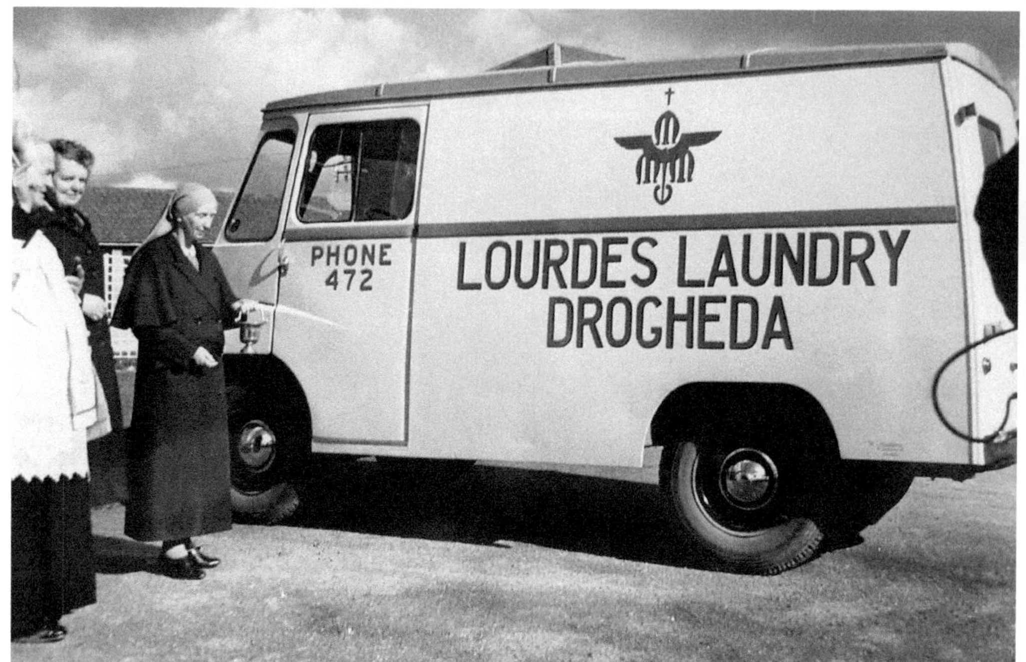

Mother Mary Martin assists in the blessing of their laundry van in the early 1950s. (Courtesy of the Medical Missionaries of Mary)

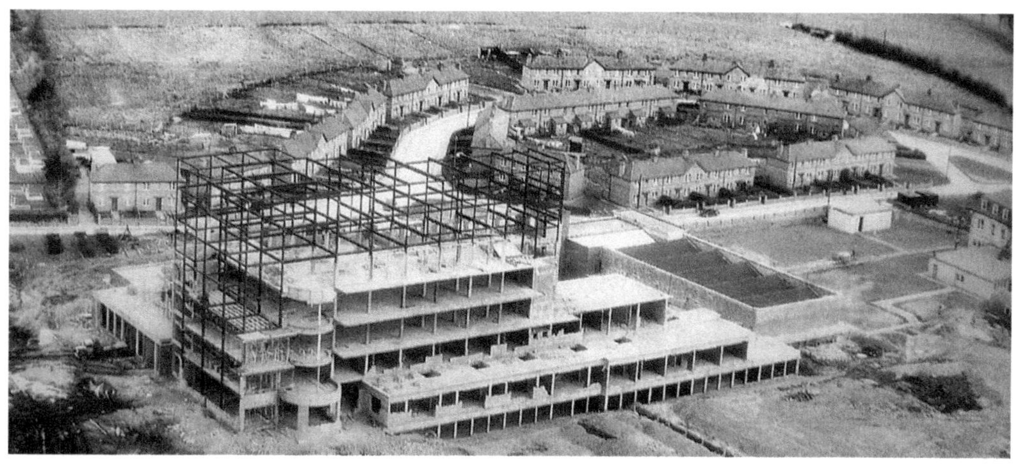

The east wing of the Lourdes Hospital takes shape. (Courtesy of the Medical Missionaries of Mary)

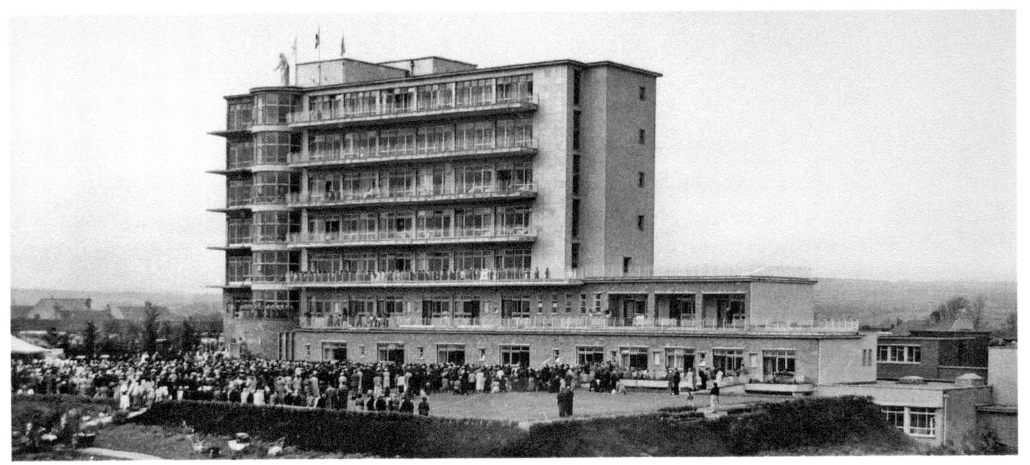

The east wing of the Lourdes Hospital was officially opened in 1956/57. (Courtesy of the Medical Missionaries of Mary)

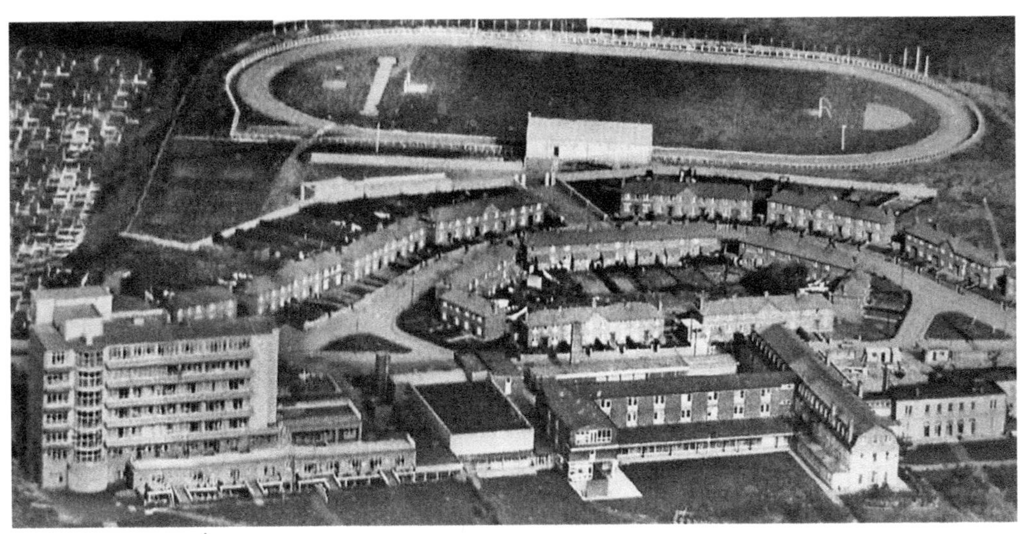

Mid-1960s aerial view of the Lourdes Hospital and convent. (Courtesy of the Medical Missionaries of Mary)

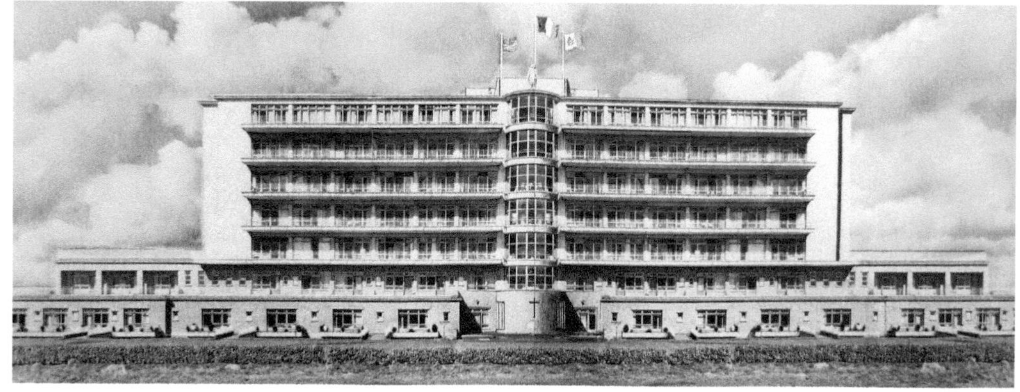

The completed east and west wings of the Lourdes Hospital. (Courtesy of the Medical Missionaries of Mary)

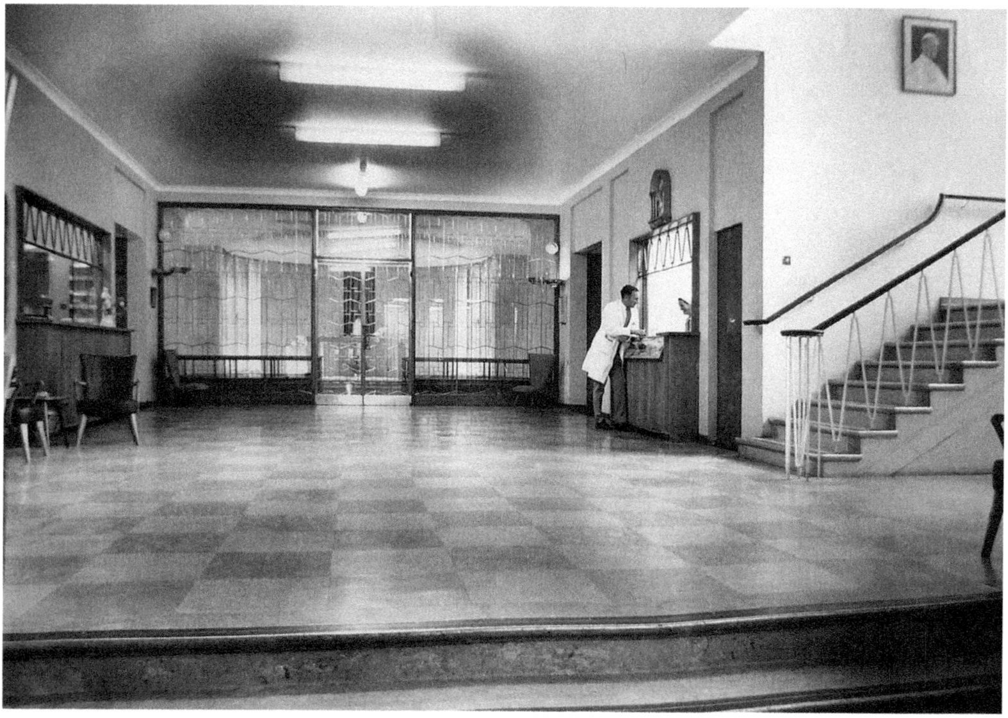

The little oratory was in the hallway between the two wings of the Lourdes Hospital. (Courtesy of the Medical Missionaries of Mary)

Opposite, top
Young missionaries in front of Beech Grove. (Courtesy of the Medical Missionaries of Mary)

Opposite, bottom
Beech Grove (left) and the Maternity Hospital (centre and right). (Courtesy of the Medical Missionaries of Mary)

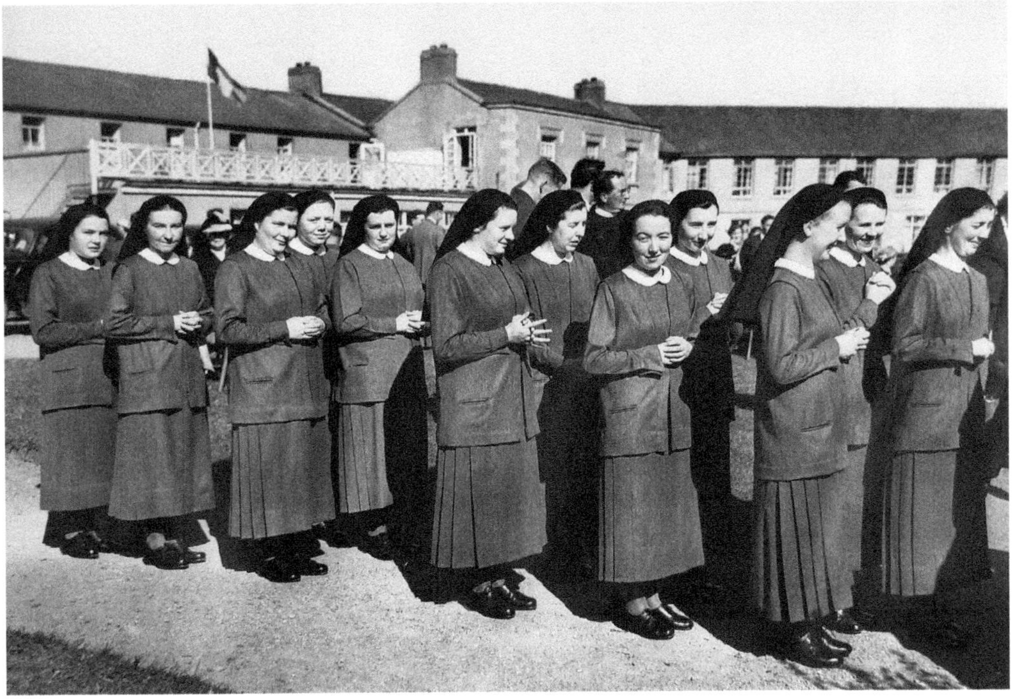

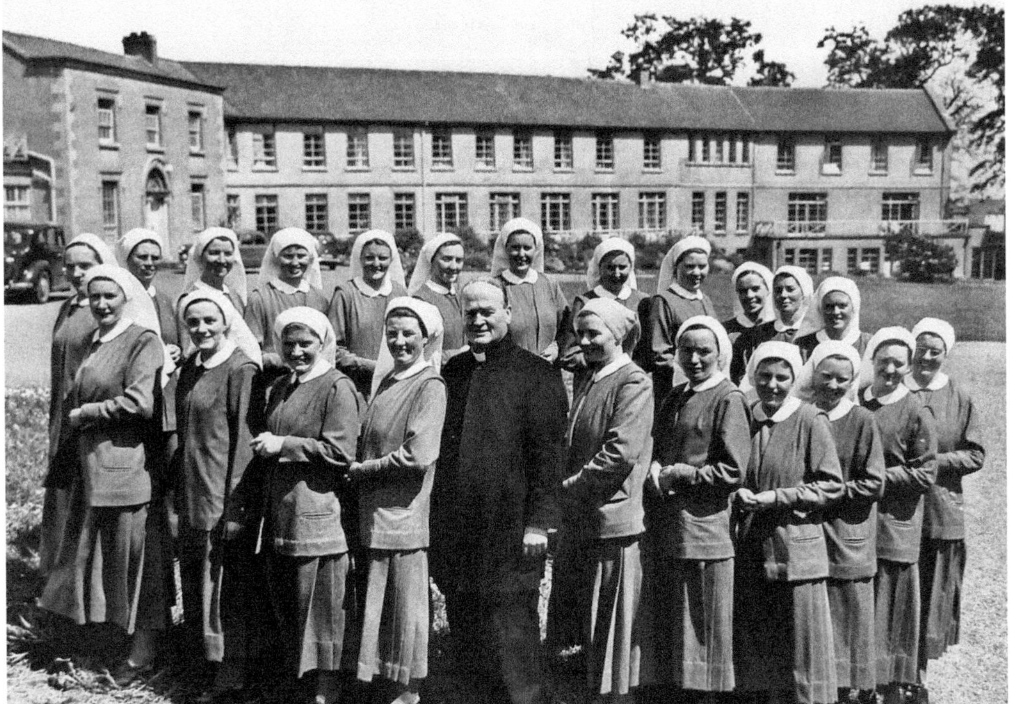

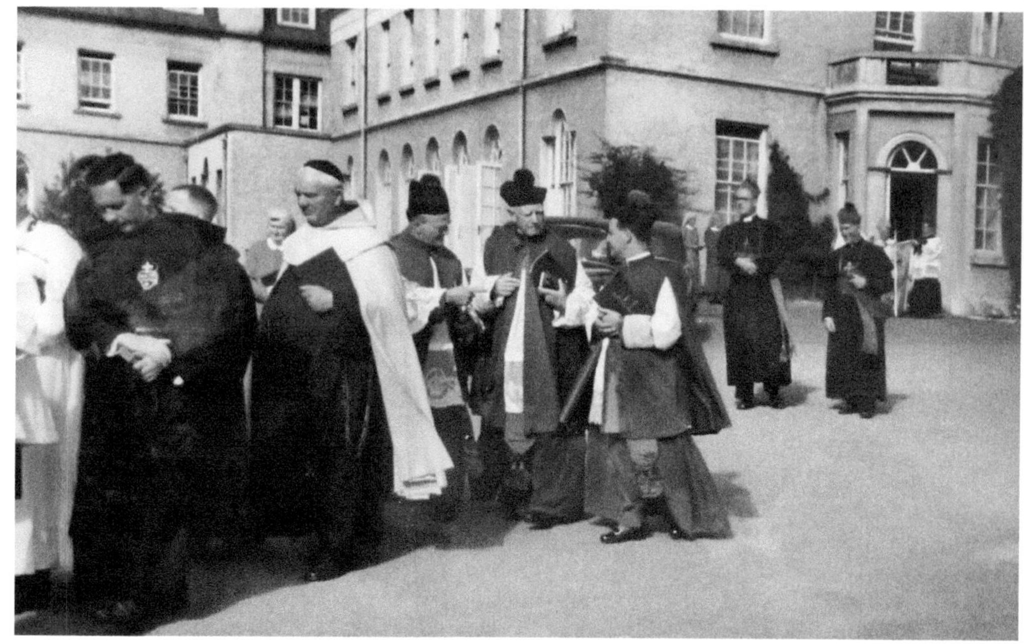

A clerical procession outside the convent/novitiate. (Courtesy of the Medical Missionaries of Mary)

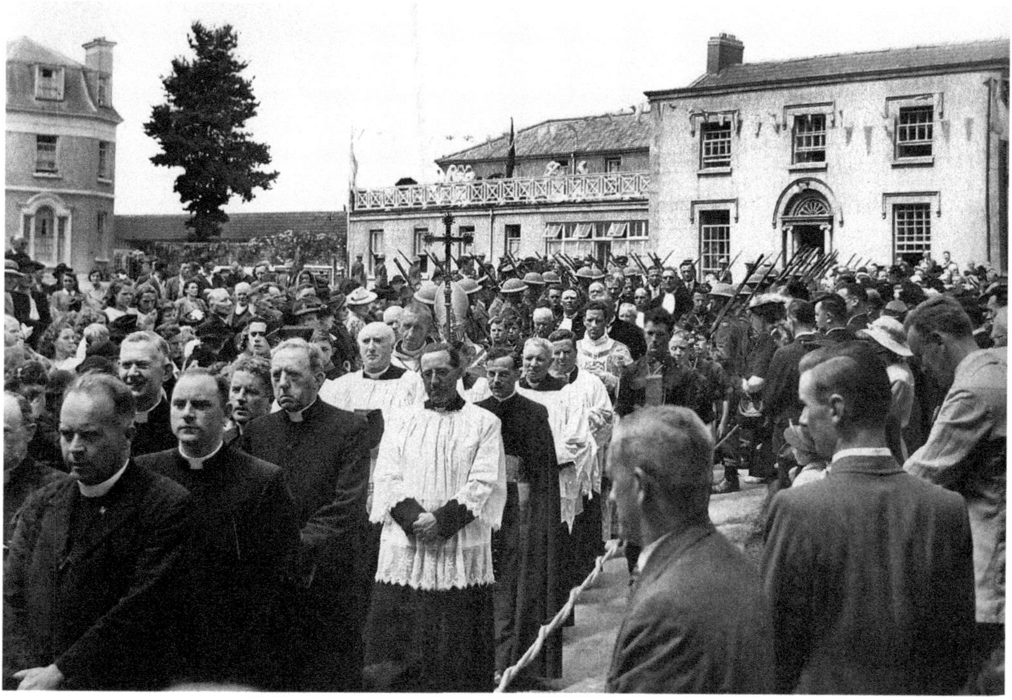

A procession in front of Beech Grove, with the Army/FCA in attendance. (Courtesy of the Medical Missionaries of Mary)

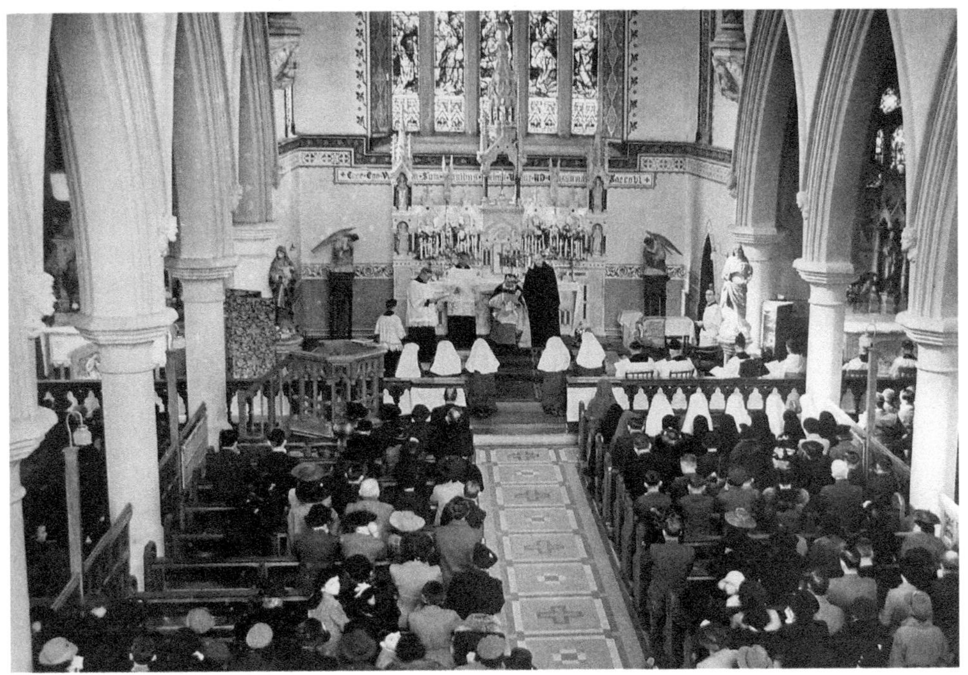

Medical Missionaries of Mary being professed in Collon in 1938. (Courtesy of the Medical Missionaries of Mary)

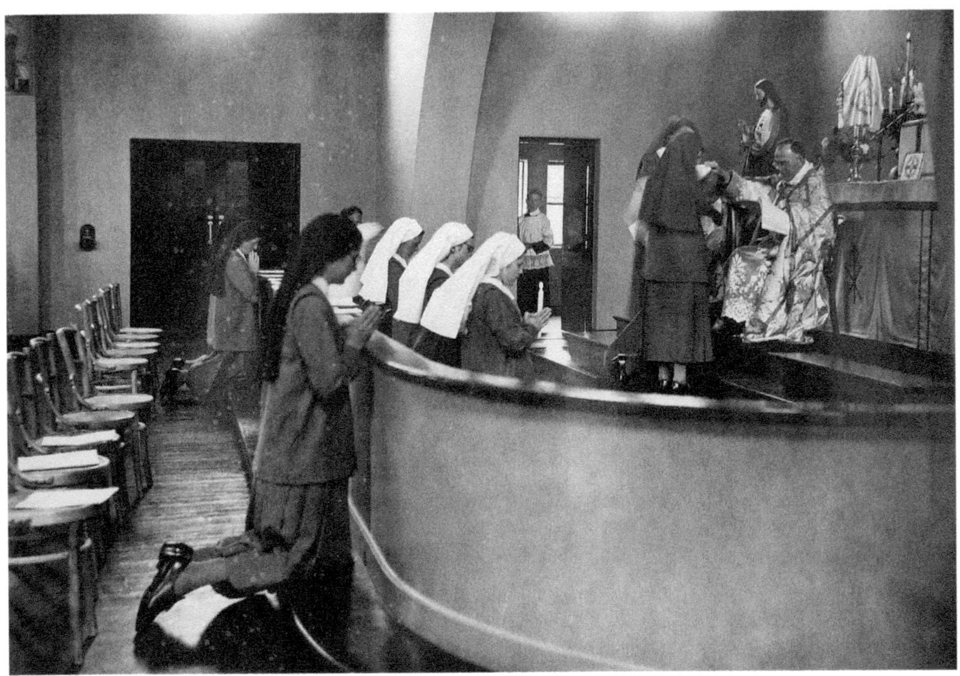

Medical Missionaries of Mary being professed in the Lourdes chapel-of-ease, 1942. (Courtesy of the Medical Missionaries of Mary)

Lourdes nursing graduates in 1973, with Sr Clair O'Leary, Sr Barbara MacNamara, Mary Kieran, Sr Elizabeth Dooley (Matron), Sr Noreen Smyth. (Courtesy of the Medical Missionaries of Mary)

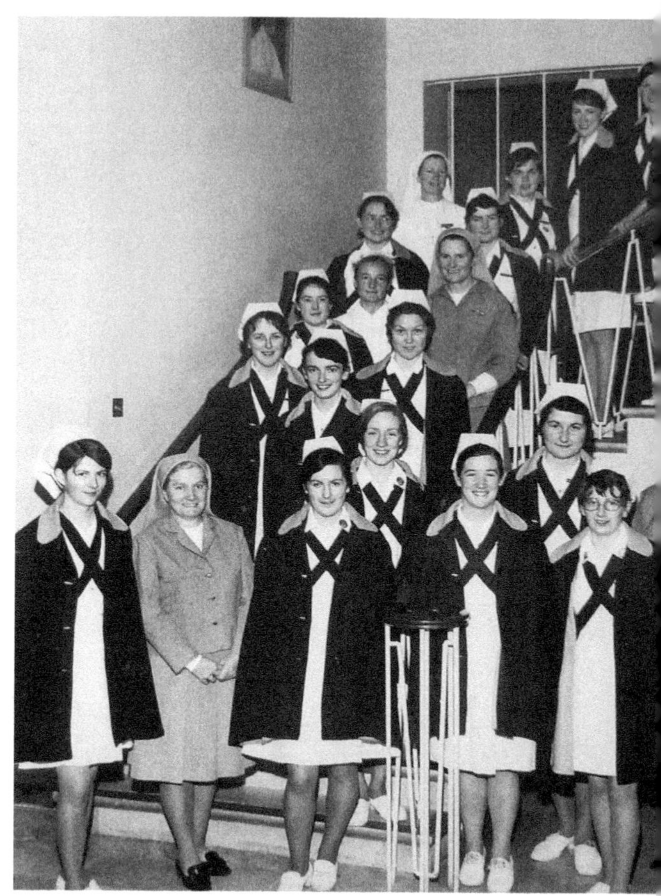

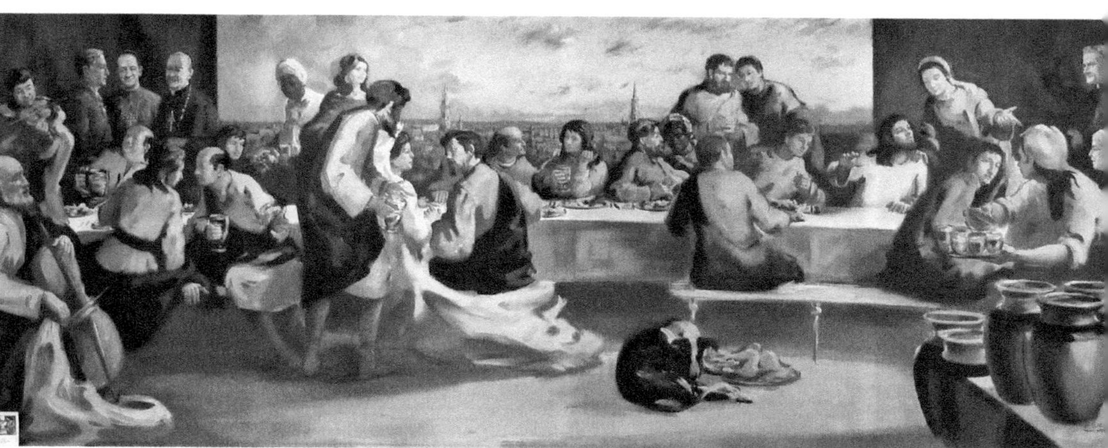

The large oil painting by Owen Walsh in 1967, which takes up one wall of the nuns dining hall, depicts The Marriage Feast of Cana, with Drogheda in the background. Included on the right are Jesus Christ and his mother Mary, with Cardinal Cushing of Boston and Mother Mary Martin watching them. At the rear left is architect, Des Martin (brother of Mother Mary Martin), Monsignor A. Riberi, and Cardinal W. Conway.

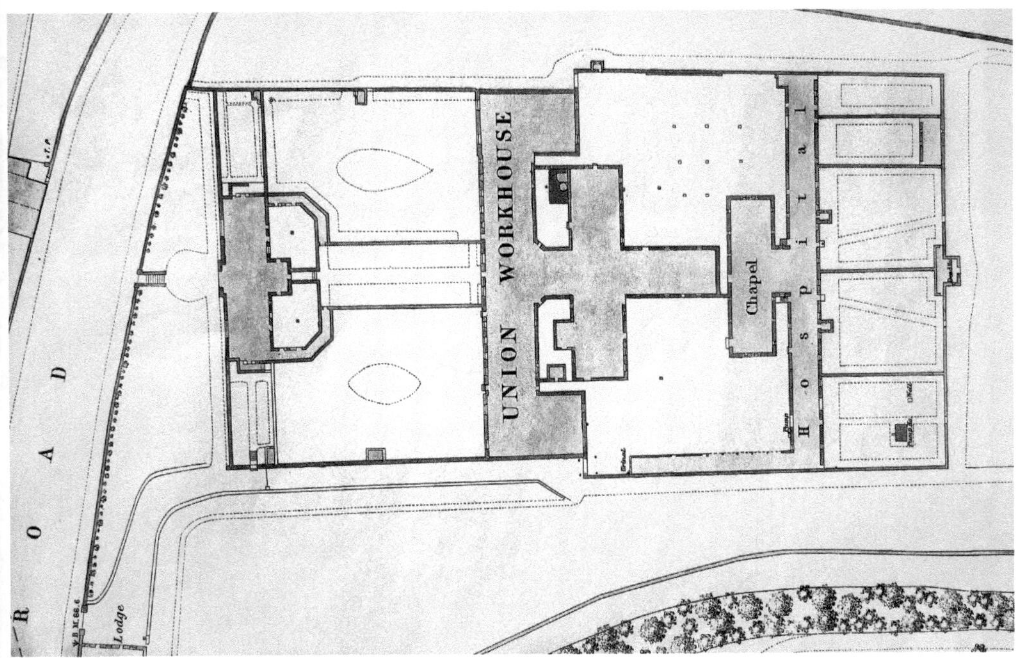

A 1872 plan of the workhouse on the Dublin Road. On the left was the admissions block, in the centre was the main accommodation block, and a hospital and chapel to the right. At the very end of the complex was the dead house or mortuary. The lodge was at the bottom left. (Courtesy of Trinity College Dublin Map Library)

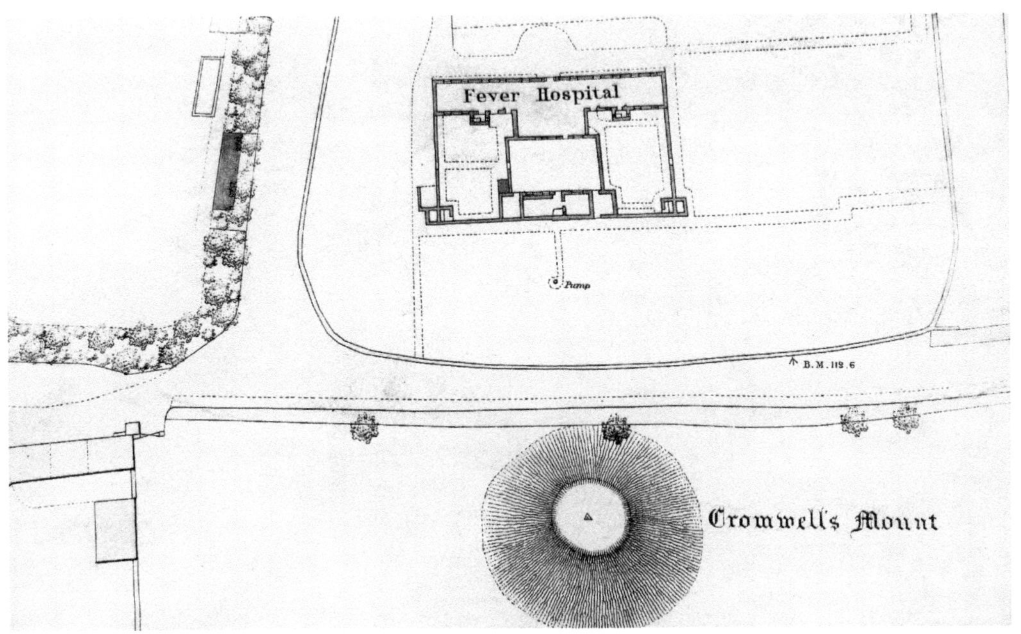

At the very south-west of the workhouse there was a fever hospital, built in 1847. Another one was added to its right in 1881. (Courtesy of the National Archives)

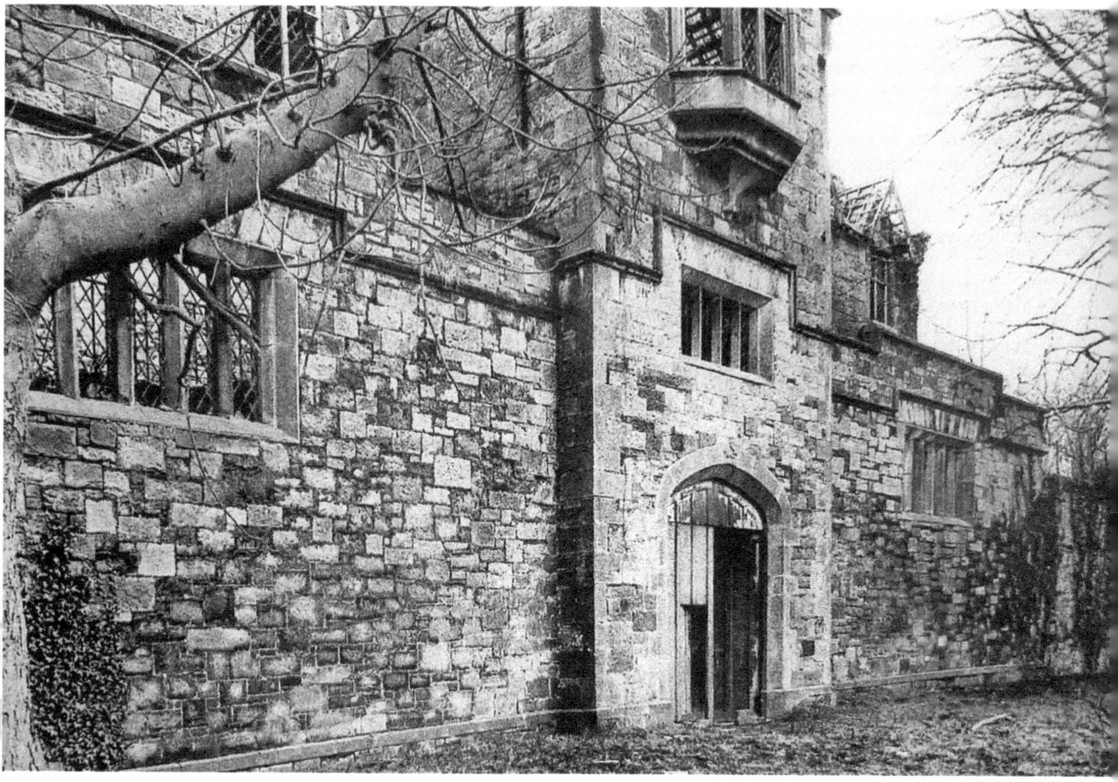

The front of the unusually designed admissions block of the former workhouse. (Courtesy of Des Clinton)

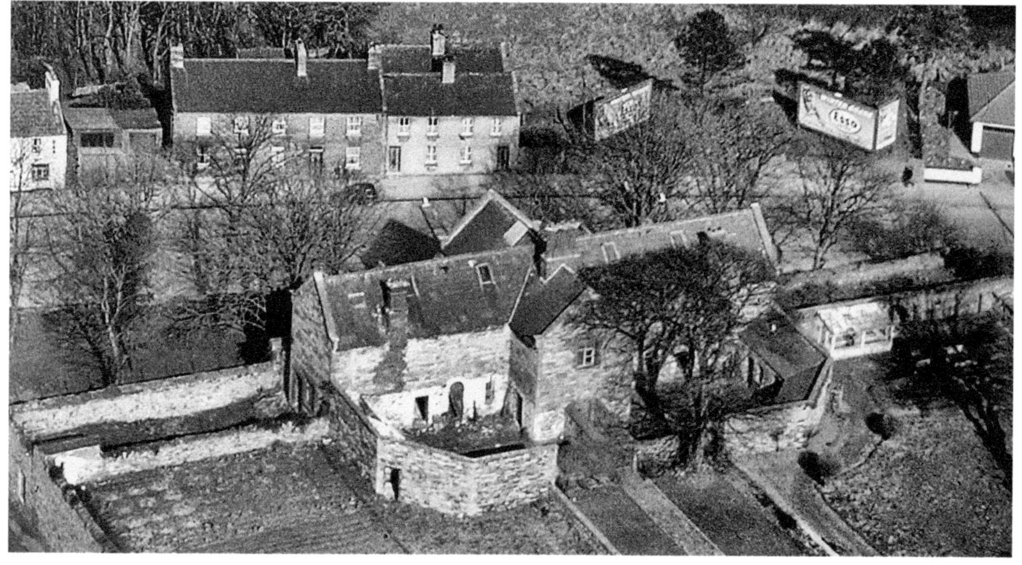

An aerial view of the rear of the admissions block of the workhouse in the 1950s, which was not as attractive as the public front view. (Courtesy of the National Library, Morgan Collection)

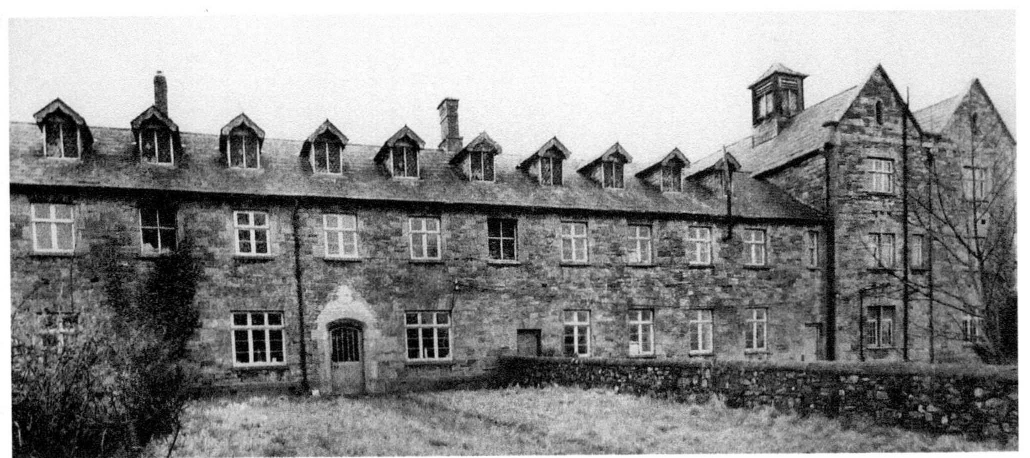

The main accommodation block in the workhouse. The dormitories were in the gabled wings at each end of the block. (Courtesy of Des Clinton)

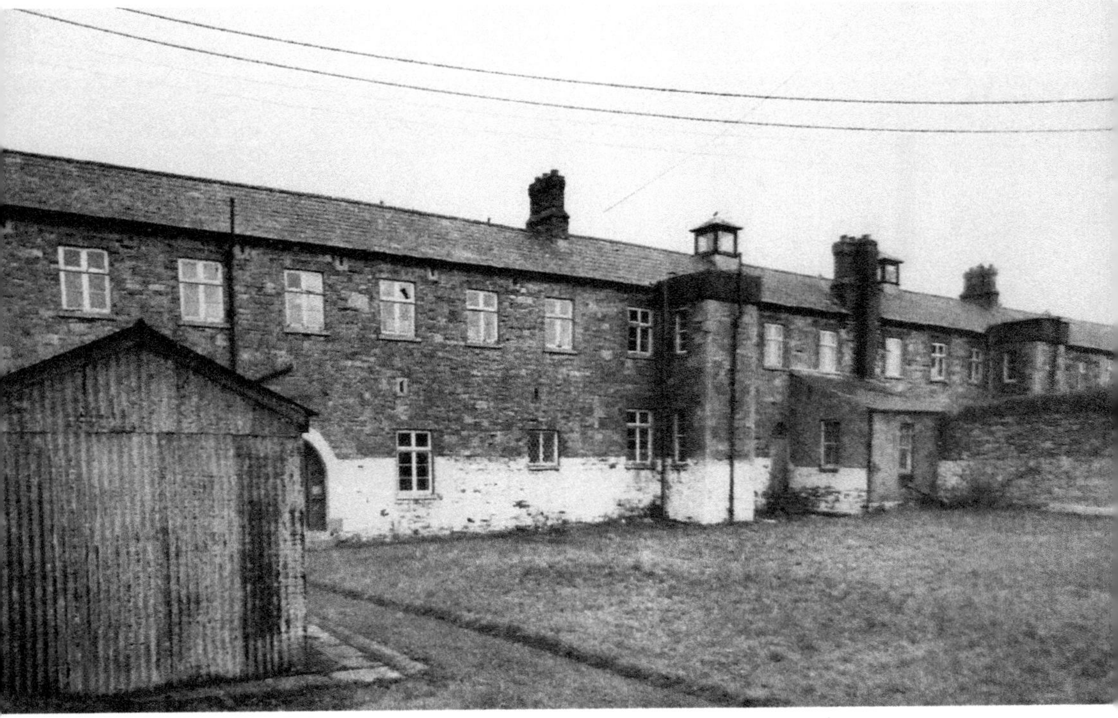

The rear infirmary of the workhouse. (Courtesy of Drogheda Museum Millmount)

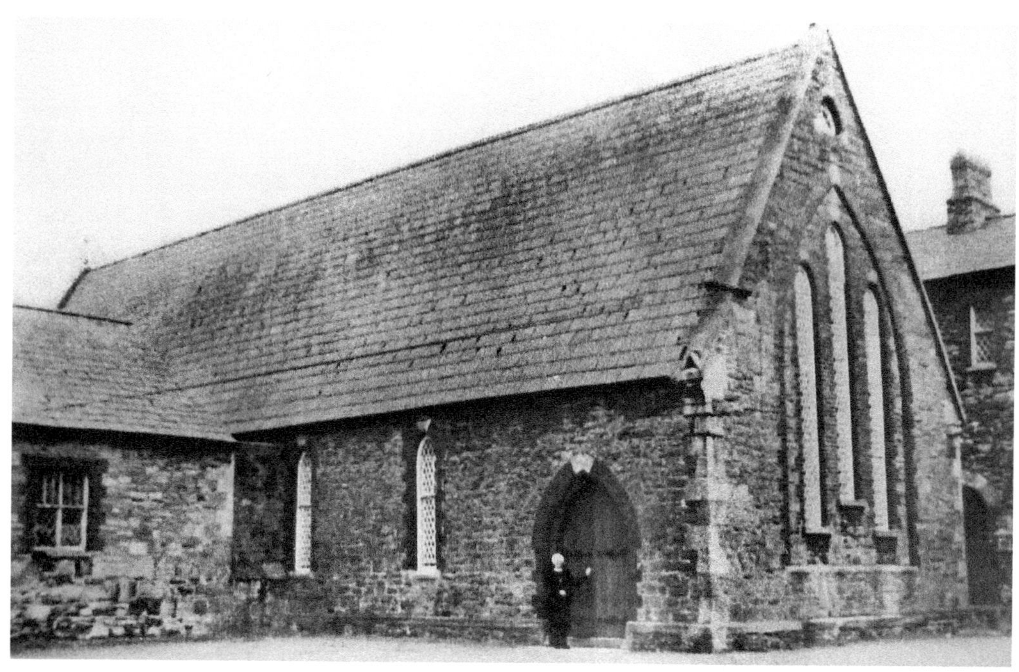

The workhouse chapel was more usually incorporated into the dining link between the main block and the rear infirmary. (Courtesy of Drogheda Museum Millmount)

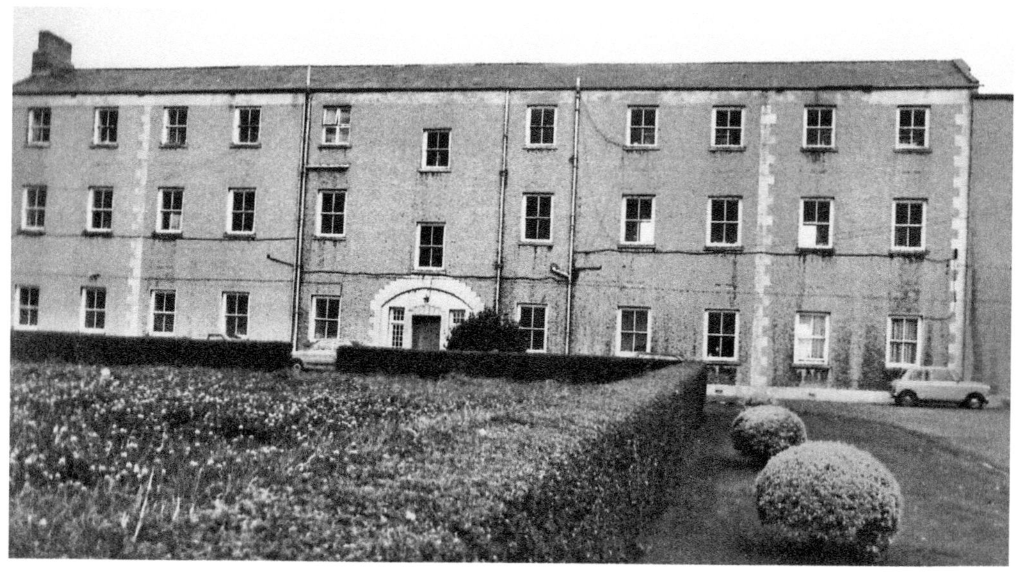

The former fever hospital of the workhouse is now a HSE Nursing Home. (Courtesy of the Sisters of Mercy)

Bullys Acre is the forgotten Christian cemetery for the workhouse.

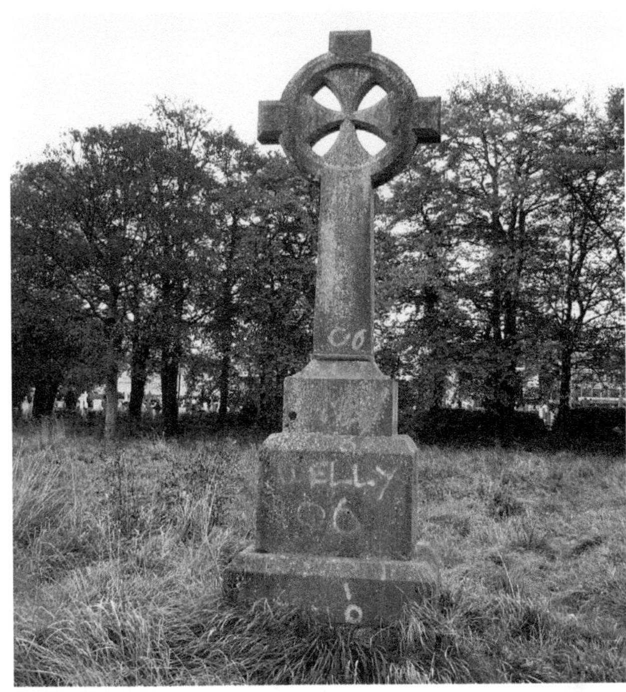

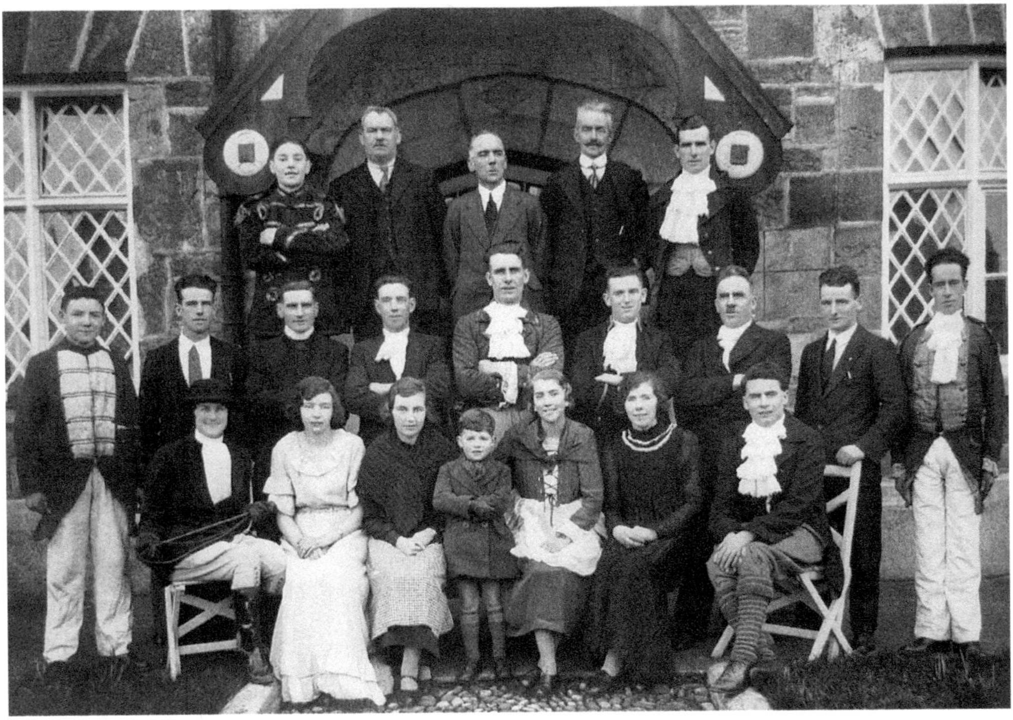

In 1934, *The Colleen Bawn* was staged in the Whitworth Hall by St Mary's TAS Dramatic Class, in aid of St Mary's Church Electric Fund (to convert from gas to electric lighting). Here, the cast pose in front of the lovely workhouse lodge. (Courtesy of the Sisters of Mercy)

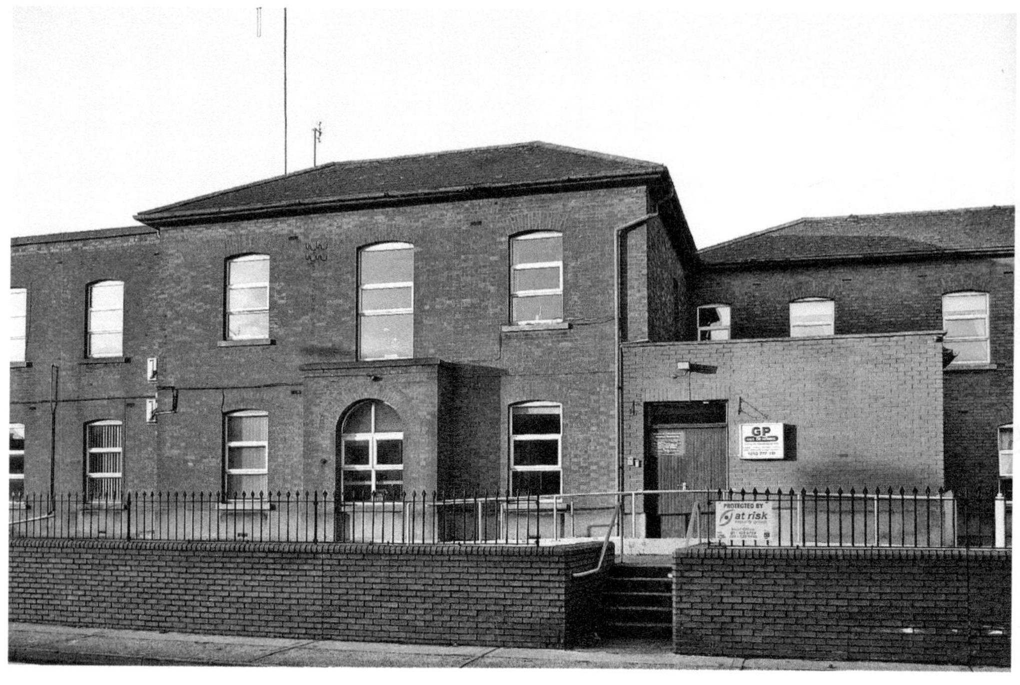

DROGHEDA COTTAGE HOSPITAL.

Patronesses :

THE VISCOUNTESS GORMANSTON, THE LADY RATHDONNELL.

President :

THE LADY BELLEW.

Vice-Presidents :

HON. MRS. PERY, MRS. OSBORNE, MISS SMITH, MRS. BALFOUR.

Members of General Committee :

MRS. BRANIGAN.
MISS BRODIGAN.
MRS. CHESTER-WALSH.
MRS. CARBERY.
MRS. JAMES DAVIS.
MISS LONG.
MRS. LYONS.
MISS M'CLINTOCK.
MISS M'DONNELL.
THE MAYORESS.
MRS. PENTLAND.
MRS. ROCHE.
MISS F. B. SMITH.
MRS. G. C. SMITH.
MRS. WALKER.
MRS. HILL.

Ex-Officio Members :

DR. REDMOND.
DR. MAUNSELL, } Consultants.

DR. J. V. BYRNE,
DR. L. V. HUNT,
DR. J. V. TALLAN, } Staff.

AND HON. SECS.

Executive Committee :

MRS. WALKER.
MRS. OSBORNE.
MRS. BRANIGAN.
MRS. ROCHE.
MISS M'DONNELL.
MISS LONG.
MRS. CARBERY.

MISS SMITH.
MISS F. B. SMITH.

Ex Officio Members :
CONSULTANTS,
MISS SIDNEY SMITH, } Hon.
MISS ROSA SMITH. } Secs.

Above The Cottage Hospital in Scarlett Street is now run by the HSE.

Left The 1910 Cottage Hospital Report. (Courtesy of Drogheda Museum Millmount)

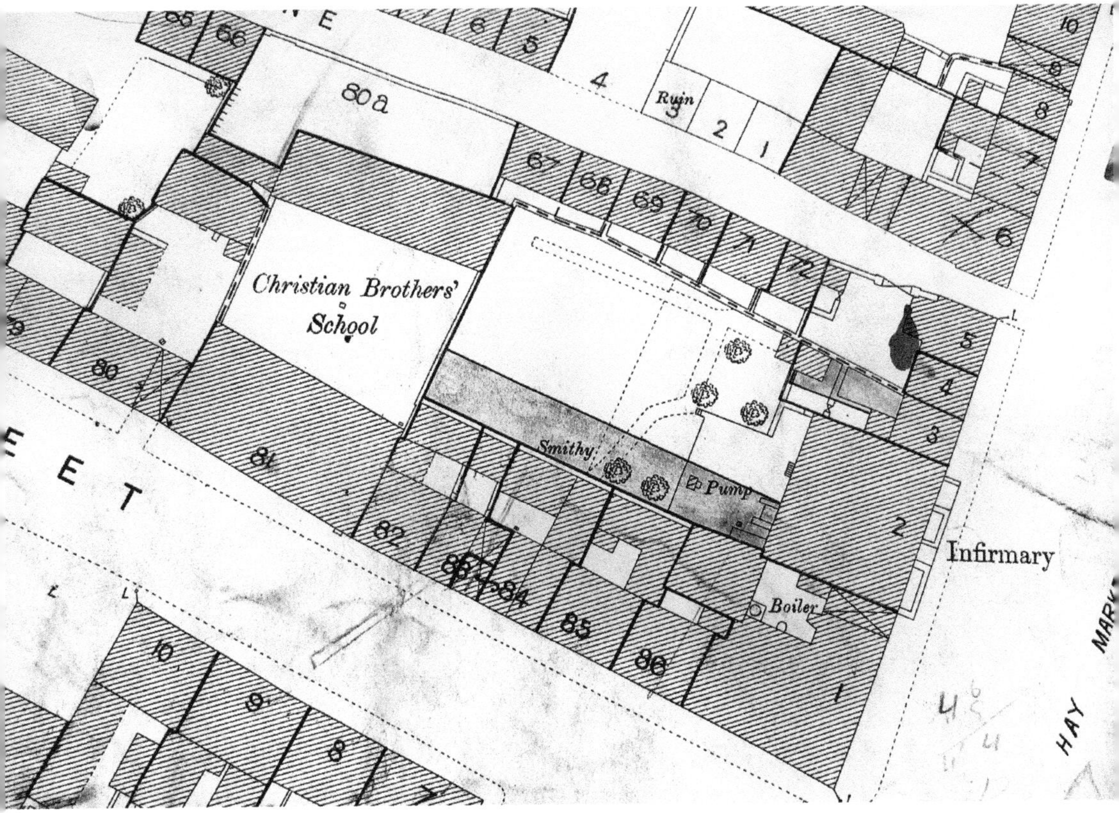

An old plan of the infirmary/hospital in Georges Street, backing onto the CBS school in Trinity Street. (Courtesy of the Valuation Office)

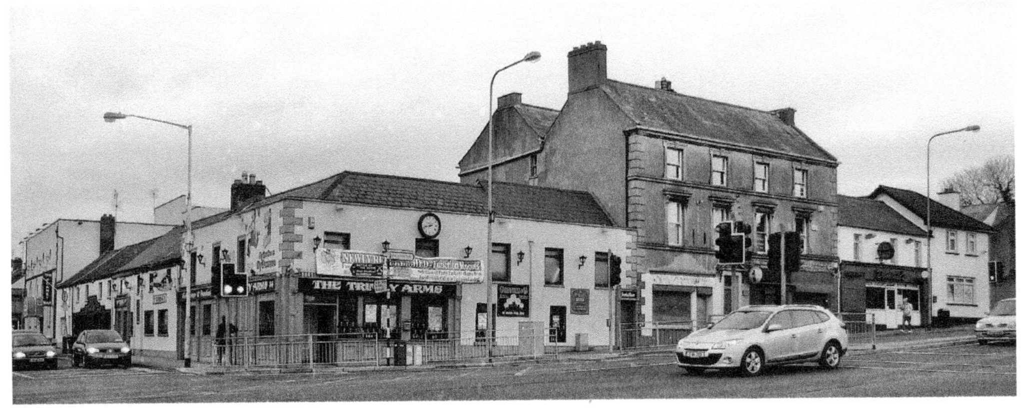

The present junction of Trinity Street and Georges Street. The three-storey building was the Infirmary. On the very left of the photo is the site of the former CBS school.

6

BUSINESS

GREENHILLS LINEN FACTORY, STRAND ROAD

John Oates built a cotton factory on Strand Road in the late 1830s. Henry Hull & Co. converted it to a linen factory, and Nicholas Flynn & Co. later bought it. Robert Usher & Co. Ltd operated the business from 1879 to 1901, after which the Allen family ran the business under the Usher name, until, in 1964, it was taken over by Ashton Bros (a Manchester company). The Allens were Quakers and their factory employed hundreds of girls. The company was famous for towels, using the brand name, 'Green Hills'.

The original building was five storeys high, 200 feet long and 35 feet wide, but almost the entire premises had to be rebuilt after a big fire in 1910. The factory closed in 1993, and the buildings are now used by a variety of businesses.

GREENMOUNT & BOYNE LINEN CO., GREENHILLS ROAD

The Boyne Mill was initially built by Benjamin Whitworth in 1865, as the Whitworth Cotton Factory. He also built the attractive brick house called 'The Sycamores' on a nearby site. His main business interests, however, were in Manchester, and in 1900 he sold the Boyne Mill to the Rt Hon. Thomas A. Dixon, MP.

The Greenmount Spinning Mill was built in Harold's Cross, Dublin, in 1807, by James Greenham, a Quaker, and the Pims family later became involved in the business. In 1922, the Greenmount Spinning Co. went into liquidation and was bought by the Boyne Weaving Co. for £25,000, thus creating the Greenmount & Boyne Linen Co. The two mills continued in both Drogheda and Harold's Cross, and shared a large red-brick warehouse at No 47 Franklin Street, Belfast. Harold's Cross closed in 1965, and is now the Greenmount Industrial Estate. The Drogheda mill closed in 1973, and following a fire in 1984 became semi-derelict, although the chimney and some buildings are still there, but disused. The multi-storey warehouse is still in commercial use in Belfast.

According to the 1911 census, it appears that the Boyne Company also owned the Westgate Mill, and St Mary's Mill on the Marsh Road.

IRISH TAPESTRY CO. (DROGHEDA) LTD, FLAX MILL LANE

The company started in 1950 in an old flax mill previously owned by Louth and Meath Flax Co., but which was originally the Yellowbatter Corn Mill. In the 1930s, there was a shoe and slipper factory here. The 5-acre site, with a house, was bought for £3,000 in 1950. The new business was a subsidiary of an older company in Newtownards, Co. Down, and was owned by Mr T.L. Meikle, and Mr Lane from Rathgar in Dublin.

The company made bedspreads, quilts, and tapestries, and had twenty Jacquard looms in 1963. They were responsible for the tapestry now hanging in St Peter's church in West Street, and which was on the altar at the Pope's mass in Killineer in 1979.

In 2003, the company moved to the Boyne Business Park, trading as Porterhouse Ltd, and still make clothes, such as coats, scarves, etc. The old mill was sold to developers for a housing scheme.

MCCANN & HILL, MERCHANTS QUAY

Samuel Lewis, writing in 1837, records that Smith and Smythe flour and corn mills on Merchants Quay, using a 50hp steam engine, could grind 40,000 barrels of wheat and 60,000 barrels of oats annually.

In 1800 John McCann opened Beamond Mill, to make oatmeal, on the Nanny River, a few miles from Drogheda.

The Drogheda Steam Mills were built in 1824, by Nathaniel Hill, at the foot of Constitution Hill, for milling flour and oatmeal. The property had a frontage of 150 feet on Bachelors Lane, and their western boundary comprised part of the old town wall at St Laurence Gate.

In 1897, McCann of Beamond amalgamated with Hill of Drogheda, and in 1898 they acquired Smith & Smythe (by now closed), on Merchants Quay, to become McCann & Hill.

DROGHEDA OATMEAL MILLING CO., MERCHANTS QUAY /CONSTITUTION HILL

The company started in 1870, and was later taken over by Charles Dougherty & Co. Ltd.

IRISH CEMENT LTD, STRAND ROAD

Irish Cement Ltd started in Drogheda in 1938, with the factory to the east of Greenhills. They moved to Platin, two miles south-west of Drogheda, in 1972, but their abandoned quarries can still be seen to the north-west of Drogheda. The former cement factory has been the site of Premier Periclase since 1980, which makes seawater magnesia from limestone and seawater, for export to factories abroad making refractory (heat-resisting) bricks.

A report of 1955 makes very interesting reading, stating that the workforce of 600 could produce 450,000 tons of cement powder a year. To produce this amount of cement, 600,000 tons of limestone was required, plus 80,000 tons of shale and clay, and 20,000 tons of gypsum. In addition, 125,000 tons of coal was needed for the furnaces, and 48 million units of electricity.

Limestone was obtained from the quarry at Killineer, and the shale from another quarry about one mile further north. The latter was carried by road to the main quarry and crushed, and both were then transported by aerial ropeway to the cement factory – a distance of 2¼ miles. Clay was quarried at Boycetown, about 9 miles north of the factory, and carried by lorry to the factory.

The limestone, shale and clay were pulverised and mixed with water, and then fed down one of three rotary kilns comprising near-horizontal pipes 12 feet in diameter and 423 feet long. Flaming pulverised coal dust met the slurry at the bottom of the kiln, resulting in clinker. The clinker was then crushed and mixed with gypsum to create cement powder.

E. DONAGHY & SONS, WESTGATE

The Ordnance Survey map of 1835 shows a linen yarn factory on this site at Westgate, and the 1909 map records it as 'Westgate weaving'.

E. Donaghy & Son (Drogheda) Ltd acquired the old mill in 1932, for the manufacture of boots and shoes. They employed 230 people in 1959 and were still trading in the 1970s. However, the historic mill is now derelict.

CASEYS BREWERY, MELL

The site was a cotton mill up to the 1860s. Then a brewery was established here – first Richardson & Sims, then Nugent & Co, which closed in 1874. In 1884 the brewery was bought by Patrick Casey Connolly, Mayor of Drogheda, and became known as Caseys Brewery. The main building was five-storeys, and there was a 149 feet high red-brick chimney.

After the brewery closed, Wilson & McBrinn from Belfast started a clothing factory here in 1926 and added a weaving mill in 1953, giving total employment of about 300, the majority being girls and women. They had a warehouse at No 206 Pearse Street, Dublin. Following a major fire in 1963, the factory was totally rebuilt. In the 1970s the company introduced its famous 'Dingos' jeans. Today, the company is still going strong in the same premises behind Topaz filling station, although now this premises is just a wholesaler's, with no manufacturing on site.

ST MARY'S MILLS, MARSH ROAD

A flax mill is shown here on the 1868 Ordnance Survey map, and then St Mary's Mills on the 1909 map. The Chadwick family were prominent in this spinning and weaving business for much of this time.

Irish Oil and Cake Mills acquired the mill in 1935, and they made edible oils, soap-making oils, linseed oils, cattle cakes and meals, and sanctuary oil (for churches).

Next door was W. & C. McDonnell Ltd, from 1950, makers of margarine, especially Stork Margarine, and they obtained their vegetable oil via a pipeline from Irish Oil and Cake. All this area has now been re-developed.

DROGHEDA CHEMICAL MANURE CO. LTD, MARSH ROAD

The Drogheda Chemical Manure Co. Ltd started in 1867 and made superphosphate fertiliser. The business was later named the Vitriol and Manure Works. Some of the buildings and plant are still standing, but disused.

DROGHEDA IRONWORKS, MARSH ROAD

Thomas Grendon & Co. was founded in 1835, but renamed Drogheda Ironworks from 1892. In their heyday, they employed hundreds of workers, making ships, barges, locomotives, boilers, and even the bridge at Oldbridge in 1869. The water tank (for the steam engines) in Drogheda Station was made by Grendon in 1873. In their later years, they were famous for kitchen ranges. The site was redeveloped in recent years.

CAIRNES BREWERY, MARSH ROAD

Cairnes Brewery was founded in 1825, and had close connections with the older Castlebellingham Brewery. They closed in the 1960s. The Cairne family home is now the Boyne Valley Hotel, and their graves can be seen in St Mary's cemetery.

J.H. WOODINGTON (DROGHEDA) LTD, MARSH ROAD

This company, which made boots and shoes, started in 1932, and lasted until 1987. They were a subsidiary of a Bristol business.

GAS WORKS, SOUTH QUAY

The original gas company was on North Quays, until it moved in the late nineteenth century to Marsh Road. It was bought by Drogheda Corporation in 1898.

LINENHALL, DOMINICK STREET

The manufacture of linen was big business in Drogheda in the eighteenth and nineteenth centuries, and a Linenhall was needed as a market house and store. The north hall was built in 1774, and other halls were added later (five by 1837). Dalton records that in 1836, 30,000 pieces of linen a year were sold here.

S. Bogue & Sons sawmills are shown on the Linenhall site on the 1948 Ordnance Survey map, and today all that is left is the Abbey open-air car park.

WHITWORTH HALL, LAURENCE STREET

This lovely brick and stone hall was built in 1865 by Benjamin Whitworth (who founded the Boyne Mills), to a design by William Joseph Barre of Belfast, on the site of the Primates Palace. It was used as a public Concert Hall, with seating for 600, plus 90 in the gallery. Unfortunately, the Trustees sold the hall to private interests in the 1880s. The building is now a leisure centre/amusement arcade, with slot machines, snooker tables, etc., and additional floors have been inserted.

The contribution of this local businessman to Drogheda was commemorated by the Whitworth Memorial Drinking Fountain, designed by Drogheda architect P.J. Dodd in 1876. It was originally positioned in the centre of the road at the south end of St Peter Street, opposite the Tholsel. The fountain was then moved to the North Quays in 1894, dismantled in the 1960s, but now lost.

OTHERS

Drogheda had numerous other businesses, including a rope factory, salt works, and whiskey distillery, in addition to many small mills, etc.

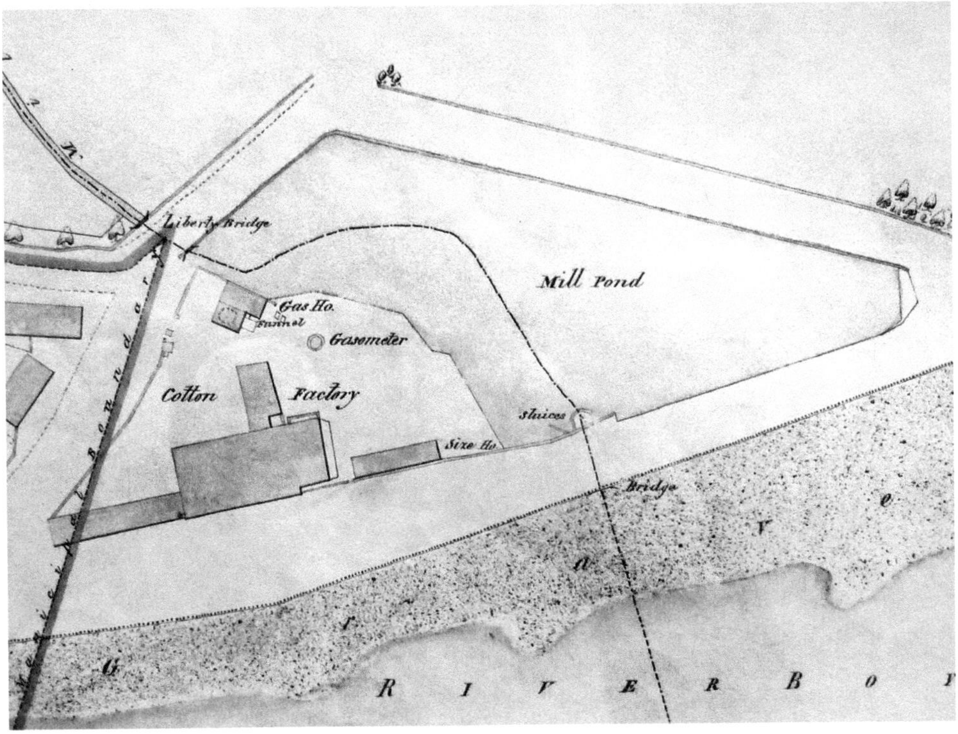

A 1847 map of Ushers Mill at the Strand Road. (Courtesy of the National Archives)

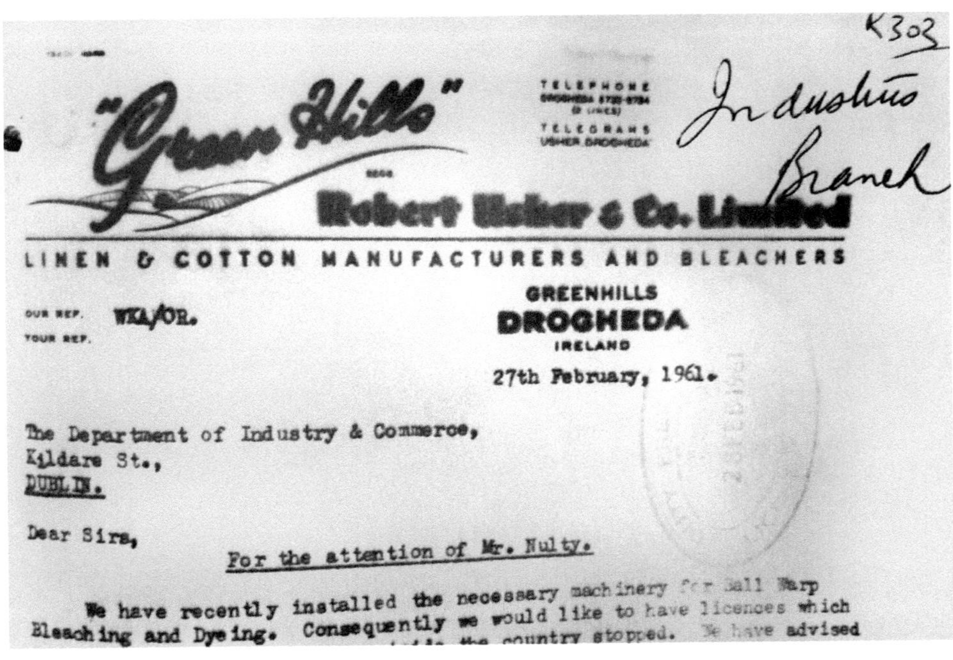

1961 headed paper for the Usher Mill. Note the 'Green Hills' trade mark for their famous towels. (Courtesy of the National Archives)

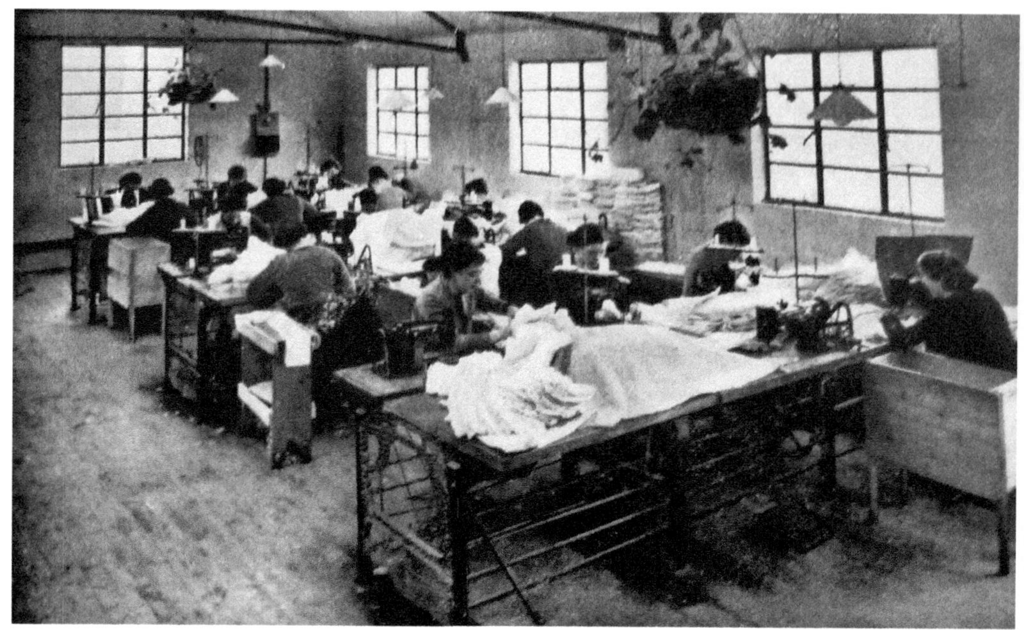

Female staff in Ushers linen factory. (Courtesy of Drogheda Museum Millmount)

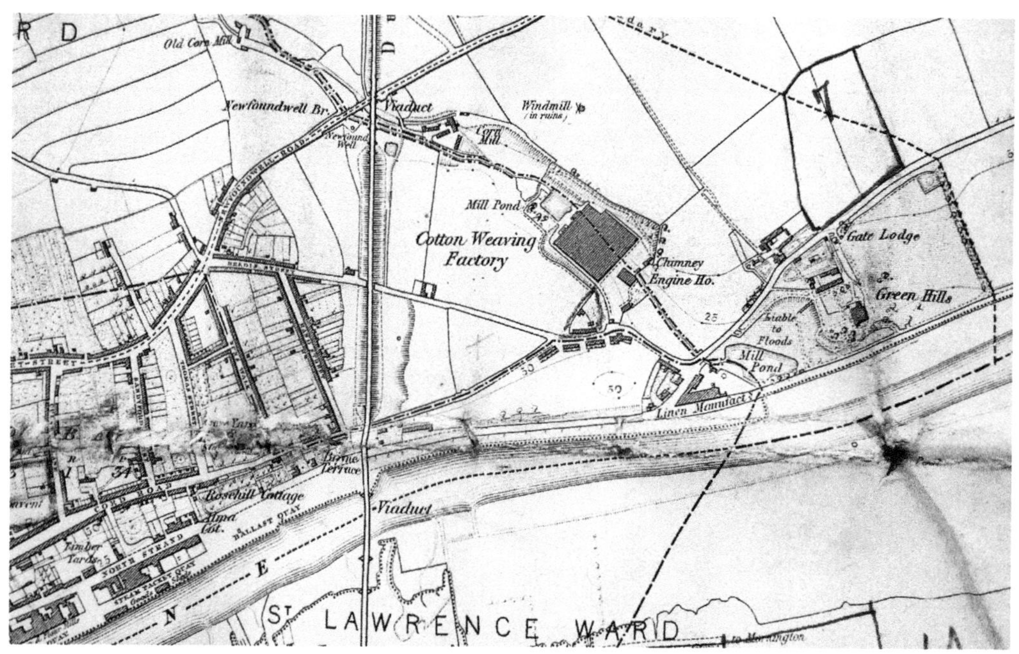

A nineteenth-century map of the Greenhills area, showing the large size of the Boyne Mills (Cotton Weaving Factory). (Courtesy of the National Archives)

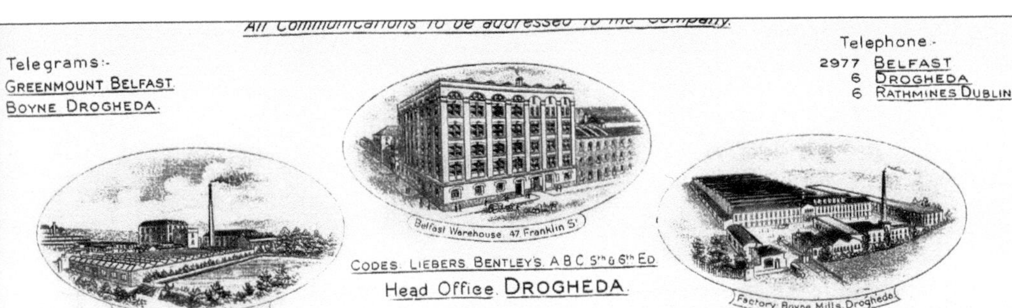

Above 1935 headed paper, with a sketch of Harold's Cross/Greenmount Mill on the left, Boyne Mill on right, and Belfast warehouse in centre. (Courtesy of Seamus O'Maitiu)

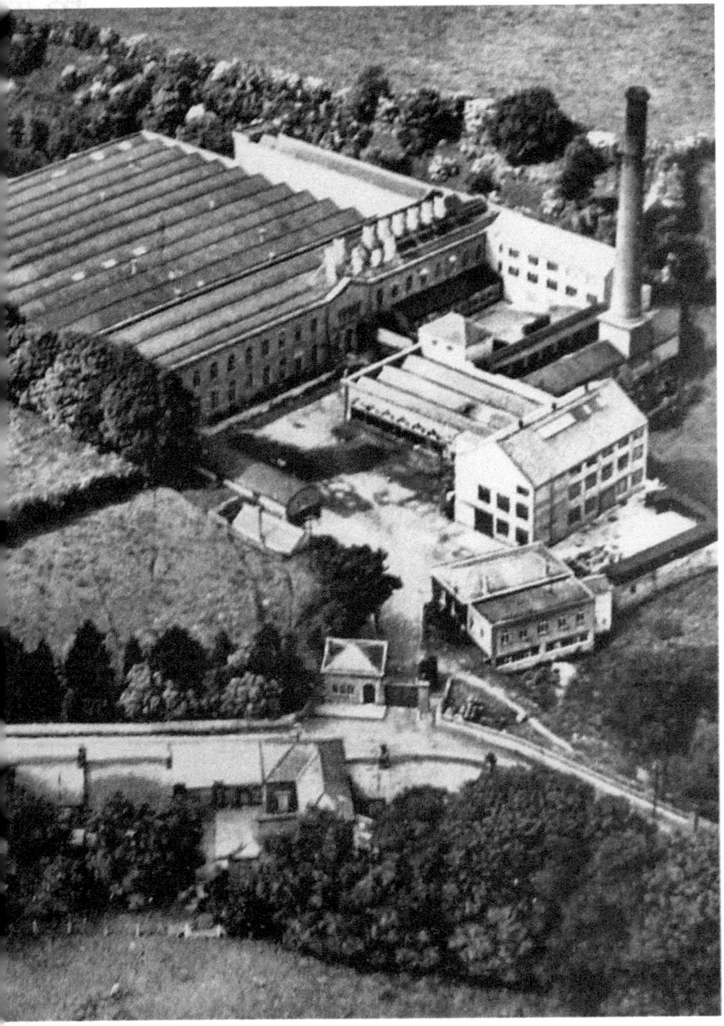

Left An aerial photograph of the Greenmount & Boyne Mill. It is now disused. (Courtesy of Drogheda Museum Millmount)

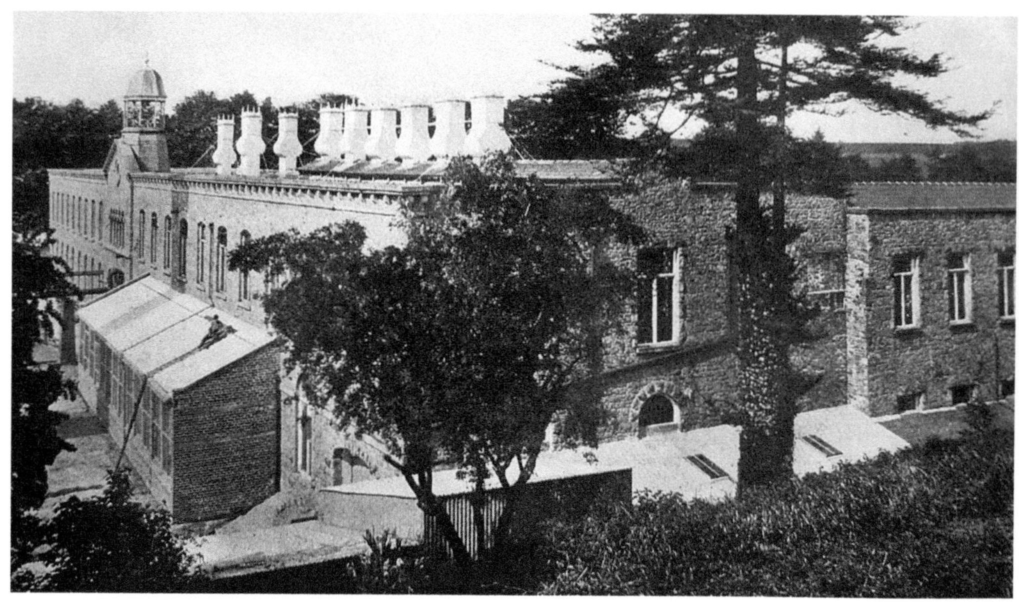

The preparing department, Greenmount & Boyne Mill, as shown in a 1924 brochure. (Courtesy of Drogheda Museum Millmount)

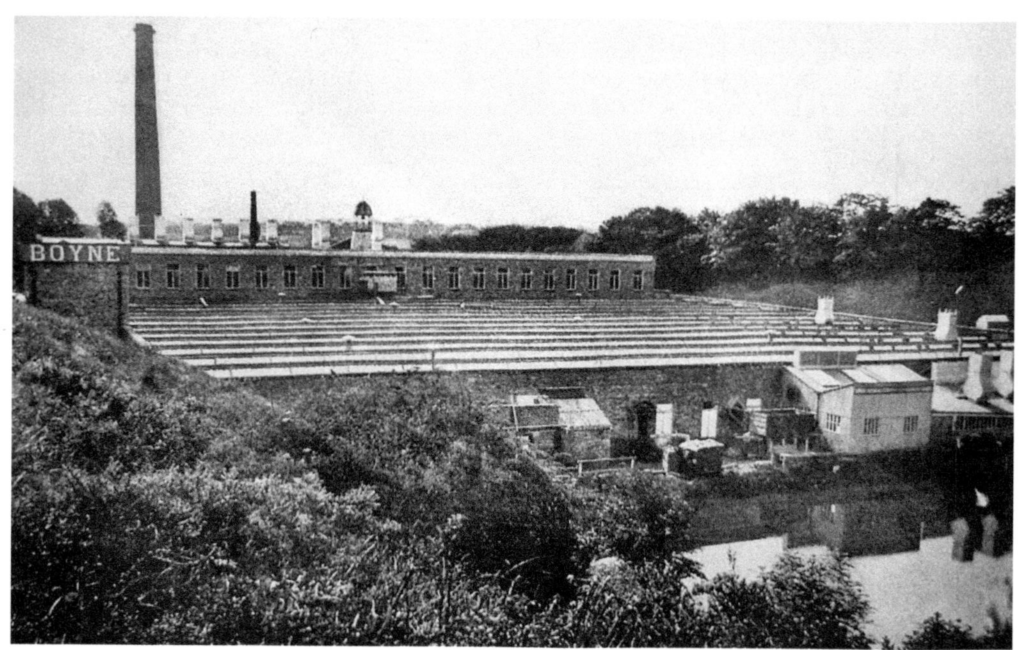

The weaving shed, Greenmount & Boyne Mill, as shown in a 1924 brochure. The mill pond is on the lower right, and formerly powered a large water wheel to drive the machines. (Courtesy of Drogheda Museum Millmount)

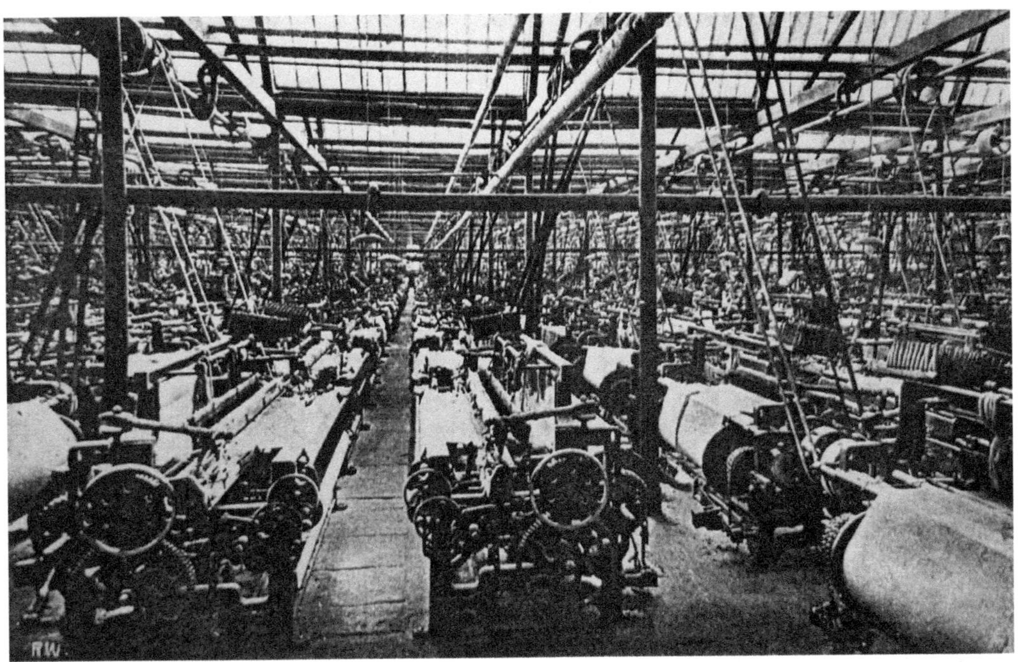

The weaving shed with its 750 looms, Greenmount & Boyne Mill, as shown in a 1924 brochure. (Courtesy of Drogheda Museum Millmount)

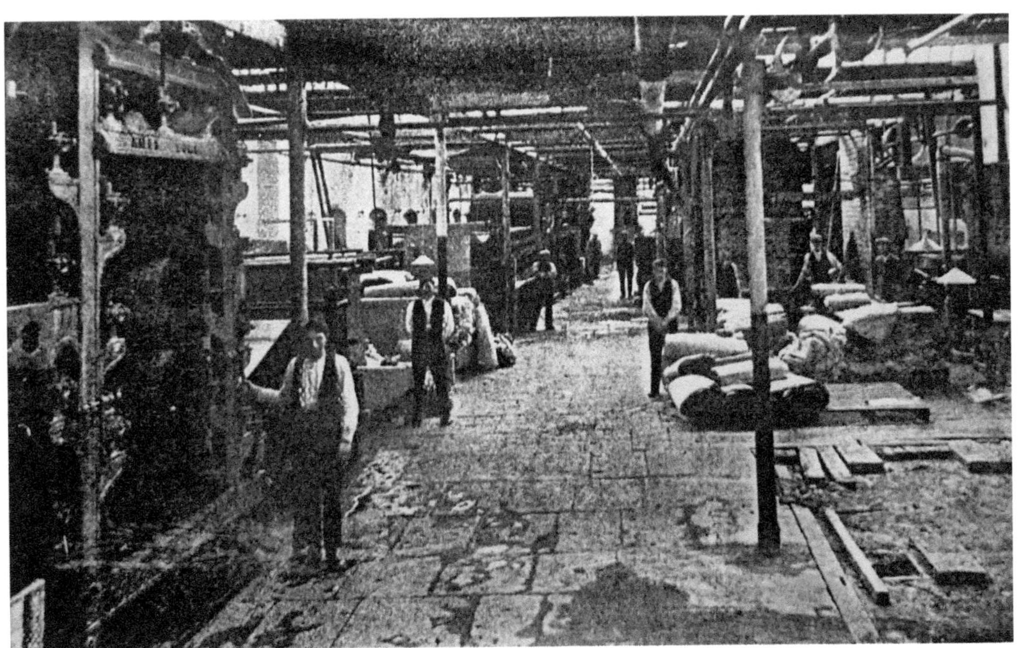

Part of the dye-house, Greenmount & Boyne Mill, as shown in a 1924 brochure. (Courtesy of Drogheda Museum Millmount)

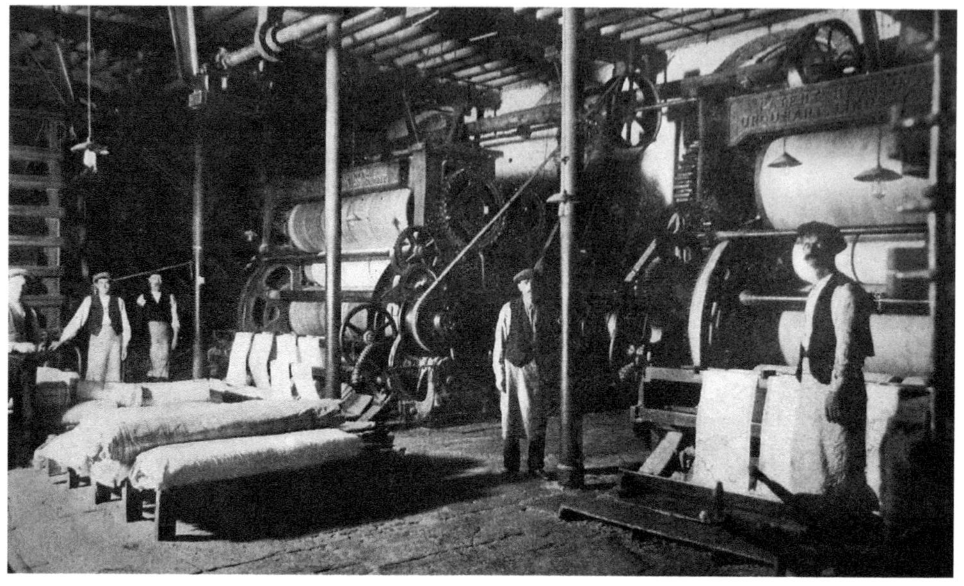

There were eight machines for hydraulic mangling at the Greenmount & Boyne Mill. (Courtesy of Drogheda Museum Millmount)

GREENMOUNT & BOYNE LINEN CO., LTD.

Manufacturers, Bleachers, Dyers, and Finishers of

LINEN, UNION AND COTTON GOODS

For Home and Overseas Markets.

Amongst the goods manufactured are

Linen and Cotton Damasks, Table Cloths and Napkins, Roller Towelling, Typed and Checked Kitchen Towels, Apron Dowlas, Huck Towelling, Damask and Coloured Border Huck Towels, Checked Glass Towelling.

Checked Dusters, Sheetings, Tickens, Dyed Dress Linens, Tailors' Linings, including

Linen, Union, Cotton, and Hair Canvas Ducks, Padding, Hollands, Buckrams, Pocketing, Bleached Drills. Bleached, Dyed and Brown Ducks. Cambrics (white and dyed). Embroidery Linens. Men's Tropical Suitings.

Also Aprons, Overalls, Cotton and Linen Frocks, Shop Coats and Dungarees. Children's wear, Sheets and Pillow Cases.

WORKS:

BOYNE MILL, DROGHEDA • HAROLD'S CROSS MILL DUBLIN

IN THE IRISH FREE STATE.

Our goods can be obtained from all the Wholesale Houses in Dublin, Cork, Limerick and Waterford.

1932

An informative 1932 advertisement for Greenmount & Boyne products, many of which are no longer used.

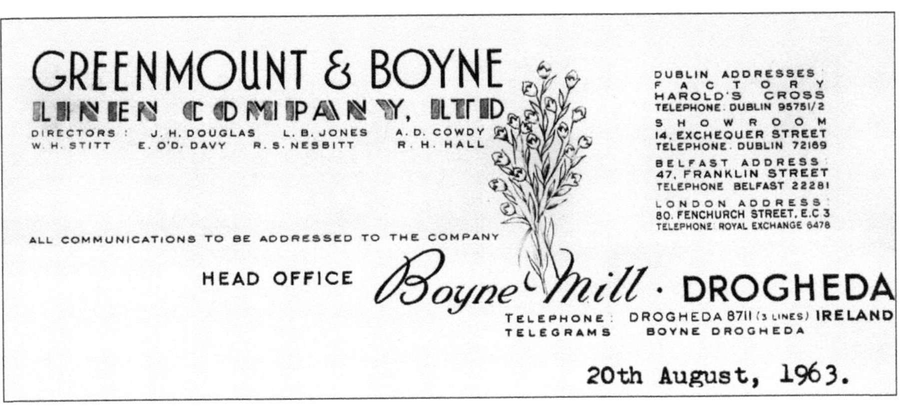

Greenmount & Boyne headed paper, 1963. (Courtesy of the National Archives)

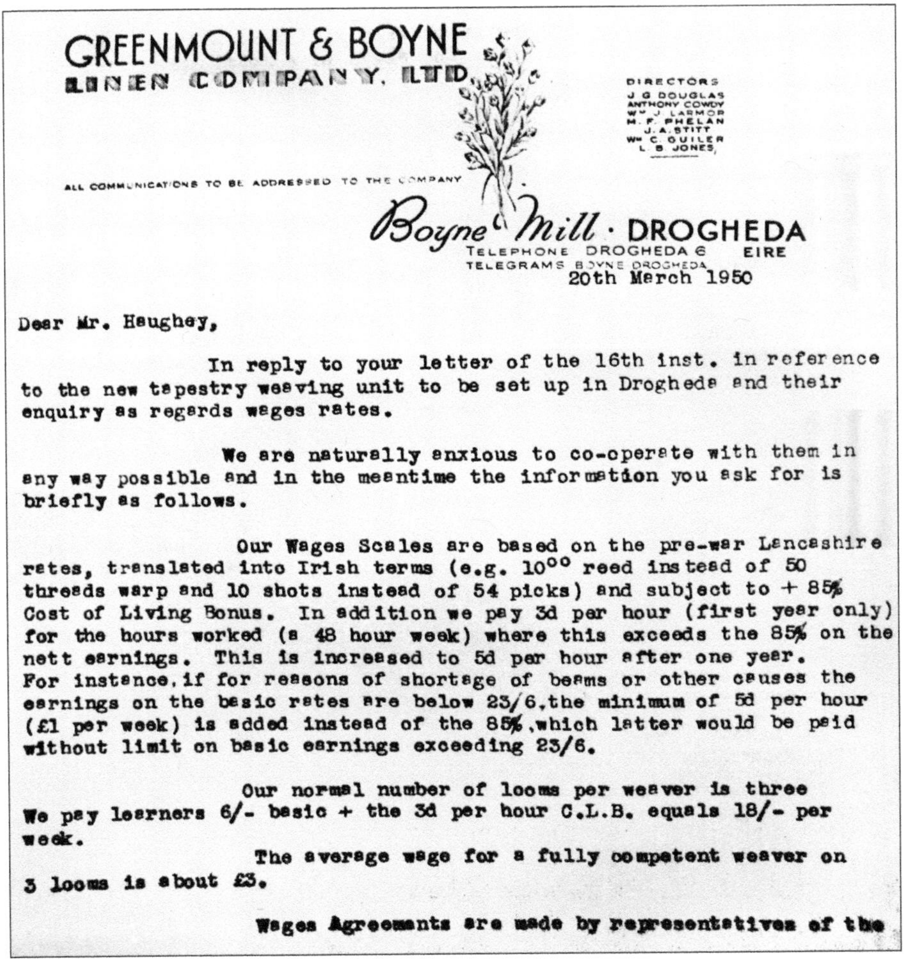

GREENMOUNT & BOYNE
LINEN COMPANY, LTD.

DIRECTORS
J. G. DOUGLAS
ANTHONY COWDY
WM. J. LARMOR
H. F. PHELAN
J. A. STITT
WM. C. QUILER
L. B. JONES,

ALL COMMUNICATIONS TO BE ADDRESSED TO THE COMPANY

Boyne Mill · DROGHEDA
TELEPHONE DROGHEDA 6   EIRE
TELEGRAMS BOYNE DROGHEDA
20th March 1950

Dear Mr. Haughey,

In reply to your letter of the 16th inst. in reference to the new tapestry weaving unit to be set up in Drogheda and their enquiry as regards wages rates.

We are naturally anxious to co-operate with them in any way possible and in the meantime the information you ask for is briefly as follows.

Our Wages Scales are based on the pre-war Lancashire rates, translated into Irish terms (e.g. 10⁰⁰ reed instead of 50 threads warp and 10 shots instead of 54 picks) and subject to + 85% Cost of Living Bonus. In addition we pay 3d per hour (first year only) for the hours worked (a 48 hour week) where this exceeds the 85% on the nett earnings. This is increased to 5d per hour after one year. For instance, if for reasons of shortage of beams or other causes the earnings on the basic rates are below 23/6, the minimum of 5d per hour (£1 per week) is added instead of the 85%, which latter would be paid without limit on basic earnings exceeding 23/6.

Our normal number of looms per weaver is three We pay learners 6/- basic + the 3d per hour C.L.B. equals 18/- per week.

The average wage for a fully competent weaver on 3 looms is about £3.

Wages Agreements are made by representatives of the

1950 wage rates in Greenmount & Boyne. (Courtesy of the National Archives)

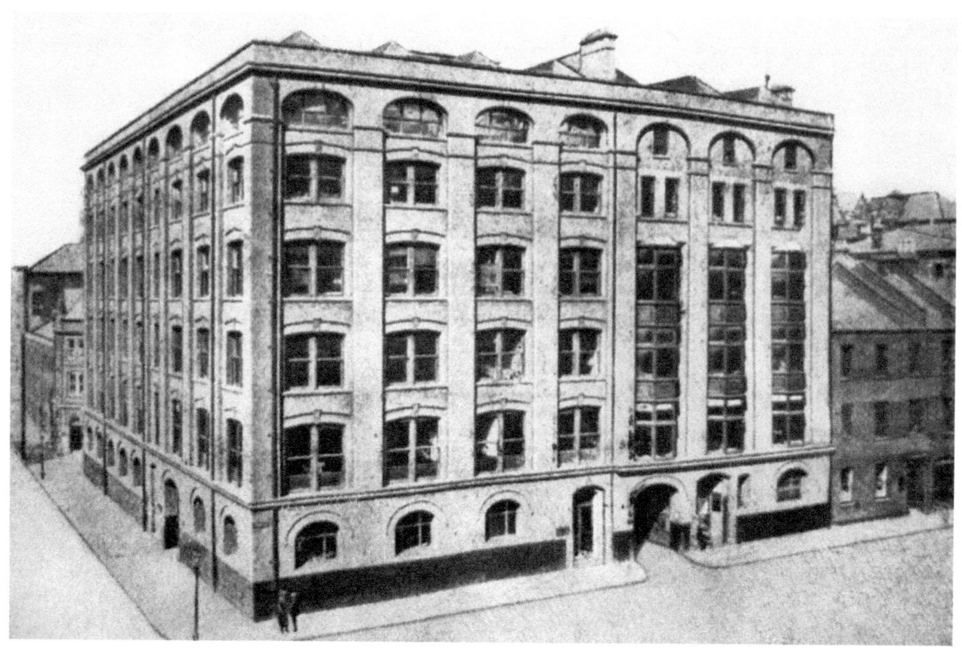

No 47 Franklin Street, Belfast, was the warehouse for the Greenmount & Boyne linen company. The red-brick building is now in alternative use. (1920s brochure courtesy of Drogheda Museum Millmount)

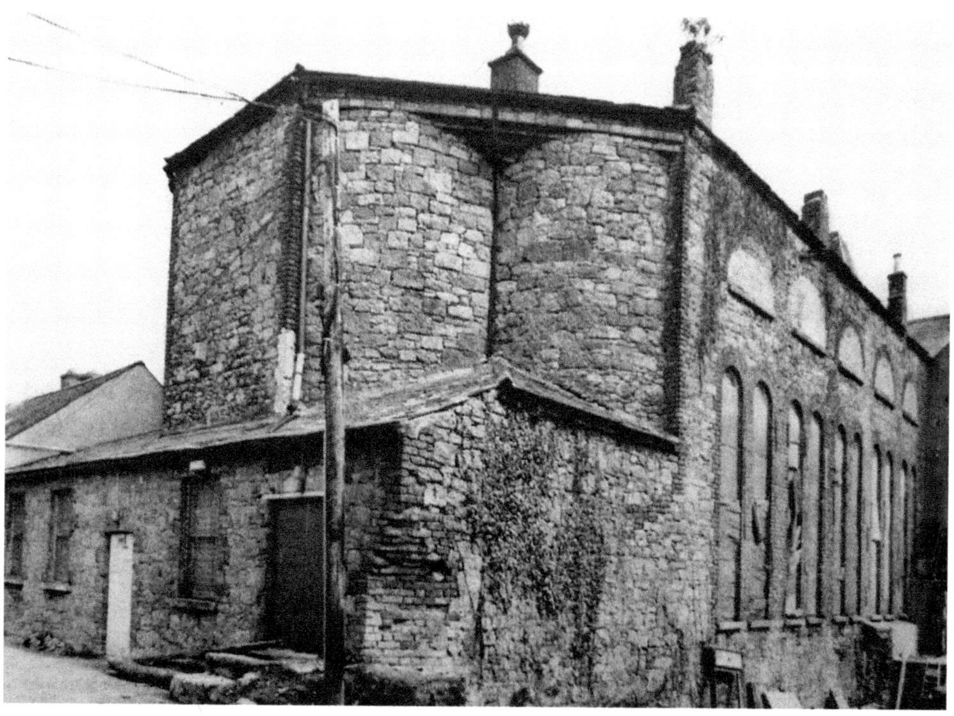

The unusual rear of the Whitworth Hall, 1986. (Courtesy of An Foras Forbartha)

Right A present-day view of the marvellous Whitworth Hall.

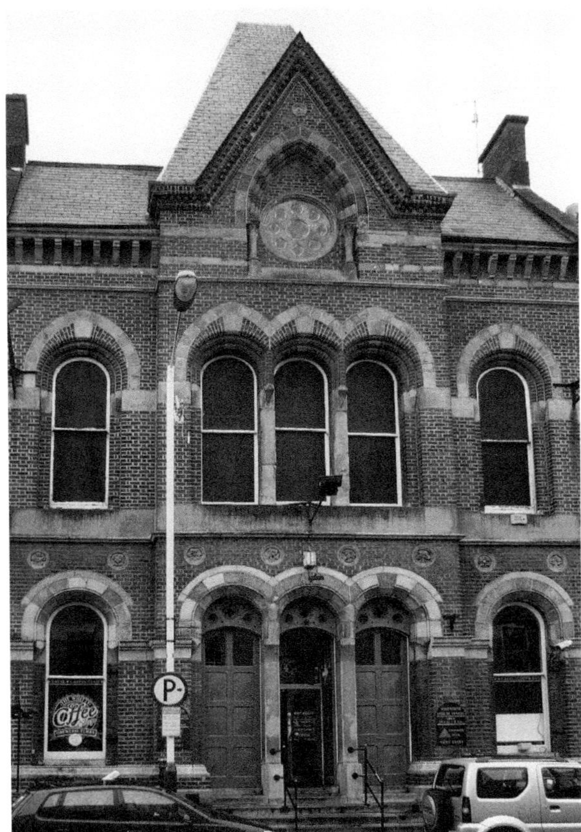

Below A plan of Whitworth Hall, where concerts were held. Note the two sweeping staircases near the front. (Courtesy of the Valuation Office)

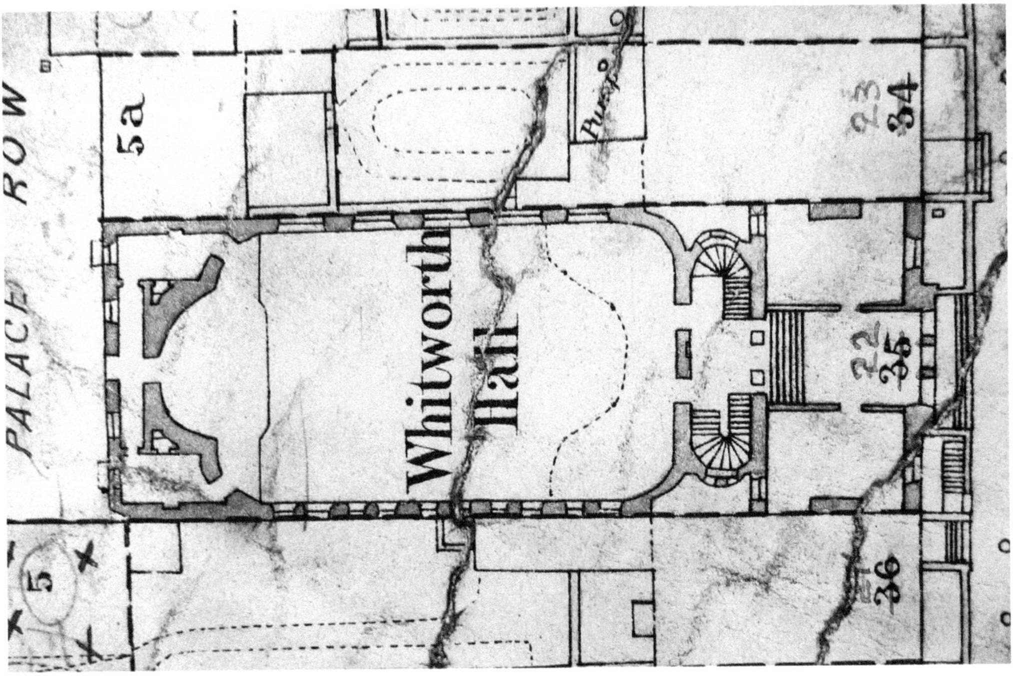

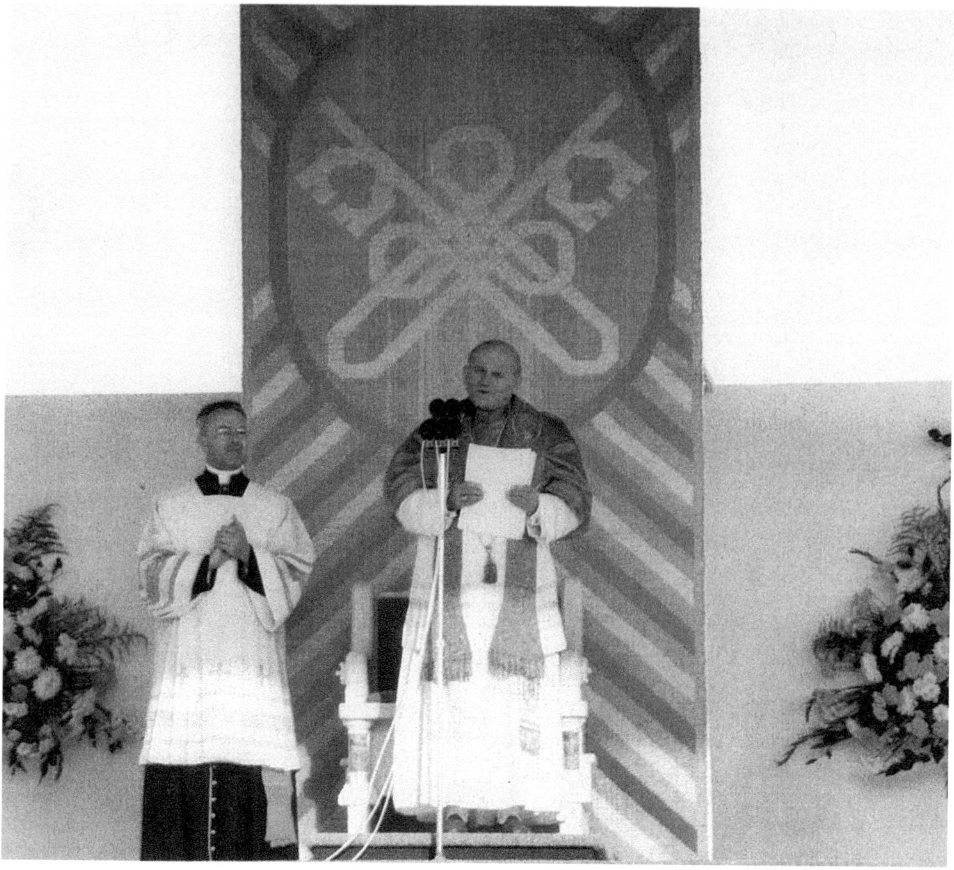

Irish Tapestries made the orange and fawn tapestry for the altar in Killineer, for the Pope's Mass in 1979. (Courtesy of Porterhouse Ltd)

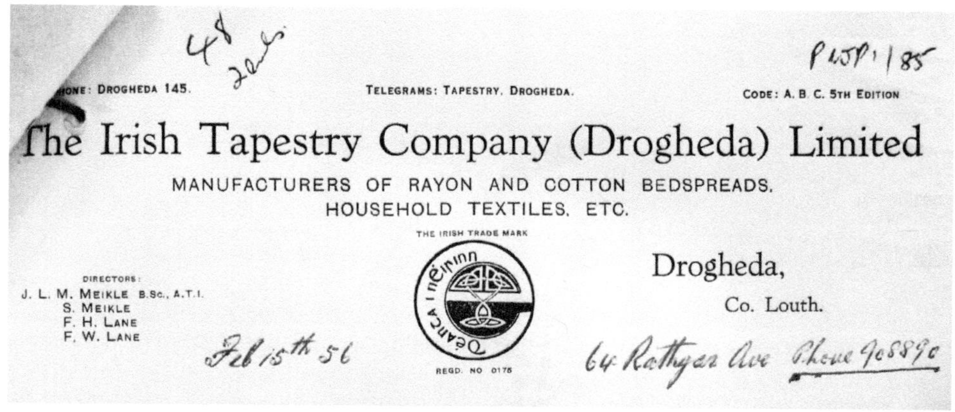

1956 headed paper, listing the directors of the Irish Tapestry Co Ltd. (Courtesy of the National Archives)

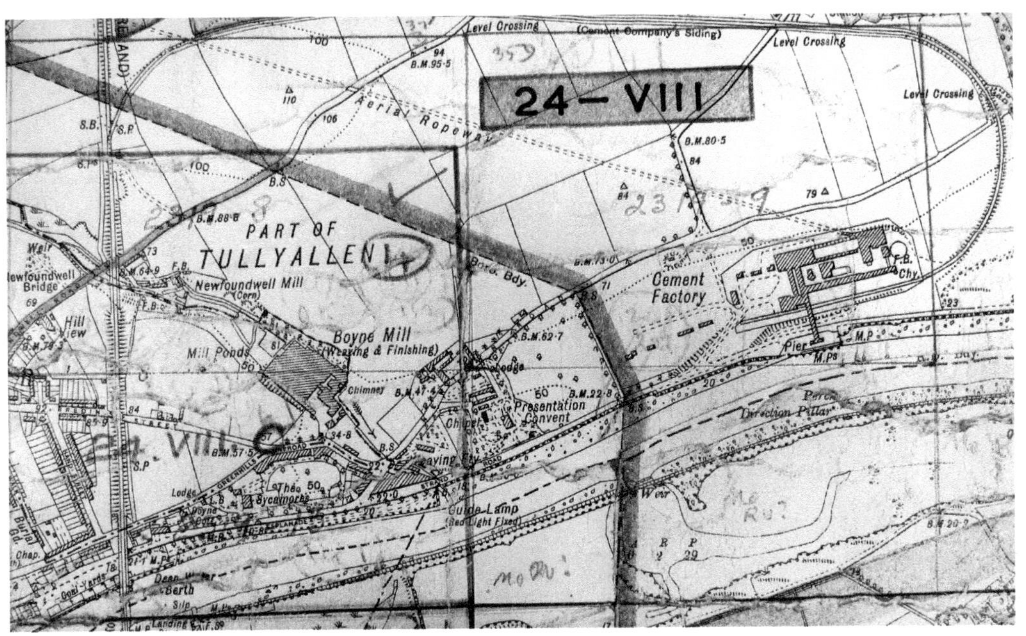

The cement factory on the right had its own railway siding, aerial ropeway, and berth on the River Boyne. It is now the site of Premier Periclase. (Courtesy of the Valuation Office)

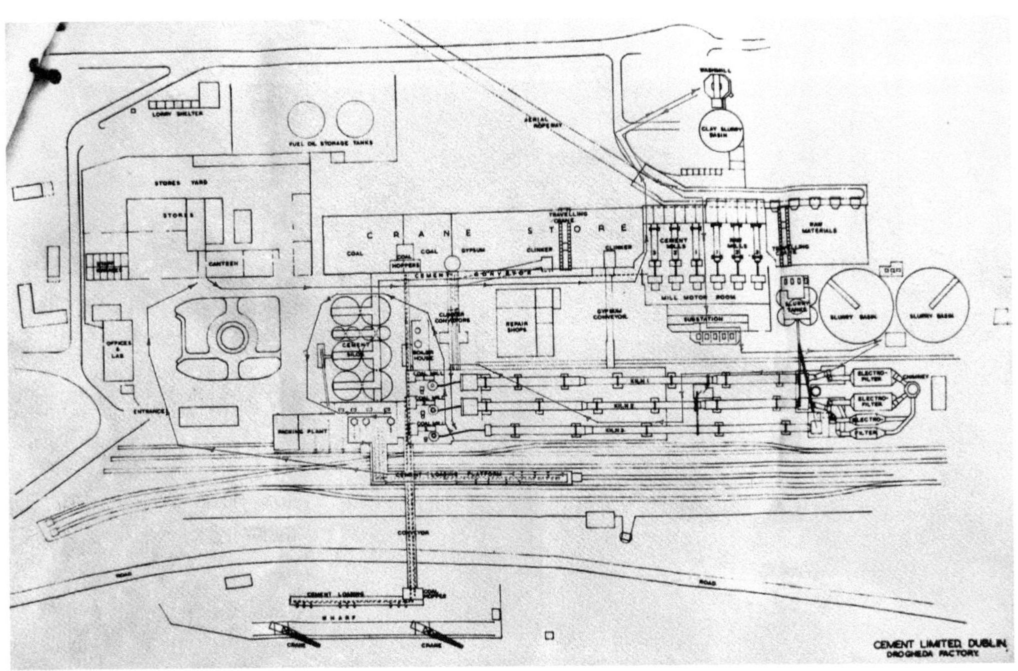

A plan of Cement Ltd in 1955, with the River Boyne along the bottom. (Courtesy of the National Archives)

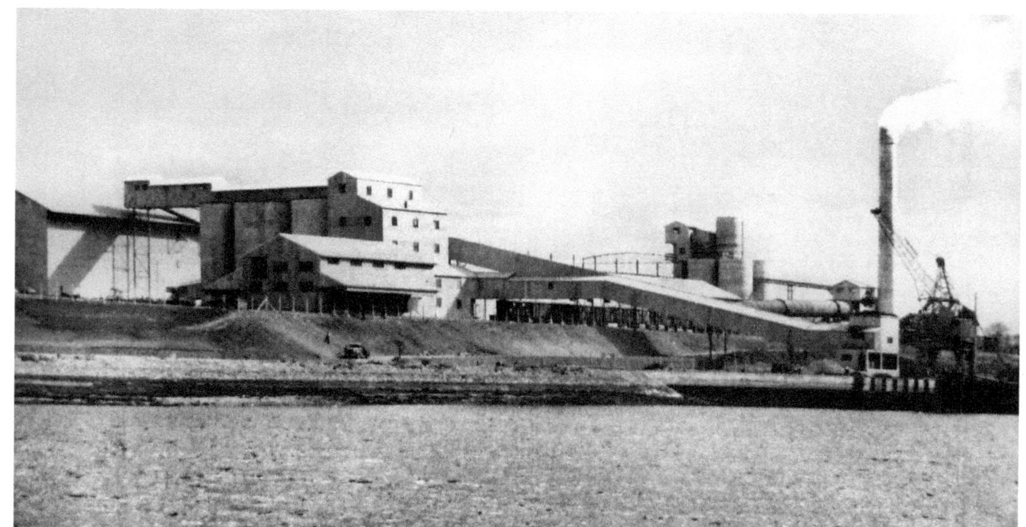

Above A view of Cement
Ltd from the River Boyne.
(Brochure courtesy
of Drogheda Museum
Millmount)

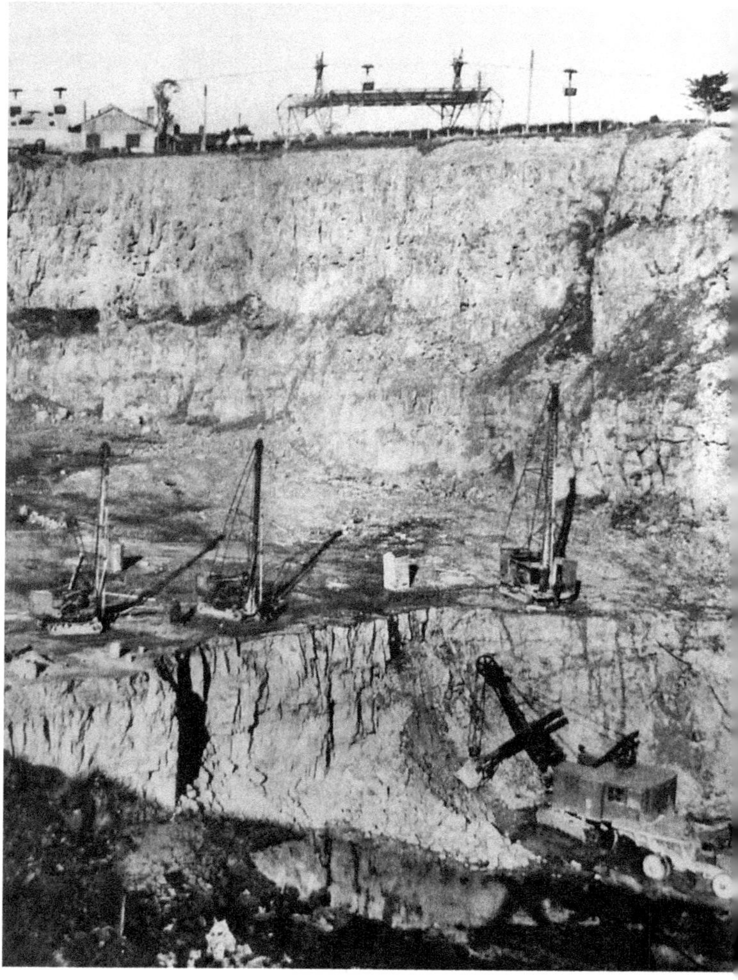

Right Limestone quarry
for Cement Ltd to
north-west of Drogheda.
(Brochure courtesy
of Drogheda Museum
Millmount)

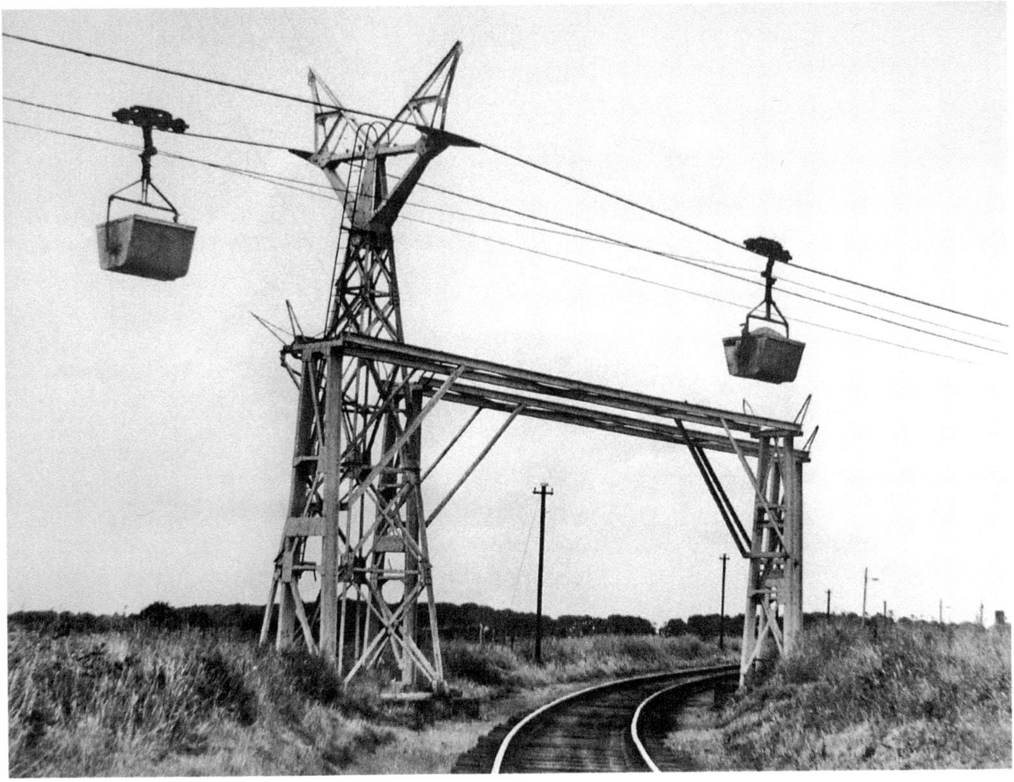

Aerial ropeway between the quarry and the cement factory, with protective platform over the railway. (Courtesy of Irish Rail)

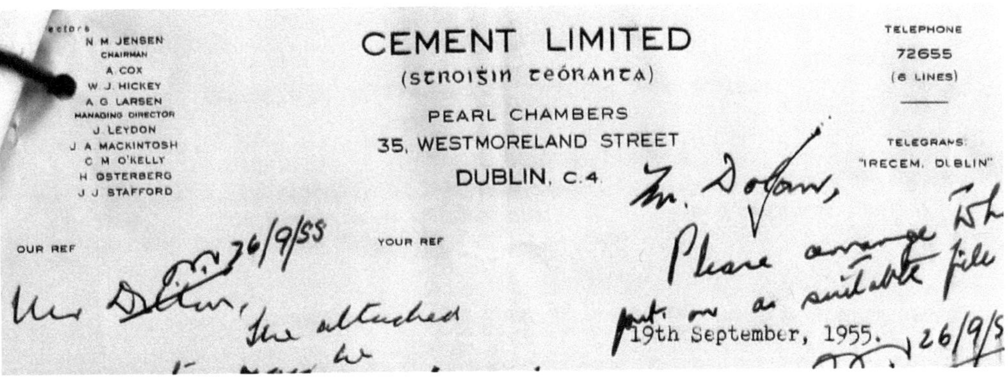

Cement Ltd headed paper in 1955, listing the directors. (Courtesy of the National Archives)

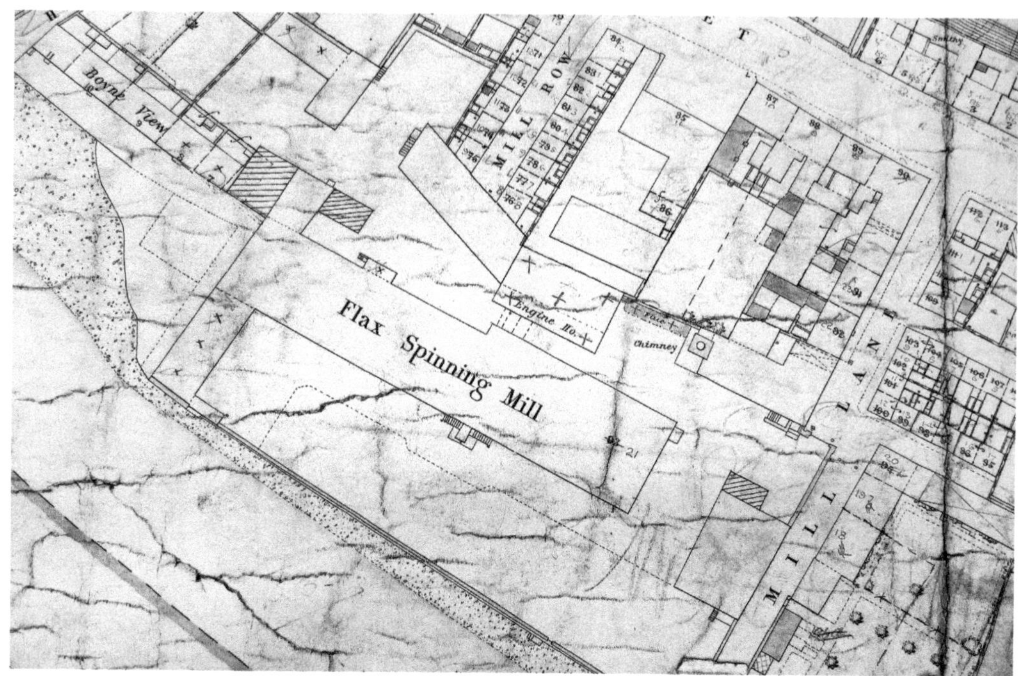

Westgate Mill was initially a linen mill, as shown on this old map. The site was then occupied by Edward Donaghy & Sons, shoemakers. (Courtesy of the Valuation Office)

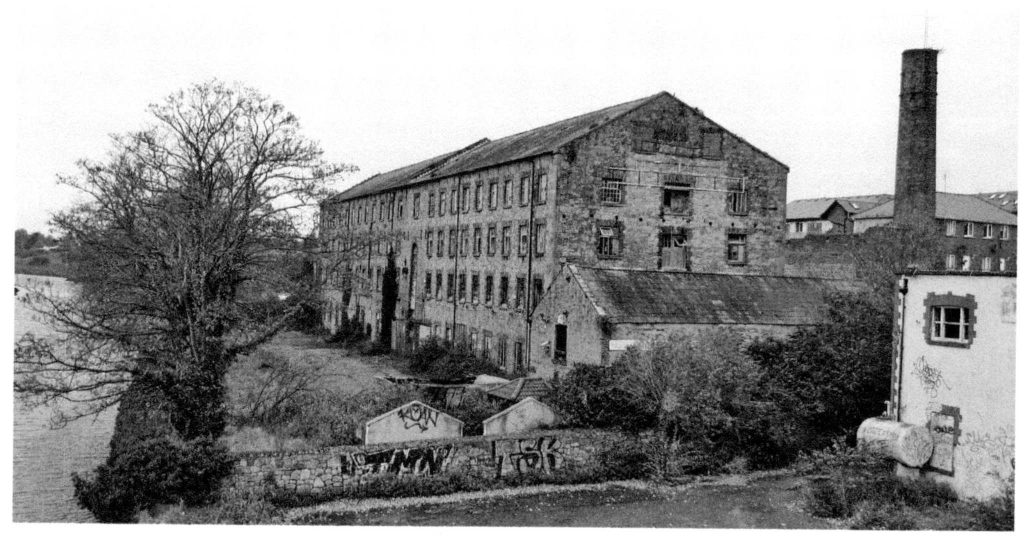

The Westgate Mill complex now lies empty.

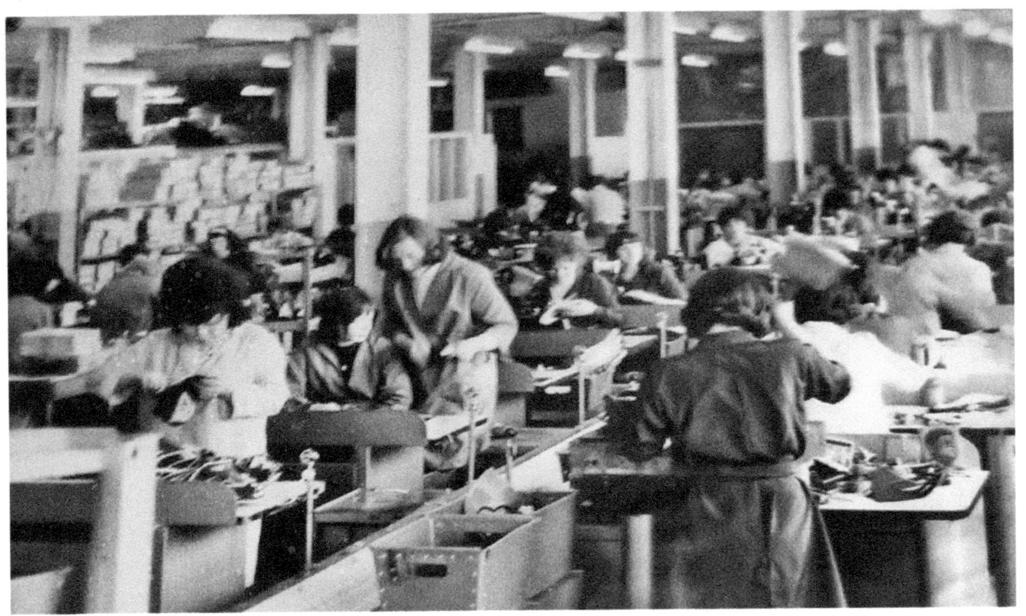

Workers in Edward Donaghy's shoe factory at Westgate. (Courtesy of Drogheda Museum Millmount)

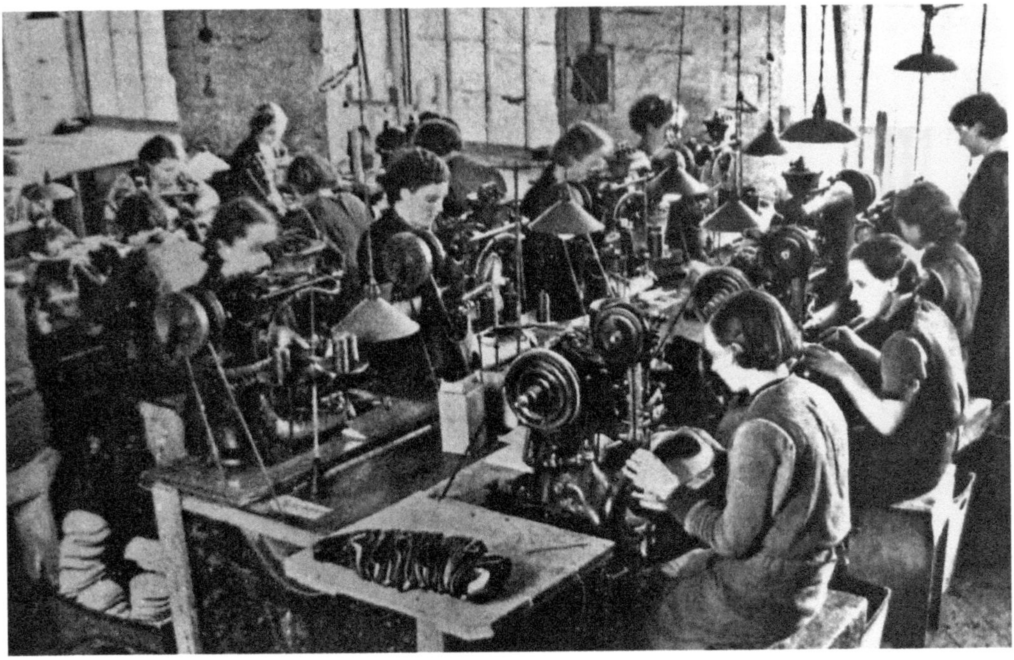

Another view of workers in Edward Donaghy's shoe factory at Westgate. (Courtesy of Drogheda Museum Millmount)

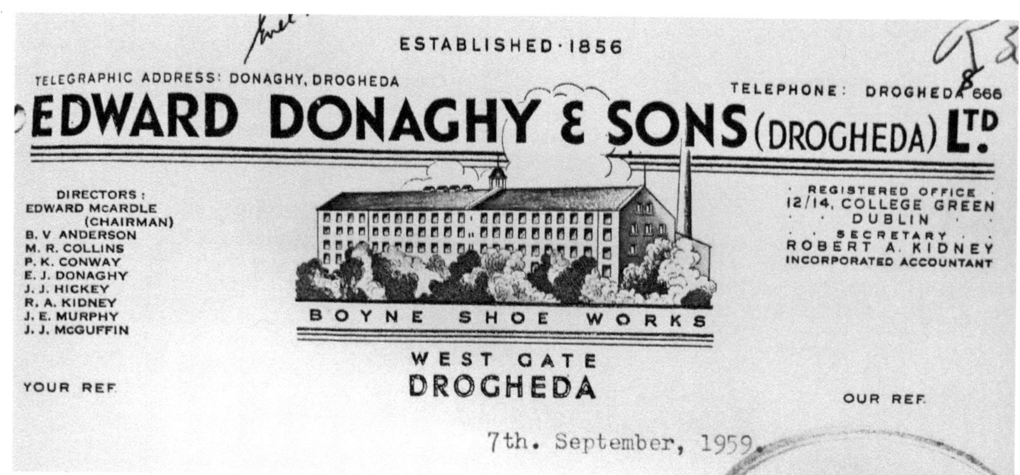

Above 1959 headed paper for Edward Donaghy & Sons. (Courtesy of the National Archives)

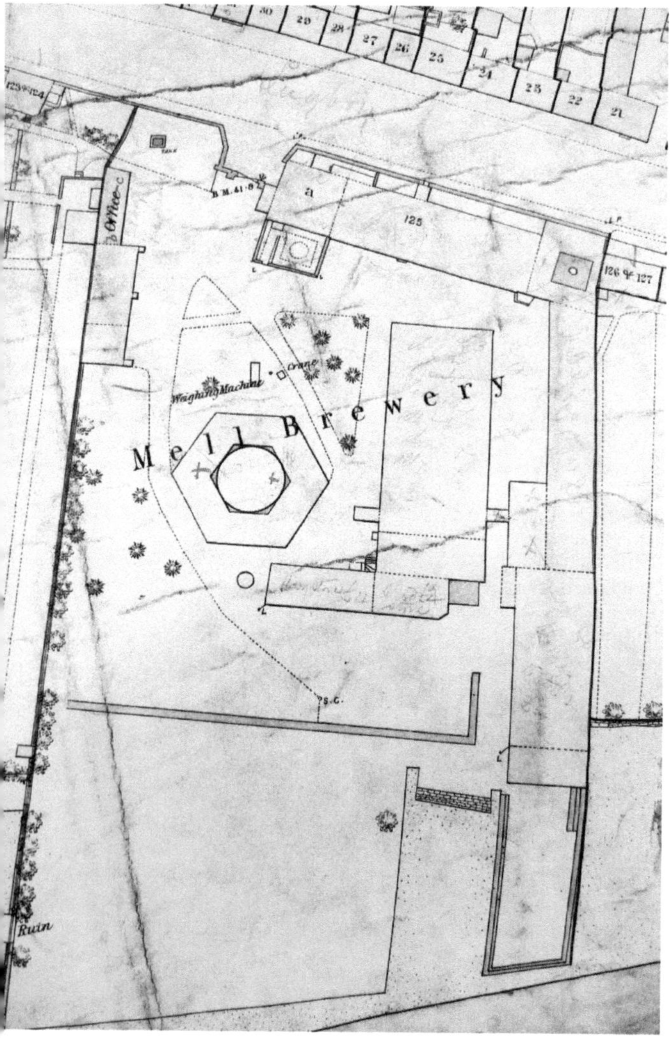

Left Mell Brewery, just west of Trinity Street, later became Caseys Brewery and now is occupied by Wilson & McBrinn clothing factory. (Courtesy of the Valuation Office)

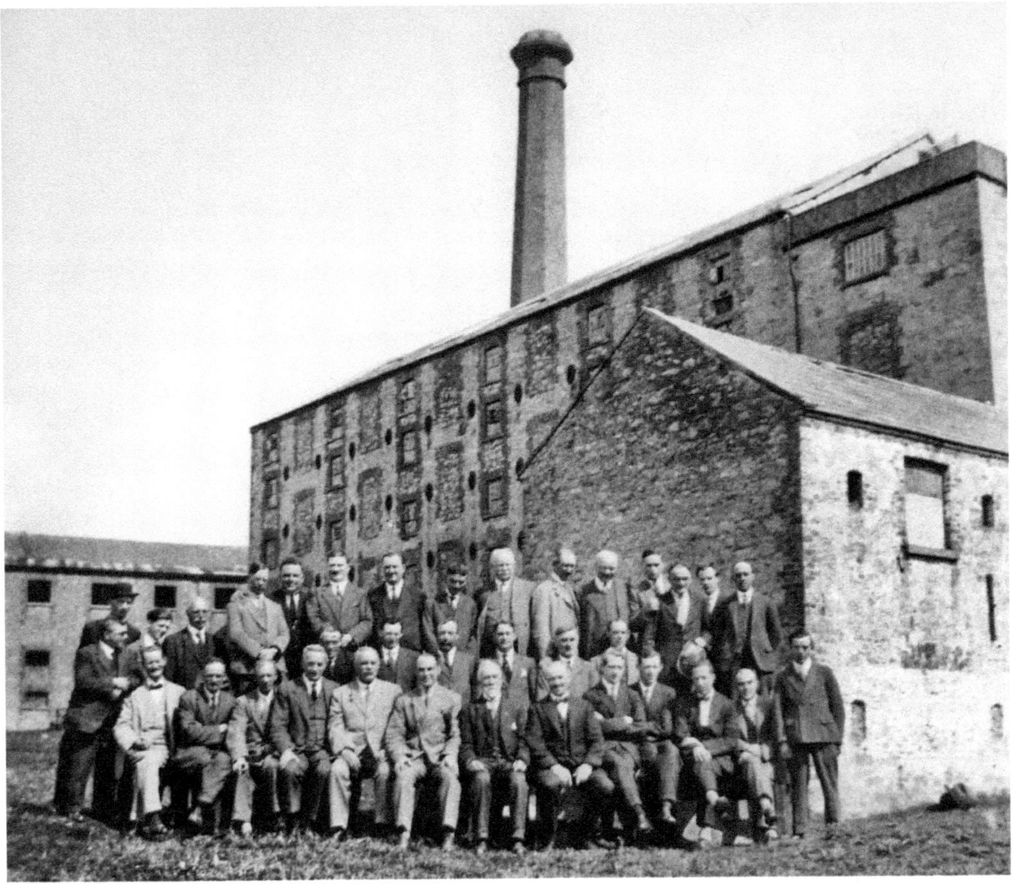

Wilson & McBrinn in front of the former Caseys Brewery at Mell, 1926. (Courtesy of Wilson & McBrinn)

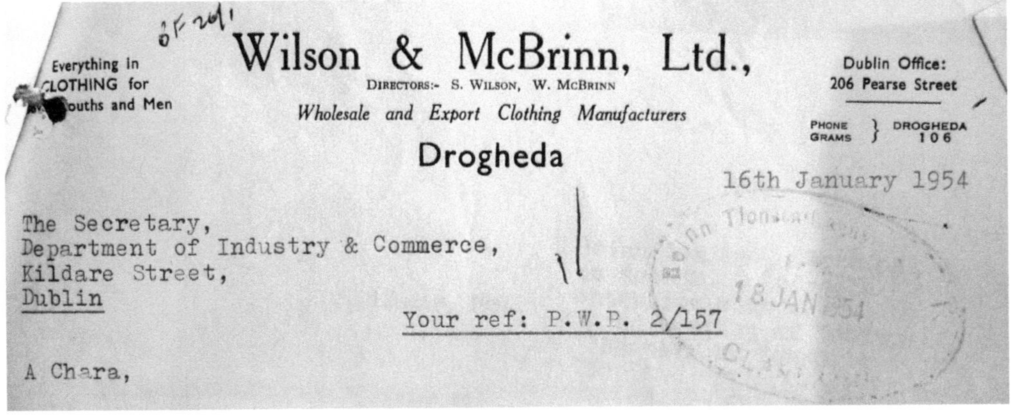

Wilson & McBrinn headed paper in 1954. Samuel Wilson and William McBrinn were the directors. (Courtesy of the National Archives)

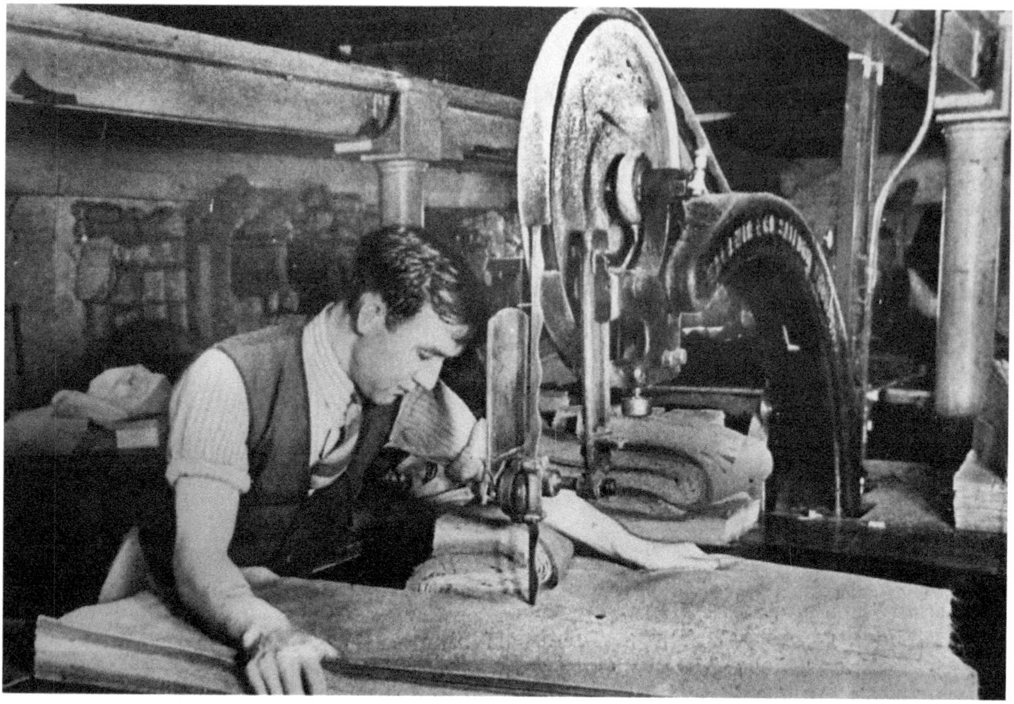

Wilson & McBrinn clothing factory. (Courtesy of Drogheda Museum Millmount)

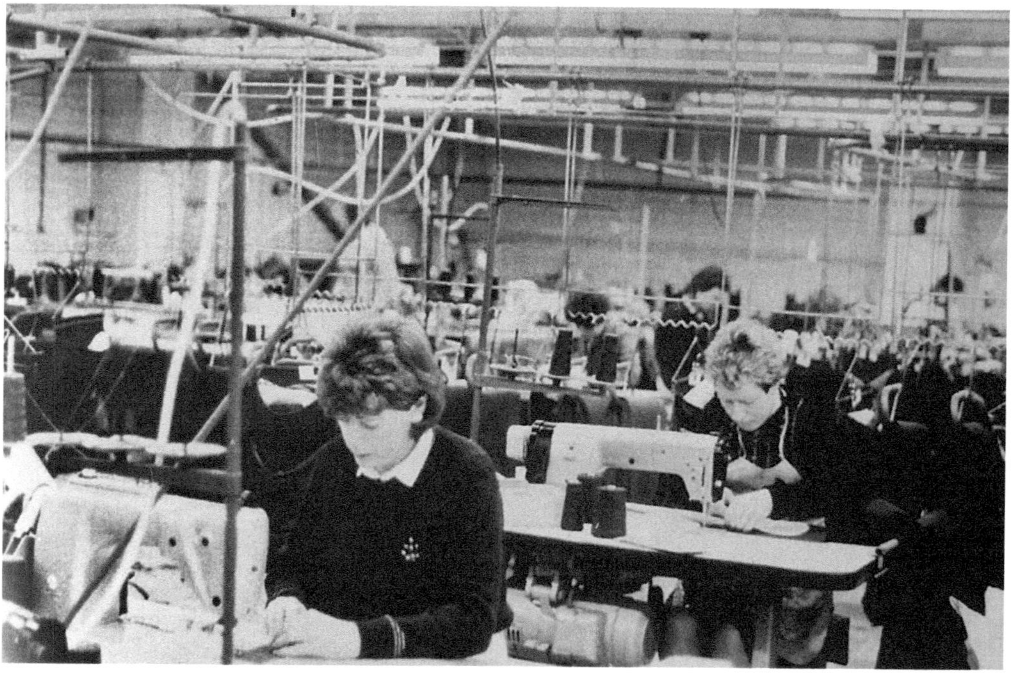

A more modern view of Wilson & McBrinn clothing factory, with machinists Ann Aspell and May Kelly. (Courtesy of Wilson & McBrinn)

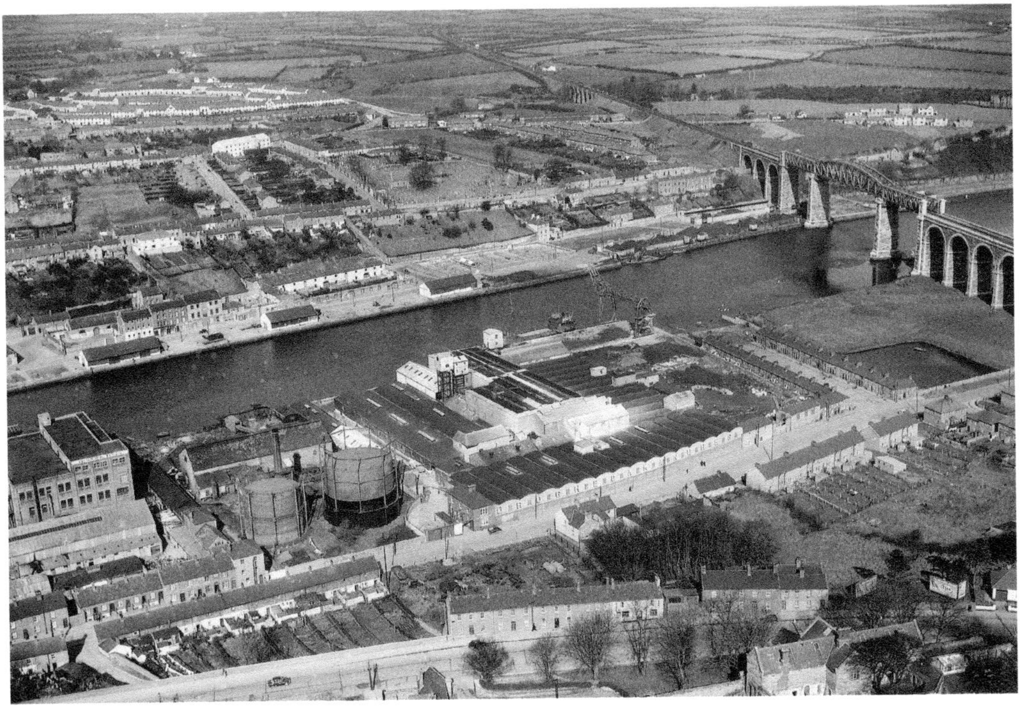

An aerial photograph of the Marsh Road area in the 1950s. Note the cylindrical gas holders of the Gas Company. The admissions block of the former workhouse can be seen at the lower right. (Courtesy of the National Library, Morgan Collection)

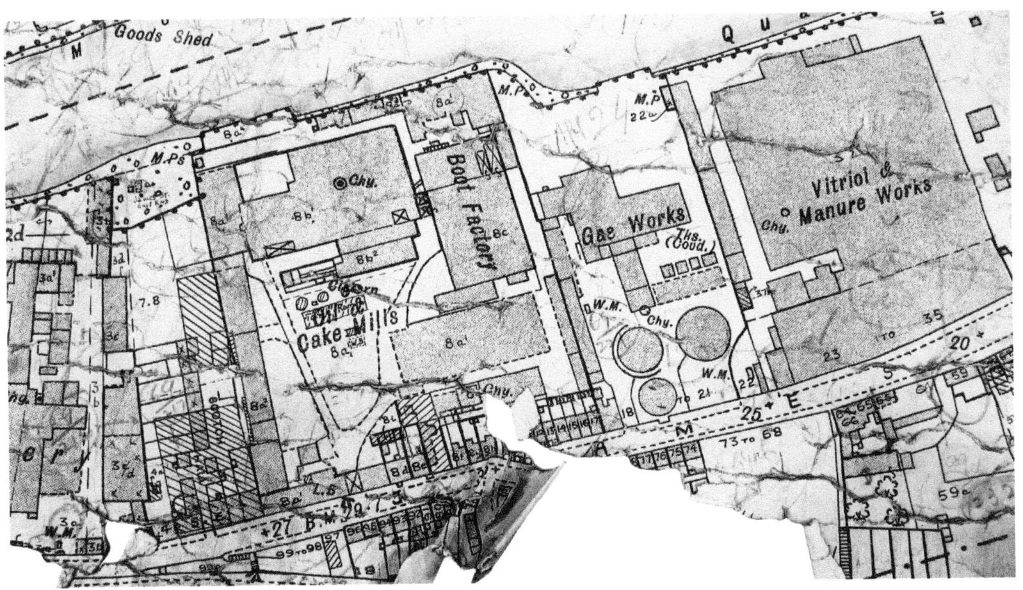

The Marsh Road was a hive of activity: Cairnes Brewery on left, then Oil & Cake Mills, then Woodington boot factory, then the town gas supplier, then Vitriol & Manure Works. (Courtesy of the Valuation Office)

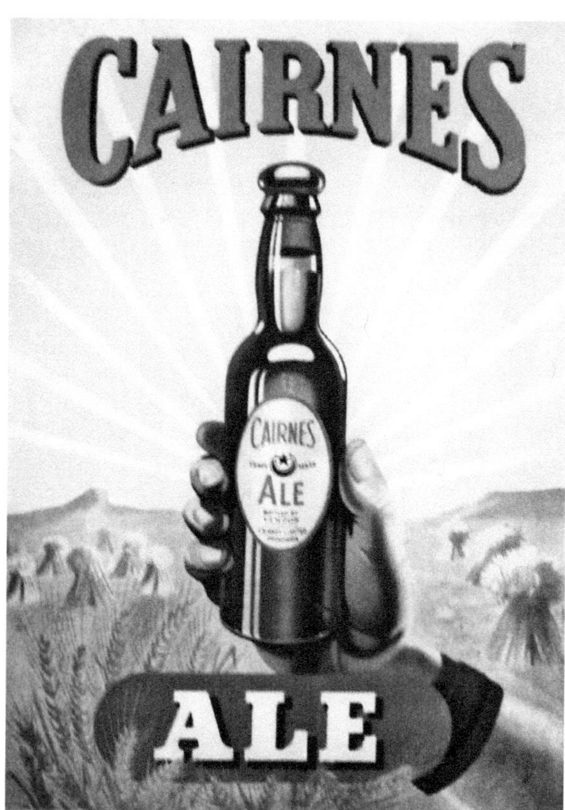

Cairnes Brewery on the Marsh Road was a big employer. (Courtesy of Drogheda Museum Millmount)

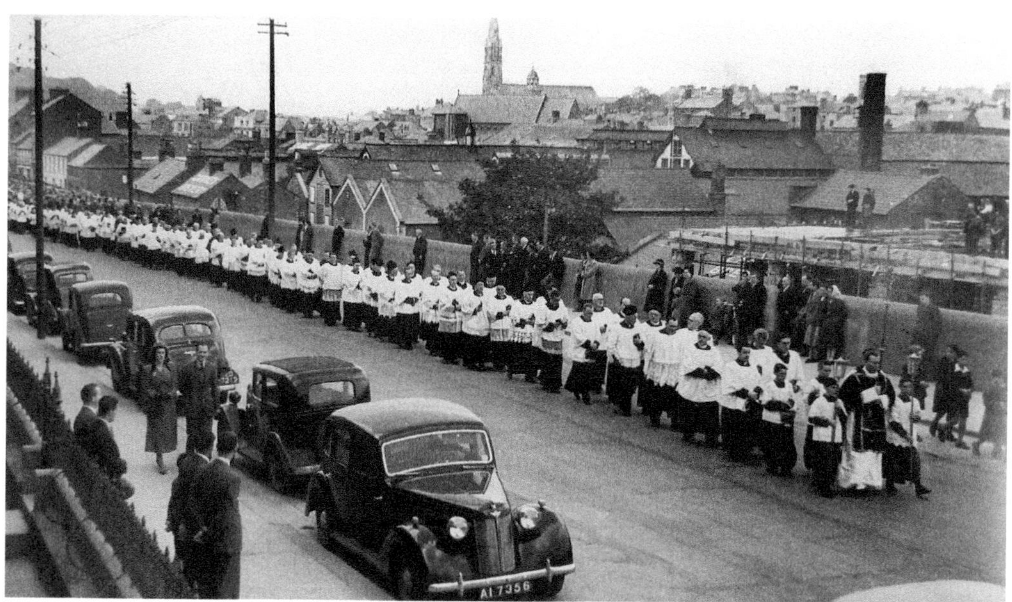

The 1949 funeral procession of the parish priest, Revd John Nulty, passes the Mercy Convent on the Dublin Road. On the right is the Stork Margarine factory being built in Scotch Hall (former cottages), and Cairnes Brewery is directly behind. (Courtesy of the Mercy Convent)

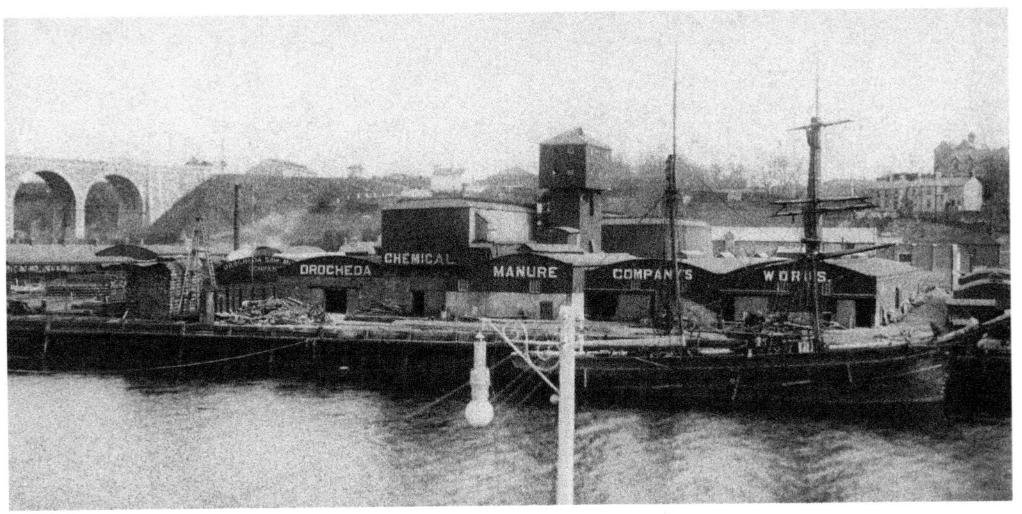

1908 view from the river of the Drogheda Chemical Manure Co. on the Marsh Road. (Courtesy of Drogheda Port Co.)

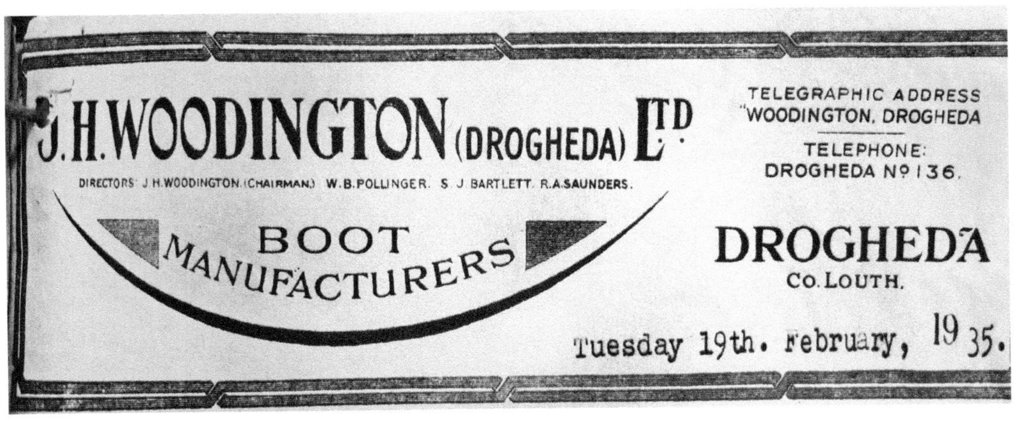

1935 headed paper of Woodington Ltd, listing the directors. (Courtesy of the National Archives)

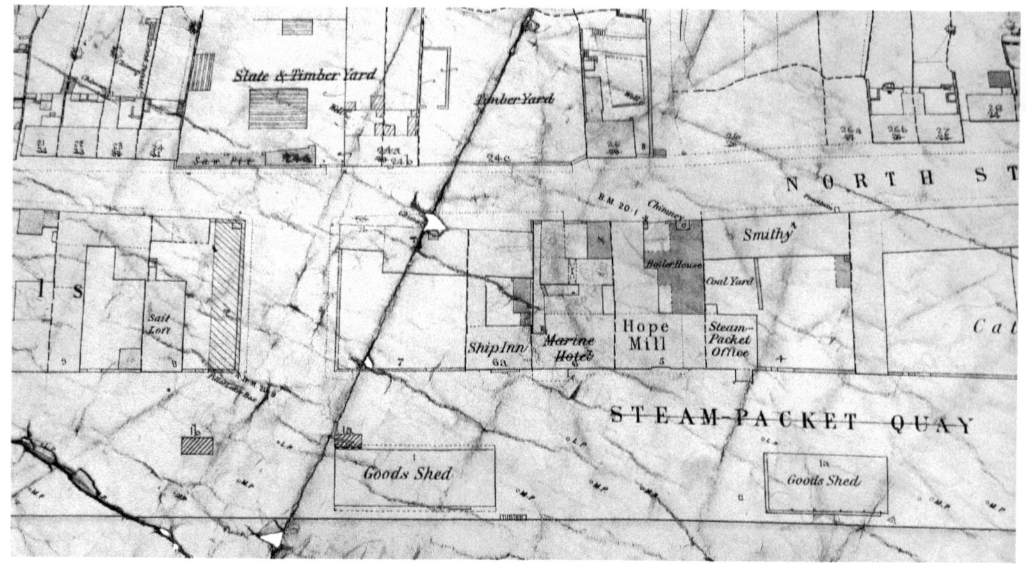

Steam Packet Quay. Note the Ship Inn, the Marine Hotel, and the Steam Packet booking office for ferries to Liverpool. (Courtesy of the Valuation Office)

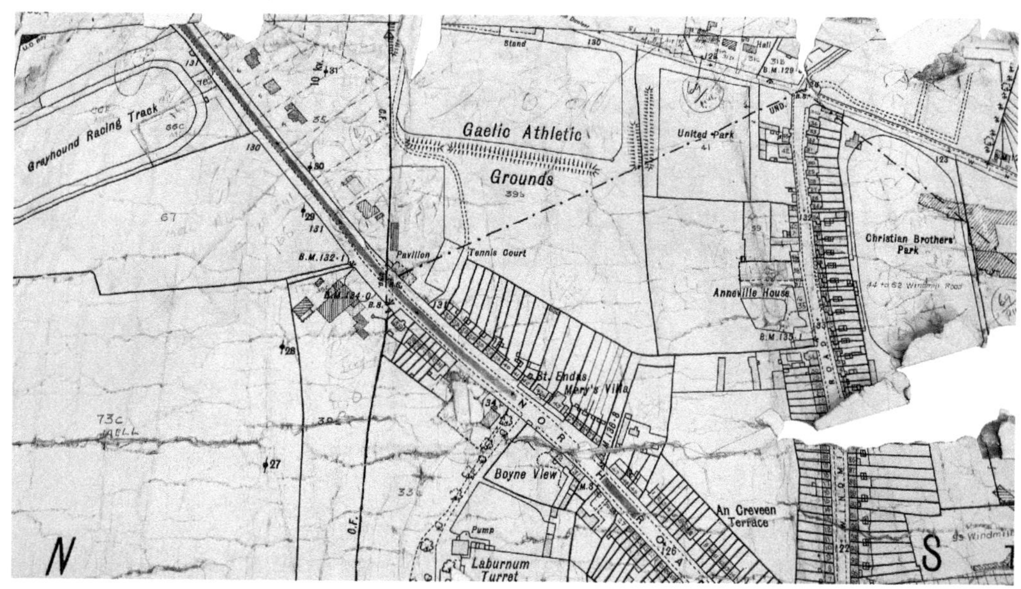

Opposite St Peter's cemetery there was the Christian Brothers running track (now part of the Lourdes Hospital), Drogheda United soccer stadium, the GAA grounds, and the Dog Track (now a housing estate). (Courtesy of the Valuation Office)

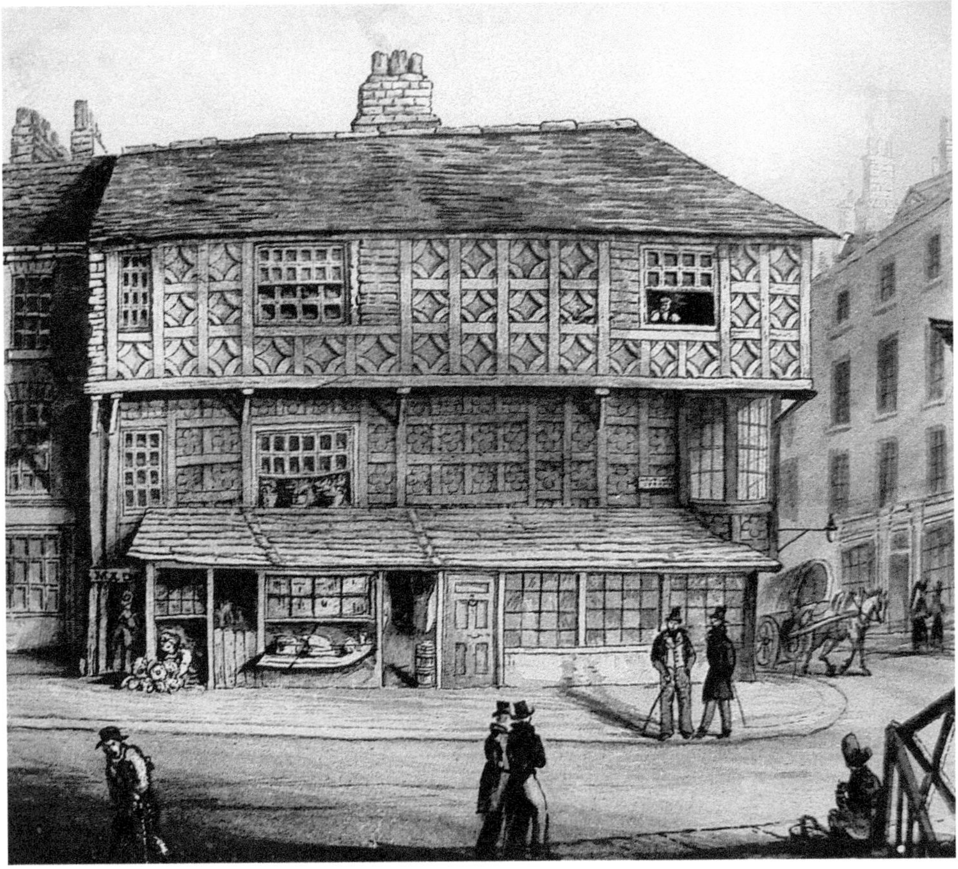

The Bathe family built this lovely timber-framed property in 1570, at the corner of St Laurence Street and Shop Street. It was demolished in 1824. (Watercolour in 1823 by Robert Armstrong, courtesy of Highlanes Gallery/Drogheda Council)

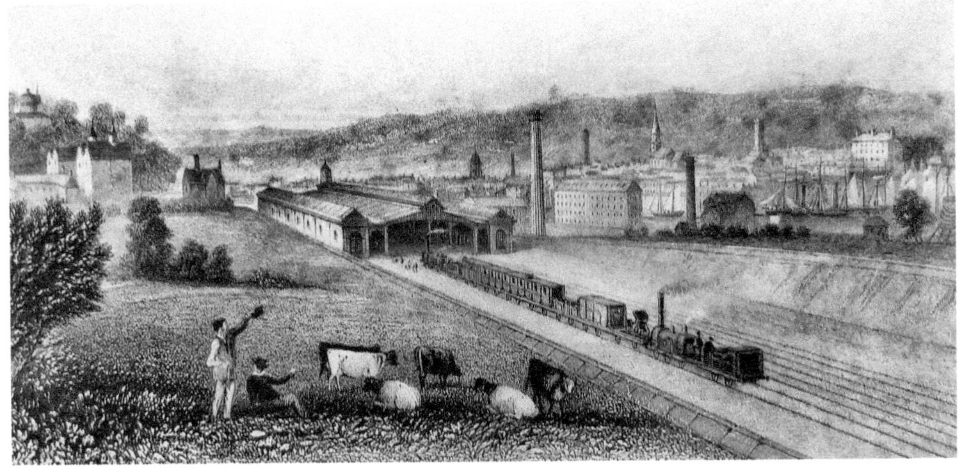

The new railway station as depicted by Dalton in 1844.

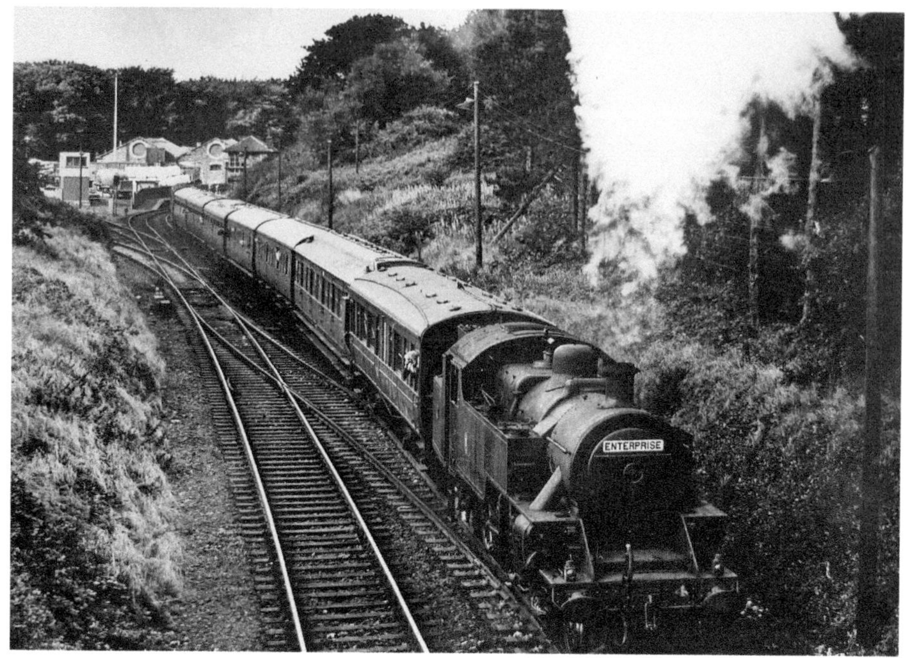

The *Enterprise* steaming between Dublin and Belfast in the twentieth century. Drogheda station can be seen in the background. (Courtesy of Irish Rail)

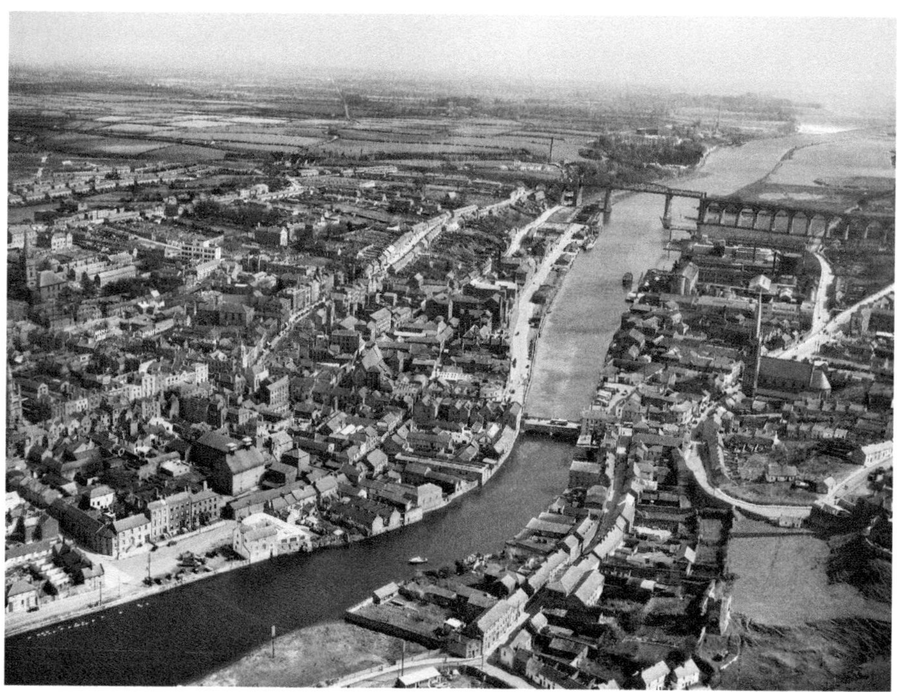

An aerial photograph of Drogheda, *c.* 1950s. (Courtesy of the National Library, Independent Collection)

OTHER BOOKS BY THE AUTHOR

Harold's Cross in Old Photographs

Mount Merrion in Old Photographs

Castlebar in Old Photographs